A RACE AGAINST
THE CLOCK

A RACE AGAINST
THE CLOCK

THE AUTHORIZED BIOGRAPHY OF
EDGAR RAY "PREACHER" KILLEN

BRIAN BONEY

Palmetto Publishing Group
Charleston, SC

A Race Against the Clock
Copyright © 2018 by Brian Boney
All rights reserved

First Edition

Printed in the United States

ISBN-13: 978-1-64111-092-1
ISBN-10: 1-64111-092-9

Dedication

This book is dedicated to my wife Jennifer, who, in addition to having beaten ovarian cancer, is battling Multiple Sclerosis. Despite her constant level of pain, she has been behind me 100 percent in this endeavor, and never discouraged me in pursuing this project.

Edgar Ray Killen, circa 1964

FOREWORD

My name is Betty Jo Killen. I married Edgar Ray "Preacher" Killen in 1997. I was aware of the allegations concerning his role in the "Mississippi Burning" murders before I married him. I also knew that he was a good man, an extremely hard worker, and adamant about his Christian beliefs. He was generous, charitable, and had a good word for everyone he encountered.

He was also hounded by the media and vilified on a constant basis. It is easy for people to play into rumors and speculation, which is exactly what the media excelled at when it came to Edgar. Looking back on the events leading up to his trial and conviction, it is so clear now that he was almost doomed to be convicted for crimes he had no part in.

This case had been the subject of movies, books, documentaries, and news articles for four decades. No physical evidence connected Edgar to this crime. The prosecution, judge, jury, and much to our dismay, even Edgar's defense team used questionable tactics and testimony to put Edgar in prison for 60 years at the age of 80.

It is my opinion that this book is the first book to truthfully tell Edgar's story. I began reading this book when the project was first started and have followed it through until the time of publishing. It is as accurate as possible considering the passage of more than 50 years since the murders occurred. I can say it is a far more accurate version the jury was presented with, and more honest than some of the jury members that decided Edgar's fate.

I am comforted to know that the true story is finally revealed, and that Edgar is now in a place where he is no longer suffering physically, mentally, or emotionally. I hope the reader can see Edgar for the truly good man that he was and that you will keep him and his family in your prayers.

Mrs. Betty Jo Killen
Neshoba County, Mississippi
February, 2018

—⚬—

I WAS CONTACTED IN JUNE OF 2017 BY BRIAN BONEY. He had gotten my phone number from a neighbor who listened to Mr. Boney's plan of writing the biography of my brother, Edgar Ray "Preacher" Killen. He tried calling me and for whatever reason, I was unable to answer. I later listened to his voicemail and called him back.

He told me of his agreement with Edgar to write this book and he wanted my input if I was willing to share it. There have been many stories told of my brother, most of them inaccurate, and a lot of them were complete lies and fabrications. Mr. Boney stressed that he not only wanted to write this story, he wanted to help Edgar return home to spend the remainder of his life with his family. It was clear he had done his research and was well versed on the case. It also helped that he had a visit with Edgar, retained an attorney, and offered to send me copies of letters written to him by Edgar, a copy of their contract, and a copy of what he had written up to that point.

I was inclined to agree with this project, and after I received the items he sent to me, I was in complete agreement. I finally met with Mr. Boney, as well as his wife, Jennifer, his daughter, Emma, and Jennifer's faithful service dog, Nina, in September of 2017 when they came to Philadelphia, Mississippi. We went to the Neshoba County Courthouse, the old jail, and the location where the trio of civil rights workers were shot. I also took them by Edgar's old home place. We had a good day and enjoyed ourselves. It took a few minutes to gain the trust of Nina being so close to her "momma", but she eventually warmed up and offered a wagging tail and friendly lick.

Edgar passed away on January 11, 2018. I know Mr. Boney wanted to help Edgar return home before he died, but it just wasn't possible. Mr. Boney and his friend, Brad Mock, came to Edgar's funeral service and showed our family the utmost respect and consideration. I am glad this story, the true story, is finally being told. I have read the contents of this book and I can attest they are as accurate as possible considering the passage of fifty years, the deaths of many who may have contributed to this effort, and the reluctance of some to tell what they know.

It is my hope that this story sheds a new light on my brother and the events surrounding his trial and conviction. This is the most accurate and truthful version that has been written thus far.

J.D. Killen,
Neshoba County, Mississippi,
February, 2018

PREFACE

THIS BOOK IS VERY LIKELY TO CAUSE accusations of racism, hatred, insensitivity, and political incorrectness. My response to that: *too damn bad*. If reading this hurts your feelings, stop where you are and put this book down. This story has been told many times over—in print, documentaries, on TV newscasts, in the Hollywood movie *Mississippi Burning*, and in several media outlets that covered the Edgar Ray Killen trial in 2005.

What has not been told, up until now, is Edgar Ray Killen's version of the events, events that have plagued him for more than fifty years, and caused him to be sentenced to sixty years in prison at eighty years old. Please make no mistake about it, I have written this story after having reviewed many transcripts and FBI reports, and conducting interviews with a well-known attorney who has represented many members of the Mafia —and Edgar Ray Killen himself. I truly believe this man was railroaded for political gain and public appeasement.

I make no excuses for criminal activity, nor do I condone it, regardless of who the victim is or the perpetrator's reason for having done it. I have spent almost thirty years in law enforcement and have served with and worked alongside officers of all races. I base my judgment on these officers—and all people I know—on personal integrity and character. If I did not believe that Edgar Ray Killen was innocent and had been used as a political scapegoat, I would have never typed the first word about him. If you choose to read this story in its entirety, please read it with an objective point of view and give fair consideration to the facts as they are presented.

Edgar Killen maintains his views of segregation, and that is his right. He was raised in a time and place where that was a normal and accepted way of life by both whites and blacks. However, he maintains he is not a racist, nor does he hate anyone because of their skin color. After visiting him in person and receiving dozens of letters from him, I know beyond a doubt that these are his true feelings. After all, at this point he has nothing to lose by expressing his opinion. While it will probably be alleged, please be open minded enough not to declare the author a racist or hatemonger for telling the story.

Killen's story is a story that *needs* to be told—it's a story that needs to be told to let people know just how vulnerable they are when the government sets out to make an example of someone.

It is my sincere hope that you enjoy this book and view it fairly and objectively.

God Bless,
Brian Boney

ACKNOWLEDGMENTS

I HAVE MANY PEOPLE TO THANK FOR the completion of this project. First and foremost, I must thank God for blessing me with the writing ability and patience to complete this project. It was far harder to complete the biography of someone who is in prison than anyone could imagine—myself included—especially when contact is limited almost exclusively to correspondence via letters.

I must also thank Mr. Edgar Ray Killen, who was not only kind enough to allow me to write his story, and, has proven to be a very considerate man who always asks about my family's well-being and keeps us in his prayers.

Mr. Shelby Bohannon, attorney at law, and his wife Linda, who accompanied me for a visit with Edgar Killen and came up with our contractual agreement for the book. Thank you both. We had a fun trip, and I will not forget what you did to make this possible.

Thanks to my friends and family who read this story as it progressed and offered suggestions and pointed out mistakes. Thanks to Mr. Louis E. Diamond, Esq. who provided insight and information on the role of Greg Scarpa Sr. as it relates to this story.

Thank you also to Mrs. Betty Jo Killen, Edgar Killen's wife, for taking time to speak with me, especially considering everything she has been through. Last, but certainly not least, thank you to Mr. J.D. Killen, Edgar Killen's younger brother, who has shared many stories of his brother with me by phone and in person. I appreciate your time, kindness, and friendship.

INTRODUCTION

EDGAR RAY "PREACHER" KILLEN WAS BORN ON January 17, 1925 in Phila-
delphia, Mississippi to parents Lonnie Ray Killen (1901-1992) and Etta
Hitt Killen (1903-1983). He was one of eight children. He was a sawmill
operator by trade and a part-time Baptist preacher, hence the nickname.
Over time, he allegedly became a member of the White Knights of the
Ku Klux Klan, and was a kleagle, or recruiter/organizer, for them.

During the "Freedom Summer" of 1964, Michael Schwerner, twen-
ty-four, and Andrew Goodman, twenty-one—who were both Jewish and
from New York—along with other young men and women, descended
on Mississippi in order to register blacks to vote. They were joined by
James Chaney, age twenty-one, who was black and from Meridian, Mississippi. These three and others began their task of getting blacks registered to vote.

On June 21, 1964, Schwerner, Chaney, and Goodman were killed.
Their bodies were found buried fifteen feet below an earthen dam forty-
four days later. This much we know to be true. The State of Mississippi
never brought murder charges against anyone. In 1966, Edgar Ray Killen and eighteen other men were tried on federal civil rights violations.
Killen was acquitted in a vote of eleven to one. The one hold-out said
she could never convict a preacher.

On June 13, 2005, Killen was brought to trial after being indicted on
three counts of murder forty years later. He was ultimately convicted on
three counts of manslaughter, and at the age of eighty while wheelchair
bound, he was sentenced to sixty years in prison. It was acknowledged
that Killen did not take part in the murders, and, was in fact not present

when the murders occurred. In addition to using the testimony from the 1966 trial, an array of questionable evidence and testimony was used against him that indicated he was the instigator and organizer of the murders.

Is Killen innocent, and in fact a scapegoat for the political agenda of others? Was he convicted out of the need to maintain "political correctness"—the need to appease the public and family members of the victims? Did the media in part cause Killen to receive an unfair and impartial trial? Was it possible for him to receive a fair and impartial trial after years of media attention in a time that was very different than 1964? This is Edgar Ray Killen's story in his words.

The media portrays him as an ignorant, racist redneck. Others portray him as a cold-blooded murderer who killed innocent people without remorse. Readers may be surprised by what this man professes to know. Government secrets, connections to high-ranking political figures, up to and including presidents and senators. Russia's Cold War battle plans. Mafia figures and entertainers. The coincidence that one of his defense attorneys, James McIntyre, was disbarred and the other, Mitch Moran, died an unexplained death, and was creamated on the same day without benefit of an autopsy. Moran's records of Killen's trial have never been located.

Everything told to the author has been researched to the best of his ability for verification. A lot of this information was hard to research due to half a century having passed, and the death of other participants, witnesses, and family members who could have elaborated, explained, or confirmed Killen's stories. What is absolutely without question is the reluctance of others in discussing Killen, or the matter in general. One thing is for certain: Edgar Ray Killen still adamantly believes in segregation, the United States Constitution as it was originally written, his religious beliefs, the evils of Communism, and he still maintains a strong dislike and distrust of the liberal media.

CHAPTER ONE

—ന—

IN 1988, THE MOVIE *MISSISSIPPI BURNING* WAS RELEASED. It starred Gene
Hackman and Willem Defoe and was loosely based on the 1964 murders of civil rights activists James Chaney, Andrew Goodman, and Michael Schwerner. I was twenty years old when the movie found its way
to the big screen, and I enjoyed it not knowing it was based on actual
events. After discussing the movie with my parents, they told me that
they remembered when those events had happened.

I was intrigued and wanted to know more, but that was before the
internet, and research was done by going to the library and reading
books and newspapers from the time period you were interested in. I
watched the movie several times over the years and developed quite an
interest in that period, particularly in the American South. Not only was
this the era of civil rights marches, demonstrations, the resurgence of
the Ku Klux Klan, forced busing, school integration, the death of Martin Luther King Jr. and the early days of the law enforcement career of
legendary Sheriff Buford Pusser, it was also the time when the South was
beginning to lose its "Mayberry" image.

The South at this point was not experiencing the crime wave of such
cities as New York, Chicago, Oakland, Los Angeles, and Newark, where
riots, looting, arson, and other acts of violence seemed to be the order
of the day. Southerners, for the most part, tended to be conservative,
hardworking people who went to church on Sundays, tended to their
families, and minded their own business. This was true for both blacks

and whites, and very few violent crimes were committed in small south-ern towns—and law-abiding people of all creeds and colors preferred it to stay that way.

In the "Freedom Summer" of 1964, members of the Congressional Office of Racial Equality (CORE) began sending members on voter registration drives throughout the South to register blacks to vote. President Lyndon B. Johnson had signed the Civil Rights Act, and the South, which was still under Jim Crow Law, viewed this as nothing short of a federal invasion on states' rights and the beginning of the second war for southern independence. The outsiders that made up CORE, and the southerners who supported them, simply were not wanted, welcomed, or tolerated.

The majority of white people, from the common working man and his family, to high-ranking southern politicians, openly expressed their displeasure and dislike of this agenda, and they did so in every imaginable setting, including on national television, the radio, and in the newspapers. Prominent politicians warned that integrating schools would result in violence, and for both races, would lower education standards, devalue their heritages, and encour-age interracial relationships that would cause harm to the children these unions would produce. While these men were commonly ridiculed by the enlightened, intelligently superior northerners for these sentiments, it seems the south-ern politicians' predictions not only came true, but the results far surpassed all expectations.

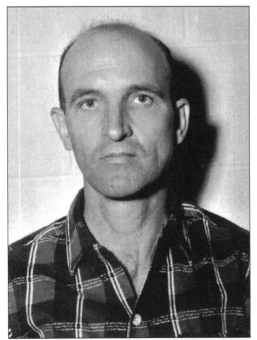

Edgar Ray Killen, circa 1967

James O. Eastland, a United States senator from

Mississippi, gave a speech on August 12, 1955 in Senatobia, Mississippi. During this speech, he stated, "On May 17, 1954, the Constitution of the United States was destroyed because of the Supreme Court's decision. You are not obliged to obey the decisions of any court which are plainly fraudulent, sociological considerations."

Eastland testified to the Senate ten days after the landmark case of Brown v. Board of Education of Topeka, Kansas, 347 U.S. 483 (1954) came down: "The southern institution of racial segregation or racial separation was the correct, self-evident truth which arose from the chaos and confusion of the Reconstruction period. Separation promotes racial harmony. It permits each race to follow its own pursuits, and its own civilization. Segregation is not discrimination . . . Mr. President, it is the law of nature, it is the law of God, that every race has both the right and the duty to perpetuate itself. All free men have the right to associate exclusively with members of their own race, free from governmental interference, if they so desire."

Senator James O. Eastland whom Edgar Ray Killen referred to as being "like a second father to me."

Senator Eastland, discussed further later in the book, was like a "second father" to Edgar Ray Killen. Eastland was also often at odds with President Lyndon B. Johnson's policy on civil rights, yet they had a close friendship. This friendship, according to Killen, gave him access to government secrets while he was employed by Eastland. It has been documented that President Johnson, who had seemingly signed the Civil Rights Act to protect blacks and to provide for them equal rights, was recorded in a White House conversation as having referred to the Civil Rights Act as "the nigger bill"—yet Johnson is still to some people championed as a civil rights hero.

By contrast, Senator Eastland in his later political career won the support of Aaron Henry, a civil rights leader and president of the NAACP. After ending his political career, Eastland remained friends with Henry, and regularly sent contributions to the NAACP. It appears that Johnson was merely wanting to gain political mileage for himself and Eastland; while he was outspoken and certainly controversial by today's standards, he was nevertheless a man of conviction, integrity, and principle, and did not forsake his standards for the benefit of a false image. It is of this man of whom Killen said, "He was like a second father to me." It just may be that birds of a feather flock together.

These times were filled with men who were staunch segregationists; men such as Mississippi Governor Ross Barnett and Alabama Governor George Wallace, who, later in his career, was endorsed by the NAACP and whom Attorney J. L. Chestnut, who was black, referred to as "the only judge who ever called me 'mister' in the courtroom." These were not uneducated men. They were well-schooled attorneys, and Wallace flew combat missions over Japan in World War II. At the far end of this spectrum, is the black civil rights hero, Malcolm X, born Malcolm Little in May of 1925. This makes Malcolm X, who has been called one of the greatest and most influential African-Americans in history, five months younger than Edgar Ray Killen.

Unlike Killen, Malcolm X was sent to prison for larceny at the age of twenty. While in prison, he became a member of the Nation of Islam. In 1952, he was paroled, and quickly became one of the group's most influential leaders. Unlike Killen, Malcolm X adopted an Arabic name, renounced his loyalty to the United States, promoted black supremacy, and promoted the separation of black and white Americans. He, too, rejected the civil rights movement, because it promoted integration. Both men seemingly agreed that blacks and whites should be separate, rejected the civil rights movement, and were against integration. Another distinct difference between them was that Killen remained employed, maintained his loyalty to the United States, and was an outspoken opponent of communism, an outlook he maintains to this day. The end result? Malcolm X is often referred to in the press as an "activist" and to some, a role-model judging by the frequent sightings of "Malcolm X" T-shirts. Edgar Ray Killen is vilified and labeled a "racist."

Yet another well-known and loved member of the black community is Louis E. Wolcott, also known as Louis Farrakhan. He was born in 1933, making him eight years younger than Killen. Like Malcolm X, Farrakhan denounced his loyalty to the United States in 1955 and became a member of the Nation of Islam. What is Farrakhan's opinion of the white race? "Blacks are superior to whites, whites were created 6,600 years ago as a race of devils by an evil scientist known as Yakub, and white people deserve to die."

What is Farrakhan's opinion of Jews? During a 1985 Nation of Islam meeting at Madison Square Garden, he stated, "And don't you forget, when it's God who puts you in the ovens, it's forever."

In 2005, he accused the government of destroying the levee during Hurricane Katrina in a deliberate attempt to wipe out the largely black sections of New Orleans. The black population, as well as New Orleans in its entirety, was forewarned to evacuate, and yet made a conscious decision to stay—but Farrakhan claimed it was still the government's fault. What was the result of these outrageous allegations? Was he made a mockery of in the media? Was his stupidity pointed out by local, state, and national leaders? Not even close. No, in 2005, Black Entertainment Television Network voted him "Person of the Year." In 2006, an AP-AOL Black Voices poll voted him the fifth most important black leader. And yet still, ninety-two-year old Killen sits in prison.

CHAPTER TWO

—༄—

IN JUNE OF 1989 I BEGAN MY CAREER in law enforcement. I have since retired and gained employment with a different agency. During my career, I served as a patrol officer, DWI enforcement officer, DARE officer, SWAT member, hostage negotiator, narcotics supervisor, patrol supervisor, internal affairs investigator and police academy instructor. I do not claim to be an attorney, but I do have a wide range of experience that has allowed me to apply the law in a variety of settings. This experience has brought me to the courtroom many times, and as a result I have gained a working knowledge of courtroom proceedings.

While laws vary from state to state, courtroom procedures and practices have a unique similarity. The elements of each crime must be proven beyond a reasonable doubt. In criminal proceedings, it is generally required that the intent to commit the crime must be proven. Searches and seizures require legal and probable cause and must be proven or conducted under a search warrant. Physical evidence is usually required, especially in crimes against persons, and witness testimony to back up the other evidence is, at a minimum, sought out. Confessions are priceless—if legally obtained—and any supporting evidence, such as video, pictures, diagrams, etc., if available, can make or break a case.

I have spent countless hours reading the story of the murders in 1964, as well as trial transcripts, interviews, and statements from witnesses, alleged participants, and informants, in addition to FBI reports from the original investigation. While reading various reports from an array of internet sources, I located a mailing address for Edgar Ray Killen, who is presently serving his sentence at Parchman State Prison in Mississippi. I have spent my entire adult life serving as a police officer, and I consider myself to be as pro-police and pro-law-and-order as a person can be. Generally, I do not play into conspiracy-theory propaganda.

Yet as I read some of the information on the Killen trial, and the allegations not only against him in the original trial, but those in 2005 as well, I could not help but think that there might be more to the story than meets the eye. In December of 2016, I mailed a letter to Edgar Ray Killen. This was due to curiosity about him personally, and I was intrigued enough to want to write his story—if he was willing to share it with me. I stressed in my letter that I was not seeking information about the criminal allegations against him. There were many references to him having maintained silence on those charges for over forty plus years, and I had no illusions that my letter to him would result in the proverbial smoking gun.

I could not help but think that it was quite possible that an *innocent* man—especially a ninety-one-year-old innocent man—could very well be spending his remaining days in prison away from his family and home. I had no clue as to what response my letter would generate, if any, especially considering that he had been portrayed in the media as ornery and cantankerous. A few days later I was surprised to receive a response from him. His letter, contradictory to what had been shown of him in the media, was well written, legible, and intelligent.

He immediately thanked me for writing to him and went on to complete a very polite correspondence. His manner of expressing himself was reminiscent of my grandfather, who ironically shared the same birthday with Killen, although my grandfather was born in 1917. Much like my grandfather, Killen professed a strong faith in God, even thanking me for wishing him God's blessing and protection. I had read where he was still operating a sawmill at the age of eighty, and much like my grandfather, I thought Killen to be one tough, old guy. This sort of work ethic might very well be a thing of the past, but for Killen's generation it was pretty much the norm. His generation survived under the pretense of "if you don't work, you don't eat." No giveaway programs or government subsidies. Killen is without doubt a product of his generation as well his environment, and the values, practices, standards, and beliefs of the area in which he was raised.

I instantly thought about the times I had said that Jesus must spend a lot of time in jail, because a lot of people find him there. These are the cynical thoughts of a cop who has seen criminals instantly get religion when the jail door slams behind them—and then suddenly lose that religion as soon as they are released and able to prey on the public again. Within the first paragraph, Killen made religious references, and knowing that he had been an ordained Baptist preacher for longer than I had been alive gave credibility to his claims of religious beliefs and dedication.

In the same letter, he expressed his disdain for the media, which, as a police officer, I understood, especially considering the image portrayed of law enforcement officers who must make split-second decisions in life-threatening situations. I have seen many officers degraded and their careers put in question because of unscrupulous reporters who wanted to sell a story. If the media will do that to law enforcement agencies and their officers, is it too hard to imagine it being done to a solitary, reputed "Klansman"?

He went on to express his belief in the US Constitution (as it was originally written; 1776-1784), as well as his anti-communist beliefs, his admiration of Abraham Lincoln and Lincoln's statement, "Speaking of the races, I believe that one race must be inferior to the other; I prefer to believe that my race is the superior race." Quite a statement for a man who is often referred to as the "Great Emancipator."

Edgar Ray Killen and I began a steady correspondence. He has made references to having connections and knowledge of political figures up to and including newly elected President Donald Trump, whom he supports, as well as Mafia members, entertainers, and a host of other people, in addition to his knowledge of government secrets and cover-ups. His letters, especially the parts in which he mentions his 2005 trial and subsequent conviction, led me to believe my initial assumption was quite possibly right. Due to the screening of inmate mail, as well as what Killen refers to as "widespread corruption within the Mississippi Department of Corrections," along with possible federal interest in him and with whom he corresponds, I decided that if I, a career cop and aspiring author, was ever going to write a book, this was what I wanted to write about.

I retained the services of Mr. Shelby Bohannon, attorney at law, and proceeded forward. Edgar Killen warned me that I could possibly "face some heat" if I were to pursue the project. I have faced "heat" for my entire career, and I have never been one to sacrifice my integrity or the integrity of the officers under my supervision. I have never been, nor sought to be, the golden boy of the administration, and I must say I have achieved that goal many times over.

To Edgar Ray "Preacher" Killen, I say, let the two of us—under the protection and blessing of God—tell your story. I am proud to consider you a friend and a man of integrity, principles, and moral courage, unlike anyone I have met before. Romans 12.

CHAPTER THREE

—ɯ—

THE FIRST STEP IN ORDER FOR ME to proceed with the book was to secure a visit to Parchman Prison to see Edgar Ray Killen in person. He had made previous offers for me to come visit with him, however normal visits with inmates are monitored by staff. These are normal security procedures for any such facility. It is done to prevent contraband from entering the facility, attempts at escape, and unauthorized physical contact between inmates and their visitors. The safety of visitors must also be taken into consideration, as they are close to violent offenders who may harm them or take them hostage.

Main entrance to Parchman Prison, Parchman, Mississippi.

Mr. Killen was more concerned with "the enemy" hearing what we were going to be talking about. He has a strong distrust of the Mississippi Department of Corrections (MDOC). He wrote to me about some of the abuse he'd suffered at the hands of staff, their complacency for his safety, and how other inmates had threatened him under the eye of staff and suffered no repercussions. He pointed out that Mississippi is routinely listed as one of the most corrupt states in America, and MDOC is one of the most corrupt penal systems in the country, with Parchman being one of the most violent.

He also complained that his outgoing mail was routinely withheld, and receiving his incoming mail was difficult. To circumvent these obstacles and accomplish our goals in a legal manner, Mr. Shelby Bohannon employed me as his investigator, and as his employee, I was tasked with arranging an attorney/client visit, where Mr. Killen, Mr. Bohannon, and I would be present. My initial assessment of this task was that it would be relatively easy to accomplish, as prisons or jails cannot prevent clients from seeing their attorneys. These visits are not to be monitored or recorded, and they are protected by attorney/client confidentiality, which means the attorney or client is not obligated to inform the facility or its employees of the nature of the visit.

Easy enough? Not exactly. I contacted Parchman by phone, and after letting the person who answered know what I needed, I was then transferred four times. I clearly explained to the first, second, third, and fourth person what I was calling for, and what I hoped to achieve. I was beginning to think that Mr. Killen was the first inmate in the history of Parchman to have an attorney try to visit him there. Finally, employee number five identified herself as a member of the Inmate Legal Assistance Program (ILAP). Progress? Mission accomplished? No, not quite.

Although I was armed with the essential information that Mr. Bohannon said I would need, it was not enough to satisfy what should have been a routine request. Mr. Killen had written to me on prior occasions and said that the Mississippi Department of Corrections wished to silence him, as he had information that those in power at local, state, and federal levels did not want divulged. My initial inclination to this was to think that while he wasn't necessarily lying, he may very well have been paranoid, and mistrusted those in authority, especially those who controlled his every movement.

I gave ILAP my name, as well as Mr. Bohannon's contact information, address, and Bar Assocation roll number, which would identify him as an attorney in good standing with the American Bar Association. The first question asked was, "Is Mr. Bohannon licensed to practice in Mississippi?" "Well, no, as a matter of fact he's not," I replied. "However, we're representing Mr. Killen on a Louisiana matter." Was this answer satisfactory? I'm not sure, but the next thing I was asked was, "Did Mr. Killen retain Mr. Bohannon?" I then asked for clarification of what was meant by "retain"—as in, were they asking whether Mr. Killen had somehow left Parchman, driven five hours and two hundred-plus miles on some of the most God-awful, two-lane backroads in a vehicle he didn't have, located Mr. Bohannon's office, left the confines of his wheelchair, jogged into the Bohannon Law Office, and paid a retainer fee in cash (or possibly with his American Express platinum card he kept on hand)? Yep, that's what they'd meant (and by the way, Johnny Cochran wasn't available that day).

To answer this most asinine question and remain diplomatic, I simply informed the inquiring mind that I was unaware of any financial arrangement between Mr. Killen and Mr. Bohannon, but that Mr. Bohannon had clearly expressed he did in fact represent Mr. Killen and would possibly be handling this pro bono, as he'd done for several other clients. Satisfied? Nope. Next question: "What does this concern?" Answer? "I'm not sure; however, that is attorney/client privileged information. Now for the MDOC instructions to accomplish our seemingly routine request: I would need to have Mr. Killen complete an inmate request form to have an attorney visit, and then submit the form to his case manager, who, in turn, would submit the form to ILAP.

If I have not yet mentioned this, Mr. Killen was *confined* to a wheelchair in Unit 31, which is the medical ward of Parchman. It just isn't as simple as him taking a stroll over to the case manager, obtaining this form, filling it out, and submitting it. This form would also require the pertinent information for the attorney, investigator, paralegal, etc. That very day, I sent Mr. Killen a letter outlining what I was instructed to relay to him since he did not have a telephone or a listed phone number, while I wondered why ILAP couldn't take the information I'd provided them with, and have Mr. Killen verify and sign it—all problems and formalities would be out of the way.

Too easy? Too practical? I don't know, but I do know that I waited two weeks and received a letter from Mr. Killen, who told me that he'd submitted the required forms but had not been given an answer. This was relayed to Mr. Bohannon, who called Parchman and was basically met with the same fate. He was informed that Mr. Killen had not submitted the required form. A week later, no results. I sent a letter via fax to Parchman's warden and another letter by certified mail. No response, no results. In the meantime, Mr. Killen sent me copies of the forms he'd submitted, which totaled five over the course of a month, and he still had not been given an answer by his case manager or by ILAP.

Mr. Killen had told me that he had been delayed up to eighteen months in previous attorney visits. Did every inmate at Parchman experience this problem? Or were officials taking advantage of Mr. Killen's physical limitations, intentionally causing these delays? Was it because of who he is, what he was accused and ultimately convicted of, and his staunch and outspoken views on race and segregation? More than once, he pointed out that the Mississippi Department of Corrections in general, and Parchman specifically, is what he called "black controlled." A quick search of MDOC facilities showed that all have black administrators, a majority-black employees, and are primarily occupied by black inmates.

A person may be inclined to write this experience off to the grumblings of a ninety-two-year- old, self-avowed segregationist, who was accused of one of the most well-known and well-publicized crimes of the civil rights era. That aside, Mr. Bohannon had represented thousands of clients over the course of his forty years as an attorney, and said he'd never had such difficulty getting into a jail or prison to see a client. The procedure was the same: the facility verified his name, his Bar roll number, and that he was an attorney in good standing with a current license to practice. Why was Parchman the exception?

After a couple more weeks of back-and-forth contact with the prison, I was finally told all the requirements had been fulfilled. What had changed? No explanation was given. By then it was mid-April 2017. The Inmate Legal Assistance Program informed me that I only had to call and give twenty-four-hour notice. I set the date for May 22, 2017, which would allow Mr. Bohannon and I time to clear our schedules. Not wanting to risk further complications, I asked for verification that we could bring pens, paper, and a tape recorder, as we would essentially be taking a deposition. I was informed that these items were allowed, but cellphones were not. Understood. A misplaced cellphone inside a prison could wreak havoc and be a security concern. Could we bring in extra batteries for the tape recorder, just to be safe? The last thing we needed was for the tape recorder to not work after it had taken so long to arrange the visit.

The answer? "I don't know. I've never been asked about extra batteries." "Do inmates have radios that require batteries?" I asked. "Yes, but I don't know if you can bring *extra* batteries." If inmates could purchase batteries to be used in the facility by inmates, what would be the concern with us bringing in extra batteries, especially if they remained in the package until we needed them? "I don't know if it will be a problem. Just bring them, and if it's a problem, we will throw them away."

I had no desire to further complicate matters by bringing extra batteries. I made a note to purchase fresh batteries before we got there, and I would take my chances.

CHAPTER FOUR

—◊—

OUT OF AN ABUNDANCE OF CAUTION, I called Parchman on Friday, May 19, 2017 to verify that our visit was still approved, and that the facility was not on lockdown, or experiencing any difficulties that would cause the visit to be canceled. All clear. No problems. I was reminded that attorney/client visits were Monday through Friday, from 9:00 a.m. to 3:00 p.m. No scheduled time was required in advance. We left at 6:15 a.m. that morning and arrived at the front gate at 11:30 a.m. I let the guard know who we were, and who we were there to see.

The guard, with clipboard in hand, immediately told us that we were late, and that our appointment was supposed to have been at 9:00 a.m. Because we were late, she would have to get permission from the warden to clear us to Unit 31. Mr. Bohannon and I explained to the guard that we'd been informed that we did not have to schedule a specific time to visit, as long as our visit was during the normal attorney/client visiting times.

After several minutes, Mr. Bohannon called ILAP, and due to the volume of the voice of the female who answered, I clearly heard her tell him in a rather rude voice, "The problem is you are two and a half hours late." With discretion being the better part of valor, Mr. Bohannon politely informed her that there was obviously a misunderstanding in the timeframe we had been allotted and the time we would arrive. We obviously could not have given a specific arrival time due to the distance we'd had to travel, as well as the possibility of any unforeseen delays, such as accidents, weather, etc. He was promptly told that the decision was pending from the warden's office. As soon as this call was terminated, the guard at the gate told us we were cleared to proceed and gave us directions.

When we arrived at Unit 31, we were buzzed through the front gate and front door of the building without further complications. We were met at the desk by two female guards who were very polite and professional. After looking at each of our driver's licenses to verify our identities, we were brought to an office directly behind the desk, and in short order, Edgar Ray Killen came in. Despite his age and medical issues, it was easy to tell that he had experienced a lifetime of hard physical labor. His hands were rough and scarred, and his face, creased and wrinkled.

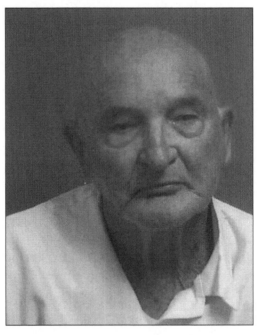

Last known photo of Edgar Ray Killen, 2017. Mississippi Department of Corrections.

From his initial appearance, a person might easily assume that Killen would be unfriendly, hard to deal with and talk to. Nothing could have been further from the truth. When we introduced ourselves, he smiled, thanked us for coming, and shook hands with us as if he we were greeting people he had known a lifetime. Mr. Bohannon had drawn up a contract prior to our trip, and the first order of business was to get this formality out of the way. Mr. Killen was readily agreeable to the terms of the contract and stated that his only concern at this point was that if our project was financially successful, he wanted his wife to be taken care of.

We began our interview, and the most natural course of questioning seemed to lead to his account of childhood. He was born in Neshoba County, Mississippi in what was known as the House Community, which he said was not identified by that name on any map, but had been called that for as long as he could remember. Given his age and the historical events that had occurred over the course of his lifetime, I asked about how his family had maintained a living during the Great Depression. His story was typical of the time and area. The family farmed, hauled pulpwood, and cut timber and anything else they could do to make a dollar. He completed high school, although a lot of his education was obtained through home schooling.

Left to right; Kenneth Killen, Edgar Ray Killen, Roy "Shorty" Killen. Circa, 1950's.

During his late teens to early twenties he began preaching in local Baptist churches, and pastored many area churches over the course of sixty odd years. He also conducted several funerals in that capacity, and that role then lead to him being looked upon as a community leader/spokesman. He also made regular radio appearances, which added to this perception. He never accepted a fee for his work as a preacher, and when asked what lead him to this calling, he said, "God knocked me on my butt and woke me up."

During this time in the South, Jim Crow laws were the normal operating procedure. Killen explained that he was raised in a time and area where segregation was simply a way of life. It had been this way long before his birth and was as much a learned behavior as was working, eating, and sleeping. Most southerners, both blacks and whites, simply wanted to be with their own kind. This practice prevented unwanted problems that would affect both races. To further this opinion, Killen clarified that he hated no person because of their race, then added, "There is no difference in the soul of a man, regardless of race. We are all two-fold beings, a body and a soul. I just choose segregation as my way of life."

During this time, his preaching earned him the nickname "Preacher." The name stuck, and he is still called by this name today. He relayed a story of driving his grandfather to a political event near his hometown, while Killen was in his late teens to early twenties. This event featured Mississippi Senator James O. Eastland as a speaker. Killen recalled that his grandfather said, after hearing the senator speak, "Edgar, you watch, that man is going places."

In years to come, Killen eventually met Senator Eastland at another event, and relayed the story of the first time he'd seen him speak—and what his grandfather had predicted. According to Killen, Eastland laughed and said, "I'm not so great." Whether this was Eastland being modest, or a lack of confidence on his part, is unknown. What is not unknown, and cannot be disputed, is that Eastland went on to become the senior US senator over the judiciary committee. By this time, Eastland and Killen had become close friends, and according to Killen, he was given security clearances that allowed him to obtain material on Eastland's behalf that Killen was read in on.

While Eastland and President Lyndon B. Johnson were often worlds apart on political issues, they had respect for each other and were close friends. According to Killen, his clearances allowed him to have access to Russia's battle plans in the event war broke out between Russia and the United States. During this time, he also became friendly with such celebrities as Louisiana humorist Justin Wilson, Mississippi comedian Jerry Clower, and was offered a position on the staff of Louisiana Governor Jimmie Davis.

In addition to these celebrities, he also became acquainted with less reputable, but no less famous, persons, such as Carlos Marcello, of New Orleans Mafia fame, Kirksey McCord Nix Jr. of the Dixie Mafia, as well as an array of CIA operatives and law enforcement officials, including FBI Director J. Edgar Hoover. Later, he would question whether these people having known his name did more harm than good.

CHAPTER FIVE

—◆—

By the early 1960s, racial integration was making its way to Mississippi. This was not well received, and whites were openly against it. Segregation was the way of life, and most white Mississippians were determined that it would stay that way. This period saw prominent politicians, such as the governors of Mississippi and Alabama, publicly announce on nationwide television that their states would never submit to federal-imposed integration and civil rights mandates. Of these prominent politicians, Senator James O. Eastland was among the most outspoken.

These men were all well-educated, and all predicted the problems that integration would cause. Lowered education standards. Increased violence among races that had been forced upon each other. Interracial marriages that would produce children that would not be accepted by either race, and affirmative action that would allow unqualified applicants to take jobs from more qualified applicants and impose quotas on businesses to hire a certain percentage of minorities, qualified or not. This would cause inferior products and business practices. If one considers what these men predicted, how far from accurate were they in terms of certain issues that America faces today? These problems aren't only applicable to the black population. How many qualified African-Americans have lost jobs or been denied employment because it was cheaper to hire illegal immigrants?

These men, much like their Confederate ancestors, were fighting a federal government that was imposing its will—state's rights be damned. If that wasn't enough, the federal government was also pushing the issue of voter rights. While this seems noble, let's put another spin on it, just for argument's sake: This was the opinion of Edgar Killen and many others in the area at that time. President Johnson had enacted and enabled the welfare class. It didn't take a lot of thought and intelligence to see that if the welfare class was allowed to vote, they would simply vote for the party that would give them the most for nothing.

Poll taxes and literacy tests were required in certain states as a voting requirement. Is this a bad thing? The liberal politicians and media would cry foul, but let's look at it from another perspective. As to the literacy test, if a voter lacks the mental capacity to cast an intelligent, informed vote, which would benefit the area's residents in the most positive way possible, what would be the likely outcome? This uninformed, unintelligent voter might simply vote for the party or candidate who would most likely provide him with the most for nothing.

How about poll taxes that dictated that those who didn't own property could not vote? Unfair? Unconstitutional? Racist? As an alternative view, if a person— regardless of race —does not *own* property, why should that person be allowed to vote on issues that only concern property owners and ultimately only *affect* property owners?

Breaking these issues down into their simplest forms, what the federal government was imposing on the southern states would essentially be akin to your local city or county government telling you that you were required, under penalty of law, to take a total stranger into your home and take care of said person's every need and want—at your expense—and you have no say in the matter. How many people would stand for this? In today's time, unfortunately, the answer is simply "Who knows?"

Such was not the case in 1964. Politicians, such as Ross Barnett, George Wallace, and James Eastland, were not accepting of this. Neither were men like Edgar Killen, and other men who had worked hard their entire lives to take care of their families. Now the freeloaders were not only going to get a free ride at honest, working peoples' expense, they were going to take over their schools, businesses, and voting polls.

Maybe . . . but not without a fight.

The summer of 1964, known as Freedom Summer, saw members of Congress of Racial Equality (CORE) come to Mississippi to register blacks to vote, and they recruited local blacks to help with these drives. Two of these CORE members were Andrew Goodman and Michael Schwerner, along with his wife Rita. They recruited a black native of Meridian, Mississippi named James Chaney to help them with their voter registration drive.

According to Killen, these two New Yorkers were not activists, but were trained Communists who were imposing communist views. Far-fetched? Impossible? The rantings of a racist? Goodman and Schwerner had trained at an Ohio training school where they were taught how to demonstrate and cause civil unrest. Killen also gave me the name of a Tennessee training school, known as Highlander Folk School, which he described as a Communist training school. I researched this school, which is still in existence, and with little effort I found that Rosa Parks had trained there *prior* to her infamous Montgomery bus ride. One may assume that her actions were a staged event, and not the result of an evil white man bullying a poor, defenseless black girl.

Sheriff Lawrence Rainey and Deputy Cecil Price. Circa 1964.

Killen, and other like-minded men, possessed the vision and fore-thought to realize that these outsiders were going to come into their areas, cause discontent between blacks and whites, and then leave, not caring what problems they had caused because they did not have to live there afterward. Therefore, the long-term ramifications were inconsequential to them. During this time, Neshoba County Sheriff's Department was headed by Sheriff Lawrence Rainey. His deputy was Cecil Ray Price.

Killen described Sheriff Rainey as "not having much formal education, but he was the best Sheriff Neshoba County ever had." According to reports, on June 21, 1964, Deputy Price arrested the trio of Schwerner, Goodman, and Chaney on speeding and investigation of having burned a nearby church. They were held for several hours while Killen allegedly assembled a team of Klansmen. When they were released, Deputy Price, who was reputedly a Klansman, along with more Klansmen, followed the trio out of town and then stopped them.

The three were forced into Price's car and brought to "Old Jolly Farm," where Goodman and Schwerner were each shot and killed. Chaney was beaten and tortured before being shot, and the three were buried fifteen feet under an earthen dam. Their car was brought to a swamp and set on fire. Forty-four days later, the bodies were discovered, and ultimately the case was solved by the diligent efforts of the five hundred FBI agents who descended upon Philadelphia, Mississippi.

This account is a synopsis, as it was relayed by Edgar Killen. Please keep in in mind that this is a generalized account, and many detailed accounts are available. The accuracy of each account is up to the reader to decide. This is Mr. Killen's version, and it generally conforms to other versions that have been released.

CHAPTER SIX

—m—

DURING THE SUBSEQUENT INVESTIGATION CONDUCTED BY the FBI, Killen and other accused participants continued in their normal day-to-day activities. The State of Mississippi refused to pursue murder charges and at that time there was no federal statute for murder unless it occurred on federal land, such as military instillations and Indian reservations. It has been reported that the federal authorities met with state authorities in the governor's office, and it was finally agreed that the federal authorities would pursue a civil rights case against their suspects.

Eighteen men, including Killen, Sheriff Rainey, and Deputy Price were indicted on civil rights violations. The trial in the case of United States v. Cecil Price *et al.*, also known as the Mississippi Burning Trial, began on October 7, 1967 in the federal courthouse in Meridian, Mississippi. Judge William Cox, who was a known opponent of the civil rights movement and against integration, presided over the trial. A jury was selected and consisted of seven white men and five white women. Defense attorneys exercised peremptory challenges against all seventeen potential black jurors.

While undergoing questioning by the US attorney for Mississippi, Robert Hauberg, one juror, a white man, admitted he had been a member of the KKK several years prior. This was challenged for cause, but Judge Cox denied the challenge. The trial had frequent crises. The prosecution's star witness, James Jordan, cracked under the pressure of alleged death threats and had to be hospitalized. The jury deadlocked on a decision, and Judge Cox invoked the Allen charge to bring them to a resolution.

Alton Wayne Roberts, the alleged shooter of Schwerner and Goodman. Circa 1967.

On October 20, 1967, seven of the defendants were found guilty. These men were Deputy Cecil Price, Alton Wayne Roberts, Jimmy Snowden, Billy Wayne Posey, Horace Barnett, Jimmy Arledge, and Samuel Bowers, who held the title of imperial wizard [in charge of state level] in the Ku Klux Klan,. None of these men were sentenced to more than ten years, and none served more than six years. Sheriff Lawrence Rainey, along with E. G. Barnett, who was a candidate for sheriff, and Edgar Ray Killen were all acquitted. The jury was deadlocked on their charges and the prosecutor decided to not retry them. The one holdout for Killen was a woman juror who said that she could not allow herself to convict a preacher.

Billy Wayne Posey. Circa 1967.

Sam Bowers, the alleged "imperial wizard" of the Mississippi White Knights of the Ku Klux Klan. Circa 1967.

Edgar Ray Killen (with glasses) and Deputy Cecil Ray Price at
1967 civil rights trial in Meridian, Mississippi.

What isn't commonly told in this case is the fact that a hitman from the Colombo Mafia family, Gregory Scarpa (also known as the "Grim Reaper"), was used as an informant for the FBI. According to Scarpa's girlfriend, Linda Schiro, the FBI had had no luck in solving the case of the murdered trio, so they enlisted the help of Scarpa. When Scarpa and his girlfriend arrived in Mississippi, they were brought to a hotel, where the FBI furnished him with a pistol and gave him $30,000 to "solve" the case.

Scarpa, accompanied by an FBI agent, went to Byrd's Radio and TV Service in Laurel. Scarpa and the agent bought a TV from Lawrence Byrd, a Klansman, as Byrd was closing for the day. Byrd helped them carry the TV to their car, where he was forced at gunpoint to get inside and was pistol-whipped. When asked about the validity of this accusation, Killen agreed that it did in fact happen, and added that Byrd was then taken to Camp Shelby Army Base, where a "gun was shoved down his throat and Scarpa went to work on him with a straight razor."

Is this the grumbling of a senile, ninety-two-year-old man? Is Killen shifting blame? Making excuses? As it turns out, the answer is most likely no. It was well established in the 1967 trial that Killen had been seen by dozens of people at a funeral home, where he was attending a wake for a relative, at the time the trio was killed. It has been established, re-established, and verified by an untold number of people that Killen was nowhere near the murder scene, and took no physical part in the murder.

There is no question that Byrd was severely beaten, in addition to that fact that Byrd signed a twenty-two-page document in which he confessed and implicated others. Former Prosecutor Chet Dillard was convinced that it was Scarpa who beat Byrd, who Dillard knew and visited in the hospital. Before his death, Scarpa allegedly told the story of kidnapping and beating Byrd (who never fully recovered, physically or mentally, from his encounter with the "Grim Reaper"), and he connected Byrd and others to the murder of the civil rights workers and divulged the location of where the victims' bodies were buried.

It has even been speculated by that unknown FBI agents that Scarpa, while employed as an informant, continued to conduct mob killings with impunity from the FBI, and may have killed as many as thirty people without repercussions. Ironically, according to this version of accounts, that meant the FBI essentially aided and allowed Scarpa and an agent to violate Byrd's civil rights while the FBI was simultaneously attempting to build a civil rights case against Killen and others.

CHAPTER SEVEN

—⚏—

THE SCARPA CONNECTION TO THE MURDERS might seem questionable to some readers, but remember, even a prosecutor agreed that the allegations were true. Edgar Killen, through his connection with Senator Eastland, was allowed to participate in late-night meetings at the White House, had security clearances that allowed him to review documents, and was able to listen to recordings made in the Oval Office and other government offices.

Senator James O. Eastland with President Lyndon B. Johnson. Circa 1964.

Killen said he was told by Senator Eastland that President Lyndon Johnson was under intense public and media pressure to end America's involvement in Vietnam. The problem for Johnson was money—pure and simple. Johnson, who was a Texas congressman in the 1940s, helped secure a contract for two brothers, Herman and George Brown, who owned a Texas firm named Brown and Root, to construct Mansfield Dam near Austin, Texas. This company eventually evolved into Halliburton, which was operated by Dick Cheney before he served as vice president of the United States. Halliburton eventually distanced itself from Cheney after numerous reports of "sweetheart deals."

During Johnson's term in office, Brown and Root was paid an estimated $380 million to build airports, bases, hospitals, and other facilities for the US Navy in South Vietnam. Johnson, not wanting to lose the money that Brown and Root was kicking back to him, needed a distraction or diversion. By now, anti-war protestors were protesting Brown and Root, citing accusations that it was part of a military-industrial complex, and protesters denounced the company for building detention cells to hold Viet Cong prisoners in South Vietnam.

The necessary distraction, according to Killen, was Johnson instructing the CIA to organize young civil rights workers, such as the murdered trio, to come to the South to be part of massive voter registration and integration projects. Johnson, himself a southerner, most certainly knew the reaction that this would garner—and the results would take attention away from Vietnam and make the focus on issues closer to home.

Should readers doubt this, let's review a few quotes from former President Johnson, who, in public, was a champion of civil rights, but never shied away from using racial slurs in private: He referred to the 1957 Civil Rights Act as "the nigger bill," and when he appointed African-American Judge Thurgood Marshall to the Supreme Court, Johnson said, "Son, when I appoint a nigger to the court, I want everyone to know he's a nigger." According to historian Doris Goodwin, Johnson also uttered this cynical statement: "These Negroes, they're getting pretty uppity these days, and that's a problem for us, since they've got something now they never had before, the political pull to back up their uppityness. Now we've got to do something about this; we've got to give them a little something, just enough to quiet them down, but not enough to make a difference. For if we don't move at all, then their allies will line up against us and there'll be no way of stopping them. We'll lose the filibuster, and there'll be no way of putting a brake on all sorts of wild legislation. It'll be Reconstruction all over again."

For the moment, let's skip ahead to nearly half a century later and take into consideration a statement made by James Stern, a black preacher from Los Angeles (who is discussed further later in the book). I spoke with Mr. Stern the day after my visit with Edgar Killen. During our conversation, he told me that he had personal knowledge of a CIA plot to introduce and promote crack cocaine within the black population of Los Angeles. Why? To take the profits and funnel them to the CIA's army in Nicaragua, known as the Contras. For further information on this, you can read about "Freeway" Ricky Ross. It would also behoove the reader to research the case of Barry Seals, who smuggled cocaine as a CIA operative and DEA informant. This was also connected to the Contras, and Mr. Seals was assassinated in Baton Rouge, Louisiana for his efforts.

Again, we will get to back to Mr. Stern as the story progresses, but for the time being, just know that James Stern and Edgar Killen are about as opposite as any two persons can be, yet they do agree on one thing: The CIA creates diversions for the gain of their own and others' agendas.

Killen also spoke of Lydon B. Johnson's involvement in the death of John F. Kennedy. According to Killen, Johnson had Kennedy killed because of Kennedy's reluctance to get involved in Vietnam. Johnson, as we have seen, stood to make untold sums of money from America's involvement in Vietnam. Before the reader gets too excited, no, Killen did not reveal the name of the actual triggerman. What Killen *did* say, was that Johnson, through financial backing of Mafia boss Carlos Marcello in New Orleans, arranged the assassination with aid from the CIA.

Why would Marcello, a known Mafia member, take such risks on behalf of the government? The answer, according to Killen, is simple. US

Attorney General Robert Kennedy, brother of President Kennedy, had Marcello deported—and Marcello wanted revenge. If he could not get Robert Kennedy, Kennedy's brother would make an acceptable alternative. The plot was carried out and the rest is history. John F. Kennedy met his demise on November 22, 1963 in Dallas, Texas.

Yet President Kennedy, as Killen tells it, was not as pure as he portrayed himself to be. It has been well documented through the years that President Kennedy was quite the womanizer and had an illicit affair with Norma Jeane Mortenson, a.k.a. Marilyn Monroe. According to Killen, when Ms. Monroe wanted more from JFK than just than a fling, she became a liability after JFK had revealed too much to her about the inner workings of the Oval Office. The answer to this problem? As Edgar tells it, the solution was rather simple: Robert Kennedy and various CIA operatives went to her residence, murdered her, and then staged the scene. Kennedy had stayed in the car to distance himself from the scene but remain close enough to verify that the mission had been completed.

This version of Ms. Monroe's death has been circulated and denied by various parties for years. Yet Killen, who was most certainly privy to such information and has nothing at this point to lose, verifies these accusations. In his letters to me, he stated that certain parties had contacted him during his incarceration and asked that he never reveal his knowledge of the Kennedy assassination. Taken into consideration the totality of the circumstances—Killen's security clearances, his working and personal relationship with Senator Eastland, and Eastland's relationship with Lyndon Johnson—I tend to believe Killen's story has quite a bit of merit.

CHAPTER EIGHT

—⚏—

I, AS A WRITER WHO WANTED TO tell the story of Edgar Ray Killen in its entirety, fully intended to fill the reader in on the details of Killen's life between the years of 1967 and 2005, when his second trial took place. Forty years is a long time to cover, yet when Killen was asked what he'd done during this time frame, he summarized it: "I operated my sawmill, preached on Sunday, and did my best to avoid the media, which would pop up once a year or so." Sometimes the simplest explanation is the most honest.

I wanted to delve further into this. Not that I doubted Killen, but I wanted a second source with this information, not only so I could verify his statements, but to see whether Killen was a constant problem for his community in general, and for law enforcement particularly.

Killen provided me with contact information for his wife, Betty Jo, who was eighty years old and living on social security. His concern was for her financial well-being. Mr. Bohannon and I agreed to a contract that would entitle Mrs. Killen to a portion of the proceeds of book sales that would go directly to her, or to whomever Mr. Killen designated. I phoned Mrs. Killen, and after some delays, we finally connected. Mrs. Killen told me that she and Edgar had only been married seven years at the time of his conviction, yet she was certain he hadn't participated in the murders in any way, shape, or form. I sent her a copy of the contract Killen and I had signed, as well as what I had written of the book up to that point. I also offered to change, correct, or edit anything I had written, should she believe it would cause her any hardship. A few changes were made, however it was nothing that would take away from the accuracy of what Edgar Killen relayed to me. Mrs. Killen was nothing less than accommodating and cordial, and it is my hope that she benefits from this endeavor.

Edgar Ray Killen and Betty Jo Killen. Circa 1997.

Edgar Ray Killen and Betty Jo Killen. Circa 1998.

Killen had also suggested that I contact the Neshoba County sheriff as well as the chief investigator for the sheriff. He holds both men in high regard, and stressed that they were good and fair men. A convicted criminal making positive statements toward law enforcement? Surely the sheriff and his investigator could provide fair and impartial insight. Not exactly. I phoned the sheriff's office and asked the lady who answered the phone if I could speak to the sheriff. She inquired as to the nature of my call. My response was that I was seeking the sheriff's input regarding his knowledge of Mr. Killen, or anything he knew about Killen from a personal standpoint.

The lady I spoke with listened politely as I explained to her that I was writing Killen's biography and was seeking stories about him from those who knew him personally. After I finished my sales pitch, the lady informed me that the sheriff would not be able to speak with me because he was "an elected official and this [was] a very political matter." Political matter? Killen had been convicted twelve years prior to my request for personal observations and recollections. What could possibly have been harmful to the sheriff, politically or otherwise, in sharing personal input and observations about a man who thought highly of him, and who was obviously no threat to him in any manner?

The next step was to send an email request to the chief investigator requesting the same information. Once again, I clearly explained what I was requesting and why I was requesting it. The response? Nothing. Here we had two professional lawmen not responding to basic inquiries about who is quite possibly one of the most famous, if not the *most famous*, accused murderers in the history of Mississippi. I guess stranger things have happened.

CHAPTER NINE

—ɯ—

Not to be deterred, I continued to seek out anyone who could provide insight to Edgar's story, regardless of how seemingly unimportant their input may have seemed on the surface. I located the name and phone number of someone who was closely connected to Killen's trial. This person requested that I not mention him by name, or even state what his role had been in the trial, as he believed he could potentially face severe unwanted consequences for sharing his input and opinion. I gave my name and background information to during the conversation, and I could tell that he was on a computer verifying my name and the information I'd provided.

Apparently, I'd passed the internet test, and he then began to speak a little more freely. I asked if he was aware that Killen had suffered severe head and brain trauma three months prior to his trial, in addition to two broken femurs after a tree had fallen on his head. The answer was, "No, nobody was made aware of that." My next question was whether the judge, prosecutor, or defense had asked for a competency hearing. Seemingly, these considerations would fall under basic court procedures 101: Was Edgar Killen able to physically withstand the rigors of a trial? Was Edgar Killen mentally able to aid and assist in his own defense? The answer to my question? "No, it was never mentioned in court."

This coincided with Killen's previous written statement to me that the trial judge, Marcus Gordon, refused to allow the jury to see Killen's private nurse treat him or provide him with any care or give him medication. It would seem likely, and prudent, that the judge would have the forethought to order a competency hearing if for no other reason than to prevent the case from being reversed on appeal. Killen's defense team most certainly should have requested a hearing, and the prosecution, in the form of Mississippi Attorney General Jim Hood, should have requested this most basic service out of caution, and maybe even fairness to the accused, who by all rights was innocent until proven guilty.

For the record, as well as for the sake of posterity, I did send an email to Mr. Hood outlining the basis of this project and requested his input and opinion. I received no response. In all fairness, I give credit to the responsibilities of his office; however, this was a landmark case, and I would assume that any inquiries would be worthy of his attention. As to Judge Gordon, I asked Killen during our visit why an experienced trial judge would allow such questionable actions to take place in his court, in a trial that garnered world-wide attention.

To start, Killen stated that he'd requested the media not be allowed to film any portion of the trial. That request was denied. Proof? Search Youtube for C-SPAN coverage of the trial. Killen also requested that his trial be judged by another judge. Why? Well, Killen described Judge Gordon as a "long time enemy" of his. During our visit, I asked him to elaborate. This is a synopsis of his explanation: Killen had known Gordon since he was a child, and had even delivered the eulogy at Gordon's parents' funerals. However, in later years, their paths crossed again.

Killen was practicing law in a time when having a license to practice law was not required, and standards differed. He was working as defense for the suspect in a shooting that had taken place, and Gordon had been assigned to prosecute the case. As Killen tells it, he questioned the witnesses who stated they'd been watching TV, when they heard shots and then witnessed the accused standing over the victim. The distance from which they had seen the accused was over a hundred yards, and it had been at nighttime. According to Killen, he questioned the witnesses who admitted the "shots" they'd heard were from the TV show *Bonanza*, and that they'd said as much to Gordon, who had interviewed them prior to Killen's visit.

The response from Gordon to the witnesses, as Killen tells it consisted of Gordon informing the witnesses that they'd heard shots at the time, regardless of the source. When this information was revealed in court, it cost Gordon the case, which prompted Gordon to inform Killen that he "better never set foot in his court again." If this is any indication, grudges must run deep in Neshoba County. Ironically, according to Killen, these witnesses were black, and yet Killen pursued the truth despite color and racial boundaries.

As Killen, Mr. Bohannon, and I were talking, Mrs. Linda Bohannon, Mr. Bohannon's wife, was taking notes, as she was his paralegal. On occasion, Killen would express his opinions and answers in what he thought was a manner "not fit for a lady to hear." Although by today's standards these statements were mild, especially considering the setting—a maximum-security prison where Killen had spent twelve years—he constantly apologized whenever he thought his answers were "not fit for mixed company." He was a true gentleman in every sense of the word, and his mannerisms reflected the times in which he was raised and the values common to that era. It was only after our visit was concluded that I realized the impression that his politeness had left on Mrs. Bohannon.

CHAPTER TEN

—✳︎—

OUR CONVERSATION EVENTUALLY PROGRESSED TO THE subject of the murdered trio of civil rights workers. Killen's response was simple: He was not there, did not plan it, did not organize it, did not order it, and did not authorize it. No lengthy explanations, excuses, or counter accusations. He simply stated that he was not there, and that much cannot be—and *is not*—disputed. There are allegations by some, who were paid FBI informants, who stated the lynch mob met at a local diner and then went to a local mobile home dealership, where the plans were finalized, all under Killen's direction.

Killen then went to a funeral home to attend a wake to establish an "alibi," since he would allegedly be the first one questioned. Just for the sake of objectivity, let's assume this scenario to be 100 percent accurate. The "hit squad" consisted of several men, which allegedly included Deputy Sheriff Cecil Price, who then followed through with the murders, burned the vehicle, and buried the bodies. In the time between when these men had left Killen's presence and when the trio was later located, did any of these men, all of whom had free will, ever once think that maybe this hadn't been the smartest of plans?

Were these men, including an armed deputy, so fearful of Killen that they couldn't have simply agreed to tell him they'd been unable to find the trio and had had to abort the plan? If Killen was in fact in charge of this plot, why did Deputy Price not report that to his sheriff, which would have led to Killen's subsequent arrest for his part in this conspiracy? It was and still is widely speculated as being true is that Sheriff Rainey knew about and had approved this plot. After being acquitted in 1967, there is no doubt that Sheriff Rainey suffered greatly from a professional standpoint.

He was never able to return to law enforcement, lost his bid for re-election, and later worked as a mechanic and security guard in Kentucky and Mississippi. He blamed the FBI for having kept him from being able to find and keep jobs. In 2002, he died from throat and tongue cancer at age seventy-nine in Meridian, Mississippi. Ironically, one of his employers, a black man, described him as a good and decent man.

Moving forward to 2005: How did a new trial against Edgar Killen come to fruition? Before we delve get into this, the reader should know that I attempted to solicit opinions from outside sources on these details. Contact was made by phone with the sons of Sheriff Rainey and Deputy Price. It was explained to each of their sons that I was writing Edgar Killen's biography, and would like their input on him or whether they might know anything about him. Neither wished to be involved. As an afterthought, I considered that their having received a phone call from a total stranger regarding their now deceased fathers and events that had altered their lives had probably been unsettling. I wrote letters to Mr. Rainey and Mr. Price to clarify that I would not be writing anything negative about their fathers or their families; I was only interested in telling Edgar Killen's story. I received no response from either man, and I pray each of them and their families do not continue to suffer from what happened.

Back to the 2005 trial: Schwerner, Goodman, and Chaney had planned to open a voter rights school at Mt. Zion Methodist Church, a small black church in Neshoba County. Every June, since 1965, the church held an anniversary to commemorate the murdered trio. Dick Molpus, a Neshoba County native and Mississippi's secretary of state, was at one of these events and urged the crowd to apologize for what had happened. No apology was forthcoming, but the controversy of the idea generated an interest in reopening the case. There was also intense pressure from the Philadelphia Coalition to hold someone accountable for the sake of Neshoba County's image. Jerry Mitchell, a journalist for *The Clarion-Ledger* in Jackson, Mississippi, somehow "discovered,"—then published—a sealed letter from Sam Bowers, former imperial wizard in the Ku Klux Klan. In this "sealed letter"—one that a reporter had apparently been able to find when law enforcement had not been able to—Bowers allegedly named Edgar Killen as the mastermind of the murder plot.

Sam Bowers. Circa 1964.

No new evidence had been brought forth since the 1967 trial. Allegedly, former Deputy Sheriff Cecil Price had agreed to cooperate with the district attorney, however Price passed away on May 6, 2001 from injuries suffered in a fall. No record of conversation between Price and the district attorney was mentioned during Edgar Killen's trial. Please keep that fact in mind, because it will be relevant later. As to Bowers' sealed letter, if he had indeed named Edgar Killen as the mastermind, why hadn't Bowers been brought to Killen's trial to testify? Why wasn't this newly discovered letter introduced into evidence? Bowers should have been easy to find, as he was incarcerated in Parchman Prison and remained there until his death in 2006—well after Killen's trial. Quite possibly, Bowers could have been given consideration for rolling over on Killen—except that privilege was only afforded to a convicted child rapist, Mike Winstead, who we'll discuss further later on.

Sam Bowers will again be discussed in a later chapter. To give fair warning, what Mr. Bowers was documented as having said lends credibility to Killen's possible innocence, and it will quite possibly make the reader further question the idea that there are extremes your government—at local, state, and federal levels—will go to in order to secure convictions on someone they've deemed a worthy target.

CHAPTER ELEVEN

—m—

ENTER MISSISSIPPI STATE ATTORNEY GENERAL JIM HOOD. Why would the state's attorney general want to personally prosecute a forty-year-old murder case, especially considering no new evidence had been found to potentially make that task easier? The answer, as Killen tells it, is simple. Hood had ambitions of garnering media favor and attention and riding that wave directly into the governor's office in the next election.

Mississippi Attorney General Jim Hood at 2005 trial of Edgar Ray Killen.

Judge Marcus Gordon during 2005 trial of Edgar Ray Killen.

The trial began on June 13, 2005 and lasted five days. The jury, which consisted of nine whites and three blacks, heard the testimony, which mostly involved role players reading the transcripts of the testimony from the 1967 trial. While this may have been legal, take into consideration the fact that reading forty-year-old testimonies from persons, who were at that point deceased, does not afford the accused or his defense the opportunity to cross-examine. It does not allow the jury to see firsthand the person who gave the testimony in order to form their opinion on that actual person. Facial expressions and body language say a lot, and can quite possibly shed a different light on matters, which could determine the fate of the accused. It is also noteworthy that the Neshoba County District Attorney Marcus Duncan played the role of a 1967 witness who had provided testimony. Why was this allowed, as he obviously had a vested interest in the case? Not to mention, that as a prosecuting attorney, he was well versed in ways to present images to a jury.

Marcus Duncan, District Attorney of Neshoba County, Mississippi during Edgar Ray Killen's 2005 trial.

The testimony from "live" witnesses for Edgar Killen essentially stated that he had been at a family gathering the entire day on June 21, 1964, which sealed the fact that in the hours before the murder,

Killen was not in the presence of any of the other accused persons. Others confirmed his presence at a funeral home that evening. Two notable pro-Killen witnesses were Harlan Majure, the former mayor of Philadelphia, and Kenneth Killen, Edgar Killen's younger brother. In Mr. Majure's testimony, he stated that Killen had a good reputation in the community. When asked if he knew that Killen was a member of the Klan, he stated he did not, and that if Killen *were* a member, that wouldn't necessarily change Majure's opinion of him. When asked if he was aware that the Klan was a violent organization, he said that statement wasn't necessarily true; he knew things about the Klan that others did not, and the Klan did a lot of good.

In Kenneth Killen's testimony, he was asked about Edgar Killen's Klan connections. This question was posed by District Attorney Marcus Duncan. Kenneth Killen's reply? "I've heard more about *your* father and grandfather being in the Klan than Edgar." Even Edgar Killen's enemy, Judge Gordon, had to snicker at that response.

Kenneth Killen testifying on behalf of his brother, Edgar Ray Killen, at his 2005 trial.

Speaking of Judge Gordon, I asked Edgar Killen why he hadn't gotten a change of venue, or at least had Gordon recuse himself due to their prior negative interactions? Killen said he had in fact asked his lead attorney, Mitch Moran, to do exactly that. Moran told Killen that the only way he would represent him was if Gordon was the judge. What was unknown to Killen was that Moran was facing legal troubles of his own in the form of drug charges.

Edgar Ray Killen at his 2005 trial.

Edgar Ray Killen at his 2005 trial.

According to Killen, Moran had agreed to essentially bungle the case from the start—which he was able to do very well—to assure Killen's conviction. Moran's reward, aside from acquiring a hefty amount of money for his legal services, was that Judge Gordon would take care of Moran's legal troubles. James McIntyre, who served as co-counsel, had in no way, shape, or form been approved by Killen. Subsequently, McIntyre was permanently disbarred from practicing law in Mississippi. Does anything about this situation stink to you yet?

Other notable "live" witnesses were Mike Winstead and Mike Hatcher. In their cases, it wasn't clear whether they'd had anything to gain, or if they had been coerced into testifying. Mike Winstead, a convicted child rapist, was brought to Neshoba County Court from Parchman Prison, and testified that when he was ten years old, he'd overheard his grandfather ask Edgar Killen if Killen had had anything to do with the murder of the trio. Killen's response, according to Mike Winstead, had been, "Yes, and I'm proud of it." Did the prosecutor take any steps to verify this "admission"? No. Did the prosecutor—or the defense, for that matter—challenge Winstead as to why he'd held this secret since childhood? No. Did Winstead only tell this story decades later when he'd stood to benefit from doing so? It seems likely this was the case.

Ironically, Winstead's brother, David Winstead, was called as a defense witness for Edgar Killen. He stated that he believed his brother was lying about hearing the conversation between Edgar Killen and their grandfather. It seems safe to assume that when Winstead was transported to Neshoba from Parchman Prison, Bowers could have carpooled with him, as he would have had firsthand testimony. Again, why was this option not explored? Could it possibly have been that Bowers would have provided testimony that would not have benefitted Jim Hood's ambitions to become governor?

Mike Hatcher, a retired Meridian, Mississippi police officer, had testified in 1967 that he effectively knew nothing, and had no involvement in the murders. His testimony was likely pivotal, in that it resulted in further suspects not being convicted, if in fact they had been guilty. However, in 2005, this story changed. Hatcher admitted under oath that he'd lied in 1967 because he didn't want to be killed. He testified that Killen had told him, after the murders had taken place, "We got rid of goatee," in reference to Schwerner. As Killen puts it, Hatcher said "we"—not "he"—got rid of Schwerner, and he assumes that by "we," Hatcher had meant the Klan. However, Killen denies the conversation ever taking place, and no one has been able to substantiate the claim made by Hatcher.

To be fair, prior to writing this portion of the story, I contacted Mr. Hatcher by phone. I explained to him what I was doing and solicited his opinion. His response: "I don't know anything about that." He did verify that he was the same Mike Hatcher who had retired from the Meridian Police Department, which left no doubt that I had contacted the same person. He didn't know anything about that? He certainly knew enough to lie under oath in 1967. He certainly knew enough to remain silent throughout his career, effectively stalling the investigation of a triple murder for forty years. How about these crimes Officer Hatcher committed without having to suffer legal consequences? Obstruction of justice, perjury, malfeasance, accessory charges? What favors were granted to Hatcher, who by his own admission (assuming he wasn't lying again), was at least as culpable as Edgar Killen?

It has been reported that Cecil Price had agreed to cooperate with the district attorney. If that is true, and if the district attorney had recorded statements made by Price—as any rookie investigator would surely have obtained—why weren't those statements introduced in Edgar Killen's trial? Certainly, they should have been at least as admissible as the forty-year-old trial transcripts that were recited by role players. Maybe Price's cooperation was merely a scare tactic. We will never know.

CHAPTER TWELVE

—⟶∿⟵—

AT THE TIME EDGAR KILLEN WAS INDICTED, the following people suspected of having active roles in the murder of the trio were still alive: Jimmy Arledge, Sam Bowers, Olen Burrage, James Harris, Richard Willis, Billy Wayne Posey, Jimmy Snowden, and Jimmy Lee Townsend. There is an old saying in legal circles, "A prosecutor can indict a ham sandwich if he wants to," and the basis of that statement is that an indictment is merely a formal charge, and not an indication of guilt. It's almost like a police officer making a probable cause arrest. The charge is filed, yet it still must be proven in court. The prosecutor has quite a bit of leeway in a grand jury setting, as it is far less than formal than court, and the prosecutor's only burden is to convince the grand jury to formally charge the defendant.

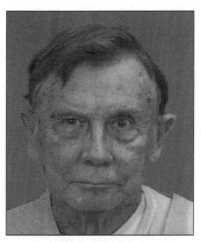

Sam Bowers, official Mississippi Department of Corrections photo. Circa 2005.

Billy Wayne Posey at the 2005 trial of Edgar Ray Killen.

*Olen Burrage, circa 1967. Burrage owned "The Old Jolly Farm" where the bodies
of the murdered trio were found buried 15 feet beneath an earthen dam, 44 days
after they were reported missing.*

It has been reported that James "Pete" Harris was accused of making
the phone calls with the intention "to gather the Klansmen." If in fact
this is true, that makes him an active conspirator. Jimmy Lee Townsend
was reported as having been in one of the cars that chased after the trio.

That would, at minimum, put Townsend at the scene, while Edgar Killen was indisputably not there. Olen Burrage owned the property where the trio had been buried late at night by means of a bulldozer, yet Burrage never heard a bulldozer running on his property in the middle of the night, and had no idea how the bodies had gotten there. He also had reportedly furnished a gallon of gasoline to burn the station wagon the boys were in when they'd been stopped, and then used one of his eighteen wheelers to go to the location where the car was burned—though large trucks on the road at late hours were not a common sight. Does this alleged involvement seem worthy of further consideration?

It would seem so, yet as one grand jury member stated, Jim Hood had not provided enough evidence to indict anyone but Edgar Killen. Given Hood's reputation, training, and experience, it seems a fair assumption that this was by Hood's design rather than the choice of the grand jury. It seems Edgar Killen was the *target*, possibly due to his outspoken views on race and segregation, although his views, while unpopular and not politically correct, certainly do not constitute criminal behavior. Also noteworthy is that none of the other suspected participants were called as witnesses by the prosecution or defense. It would seem the other suspected participants might have had more insight than a convicted child rapist—who was ten years old when he allegedly heard Edgar Killen's "confession"—or the testimony of a self-admitted liar, a retired police officer who'd stayed silent about the murders for decades. Had Hatcher have come forward, the case could have been resolved years earlier. So much for his oath to uphold the law and constitution.

On the fourth day of the trial, the jury broke to begin deciding Edgar Killen's fate. After several hours, the jury was stalled at six to six. When informed of this, Judge Gordon told the jury to consider an alternative charge of manslaughter. In trial settings, a charge hearing is held *prior* to the start of the trial. This is the *legal* way that potential charges are agreed upon by the judge, the prosecution, and the defense. It is not to be used as a means to later play "let's make a deal." Why would Gordon have offered this alternative to the jury when Edgar Killen was indicted on three counts of second degree murder? Could it be that the judge wanted a conviction that would allow him to bid good riddance to Edgar Killen, settling a decades-old grudge?

Maybe the jurors were allowing their consciences to tell them to consider the fact that this man was eighty years old, half crippled, and there was absolutely no verifiable, conclusive evidence that had been provided. Not to mention, that near the beginning of the trial, Edgar Killen had to be taken by ambulance out of the courtroom and treated for extremely high blood pressure. In theory, a defendant is supposed to have the right to be tried "by a jury of his peers." When one considers that for a moment, just who on that jury would have been considered Edgar Killen's "peer"? None of the jurors were eighty years old. None had been born and raised in similar conditions and taught the same values that he had been during the time in which these values were so common.

This man was being tried for a 1964 allegation under the standards and practices of the year 2005. The values, practices, and standards of 1964 would have been totally alien to the jurors, and it's likely not one of them was able to completely grasp the thoughts and feelings people had at that time because it was a different era.

The jury returned with their verdict on June 21, 2005. It was a unanimous vote of guilty on three counts of manslaughter. Prior to rendering their verdict, did the jury know that the penalty associated with manslaughter was a maximum of twenty years? There's a good possibility that answer is no. According to juror John Miller, had Judge Gordon not offered the alternative of manslaughter, Edgar Killen would not have been convicted of murder. Miller also added that it was quite possible Edgar Killen had been a scapegoat. Would this statement constitute "reasonable doubt?"

Killen was sentenced by Judge Gordon to three, consecutive, twenty-year terms, a total of sixty years. This was essentially a death sentence. If the jury would not find him guilty of murder, then why would they find him guilty of manslaughter? Remember, Killen was not present when the crime occurred, there was no physical evidence linking him to the crime, numerous people had verified his whereabouts before and during the time of the murders, and many others who were far more culpable than Edgar Killen weren't indicted or called to testify. Again, it would seem those testimonies would have been more credible and beneficial to the prosecution than the ones that had come from a child rapist and a lying cop—unless the prosecution knew these persons would vindicate Edgar Killen. In that case, why bother putting those people on the stand? It didn't fit into their agenda.

Going back to the jury, in the documentary *Neshoba*, juror Warren Paprocki is shown stating that the black jury members obviously did not like Edgar Killen. In most jury selections—and one can only assume Mississippi follows the same guidelines—potential jurors are pooled to determine if they can put aside their personal feelings and prejudices. If they cannot, they are normally excused from jury duty. Does "reasonable doubt" come to mind again? Did any of these black jurors lie to get selected just so they could vote guilty? The answer seems to be yes, if that answer is based on the *Neshoba* documentary, where juror Greg Griffin expresses the sentiment that he "wanted to fry" Edgar Killen, and was determined to render a guilty verdict. Where was the outcry over the prejudiced juror who had obviously lied during jury selection in order to render his own pre-determined decision?

If there was no outcry over the actions of the jurors, why wasn't there outcry over some of Mr. Hood's actions? During the questioning of a Baptist preacher concerning the preacher's opinion and/or knowledge of Edgar Killen, Hood inquired about the location of Killen's home and offered a specific road number as a reference. The preacher stated he did not know the exact road name or number, but had always referred to the road as the "Killen Road." This was, even to the average layman with basic knowledge of court procedures, the preacher's way of expressing that it was called that because many members of the Killen family resided there. Not to be outdone or outsmarted, the "Honorable" Mr. Hood asked whether the preacher had said it was called "Killen" or "*Killing* Road." Was Hood admonished by Judge Gordon for this obviously inflammatory statement intended to provoke the jury? Not a chance. Did Edgar Killen's attorneys object and ask that the remark be stricken? Not even close. When these undisputable facts are taken into consideration, is it far-fetched that Edgar Killen's allegations could have quite a bit of merit to them, and are worthy of consideration? Beyond that possibility, any of these factors could be considered potential grounds for a retrial or mistrial.

CHAPTER THIRTEEN

—ɯ—

As PREVIOUSLY MENTIONED, DURING OUR VISIT with Edgar Killen, his politeness and manners were exemplary. He could not have been more cordial and accommodating if we'd been in his home talking over coffee. I am more than two generations removed from Edgar Killen in age, yet he talked with me as if we had known each other for years. Mr. and Mrs. Bohannon, while younger than Killen, are from his same generation, and still recall when manners like Killen's were routinely displayed— and anything less was unacceptable

When we left the building where Edgar is housed and returned to our vehicle, Mrs. Bohannon made this statement: "That is one of the most polite, kind, and Godly men I have ever met. He didn't hurt anybody." I had formed this same opinion; however, I had researched quite a bit of information about Killen prior to our visit. Mrs. Bohannon, even though she was proceeding into unknown territory and had no prior knowledge of Killen, had worked in legal services for several years—and she was no pushover when it came to dealing with criminals.

When I asked Killen about his thoughts on the documentary *Neshoba*, he said he was disappointed in the way the documentary had portrayed him, especially considering that one of the producers, Micki Dickoff, had spent considerable time with both Edgar and Mrs. Killen in their home as a guest, under the guise that she was in favor of Edgar Killen being acquitted. From watching *Neshoba*, it may be assumed that it approaches things from a very left-leaning, liberal point of view. That was

Killen's view and I concur. President Barack Obama was even quoted as having said about the film, "Their legacy is our heritage." I bet Edgar Killen would have told Micki where she could put her film if he'd known Obama's opinion was going to be solicited!

Potential leftist views aside, the film was a wealth of information, as it revealed the obvious prejudicial statements made by jury members, a judge who allowed the prosecution to make inflammatory and possibly prejudicial statements in the presence of the jury, as well as a poor excuse for a defense that never challenged these statements. It is also worth mentioning again that despite his near-fatal, recent head and brain injuries, in addition to his advanced age, Killen's defense *never requested a competency hearing.* Most certainly, Hood wasn't about to do so—and risk a chance at not furthering his political agenda? What about local District Attorney Marcus Duncan? Was he unable to prosecute the case, as weak as it was, without Hood holding his hand? I guess it never hurts for a local DA to rub elbows on worldwide television with the state attorney general.

Ironically, Duncan was recently appointed to a judgeship by the governor of Mississippi. In case you are wondering, yes, the press release did mention that he helped secure Edgar Killen's conviction with Hood, twelve years earlier, and no other cases were mentioned by name out of a reported eight hundred cases he tried. Nobody else even took second place or honorable mention?

One would think the judge would consider these very real health issues suffered by an elderly man who could very well die in prison if he did not receive a fair trial. If the "Honorable" Judge Gordon didn't care how these actions could adversely affect another human and that human being's family—which apparently, he did not—how about the chance that Gordon, Hood, and Duncan might have looked like complete asses should a trial of this magnitude have been reversed because of such a remedial mistake? Had Killen's defense been worth the proverbial "plugged nickel," they most assuredly would have jumped through hoops to get such a hearing. Had Gordon denied it, an automatic appeal would have most certainly been in order. However, if the defense

56

is in cahoots with the judge and prosecutor, then you really don't stand a chance—especially if those recent near-fatal injuries prevented you from speaking coherently and being able to express yourself.

No, the fix was in. Gordon got his pound of flesh from Edgar Killen, and Hood and Duncan's careers were on the fast track. As a side note, seen in *Neshoba*, during closing arguments Hood points to Edgar Killen and refers to him as a coward. Moran and McIntyre, of course, make no objections to what was only Hood's opinion in regards to Killen's bravery or lack thereof, and the judge certainly does not reprimand Hood for giving his opinion that could have prejudiced the jury. Notably, though, Hood, brave soul that he is, apparently did not want to get too close to Edgar Killen when this comment was made. My money would have been on Edgar Killen if he'd gotten his hands on Hood, not to mention that in his prime Killen could have beaten Hood like he owned him—and made him like it. Hood doesn't appear to know what the term "physical labor" means.

What became of Edgar's "defense"? It has already been established that McIntyre was disbarred. It seems that embezzlement is frowned upon in Mississippi. How about Mr. Moran? Mr. Moran died in 2008 in Carthage, Mississippi. In a letter, Killen tells that Moran died because he knew Killen's "full story," and that cost Moran his life. Reportedly, he died from "unknown causes," and was cremated the same day he died without the benefit of an autopsy—a little strange. Stranger still, is that Moran's records on Edgar Killen seemingly disappeared. Maybe they were also cremated. Another source has it that Moran died of a drug overdose. We just might have come upon some clues to the story here.

When I googled Mitch Moran, I found a story featured on MSNewsNow.com that had Killen's attorney quoted as having said, "Edgar Ray Killen's Carthage attorney, Mitch Moran, knows what it's like to be in jail. He was arrested in September." The article goes no further; however, a phone call to MSNewsNow put me in touch with an employee who informed me that the story had been archived due to age, but he was then able to find that Mr. Moran had had some legal troubles in federal court concerning drug charges. Further research on Moran revealed that in September of 1995 he was involved in an incident referred to as "The Cali Cartel Indictments," with the headline "Massive Indictment Charges Former Justice Official and 58 Others with Racketeering."

If you were wondering if Mr. Moran was involved in this, then hopefully this quote from the article will clear the air on that question: "Criminal Defense Attorney William Mitchell Moran was also named in the indictment. Among other charges, Moran is accused of revealing the identity of a government informant to his client. The informant was later murdered." I would almost bet that Edgar Killen had known nothing of Moran's past, and that he was essentially paying a criminal— unbeknownst to him—to keep him out of prison. It begs the question that, if Moran had not minded revealing the name of an informant to a party who would have then had that informant killed, would he have been above jumping on board with Hood, McIntyre, and Gordon to purposely have Edgar Killen convicted? If the court (Judge Gordon) was aware of Moran's past, wouldn't it have been prudent to have made the Killen family aware of that? Shouldn't the jury have been informed? Maybe that would explain Moran's lackadaisical approach to Killen's defense.

This case was appealed to the Mississippi State Supreme Court as well as the US Supreme Court, and both upheld the conviction. Was either court aware of Moran's legal—and presumably substance abuse— issues? Or his propensity to be his client's worst enemy? Were they aware of the prejudicial statements made by jury members, as shown in *Neshoba*, and that apparently the lies from those jury members had resulted in attempts to keep Edgar Killen in prison? Should this case be revisited, would the judicial system disregard these facts and refuse to hear the matter?

Also, of noted interest concerning Killen's retrial: Three teenage girls who attended Steven High School in Illinois, along with their teacher, Barry Bradford, began pushing for a retrial as a school project. This effort put forth by Allison Nichols, Sarah Siegel, and Brittany Saltier was a catalyst for the retrial. This project garnered national attention and quite possibly fanned the flames of media attention which was most assuredly detrimental to Edgar as the possibility of him being innocent did not seem to be considered. Nothing like "trial by media."

CHAPTER FOURTEEN

—⁓—

THERE ARE SOME OTHER THINGS WITHIN THE *Neshoba* documentary that I feel contradict the message of peace, closure, and justice it seemingly wishes to portray. To start, Ben Chaney, the brother of James Chaney, is often referred to as "Little Ben," and portrayed as a victim. What the film fails to provide the viewer with is that Little Ben was by no means an innocent victim—or innocent of anything else. After James Chaney's funeral, the Chaneys moved to New York, allegedly due to threats they'd received in Mississippi. Little Ben enrolled in a majority-white private school, but by 1969, trouble created by Little Ben was on the horizon.

He joined the Black Panther Party and the Black Liberation Army, the very same "peaceful" groups that looted, rioted, burned, and bombed buildings, not to mention targeted law enforcement for assassination. Ben Chaney has been quoted as saying, "I hated mankind; I wanted to vent my hatred and anger on white folks. To me, they were the main perpetrators for evil in the world." In 1969, Ben and other activists—in my opinion, *criminals*—took over a YWCA because it refused to install a Black Panther Party free-breakfast program for children. Free breakfast? Who was going to pay for this "free" breakfast? The Black Panthers? Who was going to provide the labor and do the cleanup? The Black Liberation Army? Aside from these logistical problems, doesn't the YWCA or any other organization have the right to simply not participate for whatever reason they deem appropriate without being strong-armed?

Chaney even managed to organize a demonstration in New York that ended in a riot. It gets worse: Chaney said he hadn't become an activist *just* to avenge his brother's death. He thought a black revolution was imminent and he wanted to participate. In 1970, Ben and a friend went to Florida to pick up a shipment of guns to bring to a Black Liberation Army unit in Ohio. Little Ben wound up going to prison when he participated in the shooting death of four white people and wounded two others during a murder spree that covered North Carolina, South Carolina, and Florida. He was sentenced to life at eighteen years old.

He maintains that he was unjustly sentenced because he "never killed anyone." He said, "I was charged and convicted primarily because I would not tell after the acts were committed. . . . I didn't know the acts were going to be committed ahead of time. I did not go and tell the cops that this person had killed someone." Does the reader notice that Little Ben's version of their murdering, multi-state rampage, and his subsequent denial of having been an "active participant" lacking "personal knowledge" of it beforehand slightly parallels Edgar Killen's defense forty years later? The primary difference in the cases is that Killen was undoubtably *not* on scene, and did not take any physical part in the murders he'd allegedly masterminded—nobody could prove that imperative, important phrase "beyond a reasonable doubt" when it came to Killen having knowledge of the murders prior to when they happened, or afterward.

Little Ben was protected and respected by black inmates because they knew of his brother's death. He had played a role in the murder of four people and wounded two others, yet he was "respected and protected"? Doesn't all life have value? Please ponder the previous question, as it will be presented to you again later.

While Edgar Killen was running a sawmill and pastoring churches, Little Ben got his associates degree. On behalf of all taxpayers and lifelong, law-abiding, and honest citizens, I say to you, Little Ben, you are welcome for however much money we put toward your education as a reward for participating in murders.

Ironically, during his thirteen years in prison, Ben Chaney studied

Malcolm X, who at the beginning of this book was noted to have been adamantly opposed to the civil rights movement in general, and integration particularly. He also studied George Orwell's book *Animal Farm*, which, according to Killen, is nothing more than socialist propaganda. In 1983, former US Attorney General Ramsey Clark interceded and persuaded the Florida parole board to have Ben Chaney released. Now that Edgar Killen is twelve-plus years into a sixty-year sentence for manslaughter—not *murder*—do you think the US attorney general will intercede on his behalf and campaign for his release? Ben Chaney spoke of wanting those responsible for his brother's death to pay, which is ironic, because the family of the four people who were killed by Little Ben and the other participants just might feel the same way about them.

Moving away from Chaney, let us return to Judge Gordon. At Edgar Killen's sentencing, Judge Gordon was quoted as having said, "It is my responsibility to make that decision, and I have done it." At the conclusion, he stated, "Each life has value. Each life is equally as valuable as the other life, and I have to take that into consideration," adding, "Law does not take into the distinction of age."

This is a quote from the forty-eight-page FBI report on the murders of the trio. From page twenty-six: "A federal prosecution of Harris (James "Pete"), who was acquitted in the Price trial, is also barred by the Double Jeopardy Clause of the Fifth Amendment. To permit a second trial after acquittal, however mistaken the acquittal may have been, would present an unacceptably high-risk that the government, with its vast superior resources, might wear down the defendant so that even though innocent, he may be found guilty."

Obviously, Edgar Killen—who had been acquitted in 1967, and hounded by the media and others wishing to crack the case, who essentially never let him out of the spotlight—did not share the sentiments regarding Double Jeopardy. The media relentlessly pursued him, despite having chastised him already for years, and he was painted as the ultimate villain.

There is another statement from the FBI report that explains things further.

With the passage of fifty years, few persons with any direct knowledge of the facts of June 21, 1964 murders remain alive. Most of the original cooperators and confidential sources are deceased. Many of these elderly witnesses have understandably imperfect recollections. Other witnesses are reluctant to provide information. Some witnesses, despite comprehensive efforts—including pursuit of evidence to support federal prosecution for false statement (see discussion in Section VII.B.2)—to evoke truthful information from them, appeared to continue to conceal relevant information. These realities impacted the results of our investigation and current prospects of uncovering any further information useful for prosecutive purposes.

Additionally, we provide in this report our analysis of the currently available evidence relevant to a state murder charge to assist the Mississippi attorney general's prosecutive decision. We make no recommendation as to whether there is a prosecutable state murder charge. Such decision is properly the exclusive province of state prosecuting authorities.

Does the reader find it ironic that the FBI takes into consideration the "passage of fifty years" and the likelihood of "imperfect recollections"? Let's go back in time for a moment: Remember that Edgar Killen was eighty years old at the time of his trial. In terms of "imperfect recollections," would it be feasible that after having a tree fall on one's head that caused extensive brain damage, especially in the case of an elderly person, might possibly cause "imperfect recollections"? Apparently, when it comes to Jim Hood, Marcus Duncan, Marcus Gordon, or Edgar Killen's defense team—that thought hadn't crossed their collective minds. I would guess that that was by design, considering the combined years of legal experience these "honorable" men possessed.

CHAPTER FIFTEEN

—⚮—

To BEGIN THIS CHAPTER, I WOULD LIKE the reader to know that I was put in contact with J. D. Killen, Edgar Killen's youngest brother. J. D. patiently and politely listened to me explain what his brother and I had agreed to, and I made the same offer I'd made to Killen: to forward copies of letters to J. D. that Edgar had written to me, along with our contractual agreement and the work I'd completed thus far. He was readily agreeable, and a few days later he called to let me know he had received the items I'd sent to him and that I had his full approval, blessing, and promise of cooperation.

During further research of the FBI report on this case that had been submitted to Jim Hood, I noticed things written that were worthy of further mention and clarification. Before I proceeded in that direction, and with the intention to be fair to Mr. Hood, I placed a call to his office. I explained to the lady I spoke with that I was writing Edgar Killen's biography, and would like Mr. Hood's views and opinions. The lady was polite and told me that Mr. Hood would call if he was interested in speaking with me. After a week without getting a response, I assumed there was no interest on Mr. Hood's part. Well, I had at least given him his chance.

The FBI report covers the years 1964 through 2016, eleven years after Edgar Killen was sentenced. In the introduction, it is reported that this investigation focused on "whether sufficient admissible evidence currently exist[ed] to support further state prosecution against any surviving person for involvement in the murders; and whether certain witnesses [had] made recently federally prosecutable false statements to the FBI agents." They "closely coordinated with Jim Hood, the attorney general for the State of Mississippi, because of his prosecutive authority in this case."

The report also specifies that no evidence existed to support further federal prosecution; however, they did convey their findings to Hood for his consideration as to whether sufficient evidence existed to support state criminal charges. The report also acknowledges that in the 1967 case of United States v. Price, eight defendants—James Jordan, Cecil Ray Price, Alton Wayne Roberts, Horace Doyle "H. D." Barnette, Billy Wayne Posey, Jimmy Arledge, Jimmy Snowden, and Sam H. Bowers were convicted for civil rights violation.

> Federal efforts over the past three years have been extensive and exhaustive. When we began our Emmett Till Act investigation, five of the individuals believed to have been involved were still alive: Killen (prosecuted in 2005), Richard Andrew Willis (died in July 2011), Olen Lovell Burrage (died in March 2013), James Thomas "Pete" Harris, and Jimmy Lee Townsend. Harris and Townsend are still potentially culpable for state offenses related to the murders.
>
> Department attorneys and FBI agents have (1) reviewed a massive number of relevant documents assembled over nearly fifty years (including elaborate FBI confidential source files and transcripts from two 1960s grand jury sessions); (2) examined voluminous records from the Mississippi investigation that led to the 2005 Killen prosecution; (3) interviewed all surviving, willing, and competent, potential witnesses, often on multiple occasions; (4) sought voluntary information from the subjects of the investigation; (5) evaluated and assessed several tangential allegations; (6) met with the victims' families to seek their input; and most significantly, (7) made extensive use of the full panoply of law enforcement investigative tools—non-prosecution

agreements and other investigative undertakings authorized by law but proscribed from public reporting—to include a federal 1001 grand jury investigation.

Of special note in this segment of the report is the section regarding the FBI's belief that Harris and Townsend were still potentially culpable for state offenses related to the murders. As we proceed, we'll look at why these two men and others are far more culpable than Edgar Killen, but were never pursued.

Let's ponder why Edgar Killen was so blatantly targeted and ultimately prosecuted. We have covered Judge Gordon's hatred of Killen, Hood's quest for higher political office, which also seemingly applies to Duncan as well. Edgar Killen also never relented on his views regarding racial segregation, and was outspoken on that subject, reportedly even including it into his Sunday sermons when he preached. Is that a crime? No, but the powers that be didn't approve, and apparently that meant one could be held criminally accountable for expressing such an opinion. It also didn't hurt Hood's case that Senator Eastland, who had remained loyal to Edgar Killen and held considerable political power in Mississippi, had passed away in 1986. Many other key persons in the case were also deceased, thus eliminating people who could possibly have vindicated Killen—but chance always presents itself if one is patient and is willing to wait.

One thing the reader needs to know: At no time did Edgar Killen ever implicate anyone else. He has maintained his innocence without divulging other people's names. In the FBI report, which we'll look into further, even the FBI having offered to work with him did not shake his resolve on the issue.

The FBI report is included in its entirety; the reader should pay special attention to the parts covering James Thomas "Pete" Harris and Jimmy Lee Townsend, and especially take note that Harris made references to himself as having been the mastermind of the murder plot— that he and Sam Bowers had discussed the plot in detail weeks prior to when it happened. Of further interest, Harris never implicated Edgar

Killen in any part of the planning of the murder. With that having been covered, why was Killen—and not Harris—given credit for having been the mastermind? If Harris was not prosecuted, then why not call him as a witness at Edgar Killen's trial? It seems to lend further credibility to the possibility that Edgar was a scapegoat who was intentionally targeted. Further review of the FBI report establishes that Hood could have moved to drop charges against Edgar Killen, and have let an innocent man return home. It seems that sometimes a person's ego overrides their conscience.

CHAPTER SIXTEEN

—⚭—

IN THE FBI REPORT TO JIM HOOD, there is mention of two jail informants, Larry Ellis and James Stern. Not much information is available about Ellis, however Stern is a totally different matter. He and Edgar Killen were cellmates from August 2010 to November 2011 while Stern was serving time for wire fraud after having been extradited from California. One of his claims to fame is that he had brokered a "peace treaty" between rival gangs, the Bloods and the Crips, during the Rodney King riots in Los Angeles.

In researching Stern's criminal past, the following was found: In 1989, he was convicted for scheming to take out phony student loans when he was working as a pastor in training at a Los Angeles-area Baptist church. In 1990, he went to prison for writing a bad check, and in 1995 he received a sixteen-month sentence for forgery. He served two more sentences in 1996 and 1998 for similar charges. In 2007 he was convicted on five counts of wire fraud and extradited to Mississippi and sentenced to twenty-five years. At the time, he chalked his experiences up to being a bad business man—not a criminal, just bad business practices . . . with other people's money and at tax-payers' expense.

As Stern tells it, he was put in living quarters with Edgar Killen because he had no connection to Mississippi (other than having fleeced Mississippians out of their money) or its past connection to the civil rights era. Other black inmates debriefed him on Edgar Killen's infamy. Stern reports that Killen congratulated him for "fighting [Killen's] enemy" (Hood). Stern says that his Christian faith did not permit him to hate Edgar Killen. It also compelled him to act when black prisoners spit and put feces in Killen's food; instead, Stern gave his untainted food to Killen and assumed the responsibility of rolling him outside in his wheelchair for fresh air and sun.

Stern reports that, despite his compassion, Edgar Killen routinely referred to him with racial slurs, and told him, "You have what's known as a 'nigger brain,'" and "because a nigger doesn't have morals," Stern would never be able to understand a righteous man like Killen. According to Stern, even after Killen determined that Stern "didn't have morals," Killen confided in him over the next four years. He told Stern that he'd killed thirty-two additional people and named people who were still alive who had participated in the 1964 killings; he stated that his land was routinely bush-hogged to cover up the locations of the bodies of his other thirty-two victims buried there.

If this seems a little far-fetched—that Edgar Killen, a self-avowed segregationist and reputed Klan leader would confide such information to a black man—wait until you read what's next. Stern says that Edgar Killen gave him intellectual property rights to Killen's story, which was supposed to include book and movie deals. On top of this, Stern says Killen gave him forty acres of the property he owned in Neshoba County, as well as power of attorney over his estate. Supposedly the forty acres of land is the same plot of land where Killen had killed and buried some of his "thirty-two other victims." After his parole, Stern held a press conference at the Jackson, Mississippi Hilton and announced his plans to give the property bestowed to him to the not-for-profit Mississippi Racial Reconciliation Organization. He even said he planned to dedicate a one-acre plot to create a memorial to the "Mississippi Burning" victims of Neshoba County. As of this writing in July of 2017, that has yet to happen.

Stern filed suit over this issue in Hinds County, and ultimately demanded either $6 million or "an apology." According to clerk-of-court records, neither happened, and the suit was dismissed before it ever saw the inside of a court room. Consequently, relatives of Killen assured me that Stern's plans would never come to fruition on Killen land, in part because Edgar Killen owned only *twenty* acres of the alleged forty that had been given to Stern, and partly because Stern taking over any Killen property just wouldn't sit too well with them.

Should the reader doubt these allegations, and should Stern dispute them having appeared in this book, the following documents were obtained from the Neshoba County Court records. On September 28, 2011, Stern submitted a hand-written "power-of-attorney agreement" on notebook paper as proof of his claim.

> Know all men by these present that I, Edgar Ray Killen, social security number XXX-XX-7673, do hereby name, constitute, and appoint James Hart Stern, social security number XXX-XX-3726, and associates as my true lawfull [sic] representative for, and on my behalf, and in my place.
>
> My representative is further authorized to sign my signature to documentation on my behalf and in the interest of my legal affairs, and in such shall be the same as if I actually signed such document myself and shall have the same force and effect.
>
> This power of attorney shall continue in full effect throughout my incarceration in Mississippi State Prison, no matter the location. This shall supersede any previous power of attorney which may have been previously executed by me.
>
> Witnessed, the execution, here on September 28, 2011.

This document was signed by Stern and allegedly signed by Killen. Below the words "I, under penalty of perjury, have witnessed the above partys [sic] signature of free will," were signatures by inmates Junior Kimble and Bobby Allred as the first and second witnesses, respectively.

As I've previously mentioned, I am not an attorney, and make no claim to be. However, I do know some attorneys, and upon their review of this document, it's apparent Stern is not an attorney either—despite his vast knowledge of fraud and various penal institutions. The first problematic issue with the document is this: It was not notarized, which makes it worth less than the notebook paper it was written on, in addition to Stern's poor spelling and atrocious grammar. Second, Edgar Killen denies ever having signed such a document or ever giving anything to Stern, much less family land or the rights to his story.

Is it too far outside the realm of possibility that a con man like Stern could have just simply traced Edgar Killen's signature? By a very long stretch, if Killen *had* signed it, could that have been under threats of bodily harm? If he was tricked into signing the document, let's recall Edgar Killen's well-documented and undisputed brain injury, which surely could have made him easier to manipulate. As to the witnesses, just how credible were they to act as witnesses to a "legal agreement"? They were convicted felons in prison who probably weren't concerned about the penalties for perjury.

Apparently, upon his release as a guest of the State of Mississippi, Stern went to Neshoba County on May 17, 2012 with his "power-of-attorney agreement" (still not notarized), where, according to records, he had them notarized by one "Guy Nowell, chancery clerk and ex-officio notary." What's interesting is that the "power-of-attorney agreement" did not specify anything about real estate or land holdings, which at best, would make it a general power of attorney, assuming it was in fact legal. The clerk of court apparently made no effort to verify through the Killen family that Edgar Killen had agreed to this, or make any attempt to verify it through Killen himself—who I can attest is a captive audience member and should be rather easy to contact, even if that contact is delayed because it was made by way of US mail. It seems this would have been a prudent choice, considering Stern was probably unknown to the clerk-of-court staff and the notary, had a history of fraud, and the amount of notoriety generated by Edgar Killen's trial.

The rules governing the notarization of documents within the State of Mississippi (which can be found on the secretary of state's website) contain specific details regarding the necessary requirements to ensure a notarized document's validity, and those include the requirement that *all* parties must be present at the time of signing. Nowhere does it allow someone to come in with a handwritten document and have it notarized, when all parties signing said document are not signing it in the presence of the notary. Not to mention the fact that Stern was the only person of the four with anything to gain from said document and it had been written and allegedly signed almost a year earlier. Does something seem a little rotten and underhanded here? Most certainly it does, and now, for the rest of the story. Mr. J.D. Killen, Edgar Killen's younger brother, and I, went to the Neshoba County Clerk of Court's Office where we obtained copies of Stern's "power of attorney" agreement directly from Mr. Guy Nowell, the elected Chancery Clerk of Court and ex-officio notary that notarized and filed Stern's papers as "legal documents." I specifically asked Mr. Nowell if, under Mississippi law, it was legal to notarize documents without all parties signing being present and the notary witnessing each party sign the document? Mr. Nowell stated the did not know the answer to that question. Please note that Mr. Nowell is in his second term of office and it is his duty and responsibility to know the answers to such questions. In the event he did not know, he could have simply researched the Secretary of State website to answer this most basic question. I asked Edgar Killen about this matter in my next letter to him. Killen responded that Nowell was an enemy of his and in fact was a founding member of the Philadelphia Coalition, which was instrumental in his trial and conviction. In little time and with minimal effort, I was able to verify Killen's statement by simply doing a google search. As of this writing, J.D. Killen has made written complaints to the Mississippi Ethics Board, the Mississippi Secretary of State, and the Mississippi Attorney General's Office. The response from these agencies? Nothing. Did Nowell allow, condone, and become complicit in this scheme because of his personal animosity toward Edgar and his family? We may never know, but one thing is for certain; Mr. Nowell may very well one day have to answer for this. I can attest that J.D. Killen will not stand for it and I will only be happy to help him pursue this matter.

Is Reverend Stern one to file frivolous law suits? Let's look at his past allegations and the reader can determine for themselves. While he was a guest of the Mississippi Department of Corrections, he sued for second-hand smoke exposure that allegedly injured his eyes, which are sensitive to the formaldehyde found in cigarettes. He also sued Jim Hood and Hinds County Circuit Clerk Barbara Dunn, stating they had committed perjury in his criminal case and Dunn had refused to provide him with documents that would have proved Stern's innocence.

To some readers, this may not seem too important in the greater scheme of things; however, perhaps this attempt to drive the State of Mississippi further down the poverty line will be: Stern also claimed that unsanitary conditions in the prison barbershop had exposed him to HIV/AIDS, hepatitis, and other diseases for which he sought $31 million in damages. If "exposure" is worth $31 million, what is feces-laced food worth?

Stern's attempts to become a millionaire at the State of Mississippi's expense was not his only attempt to rob taxpayers. In March of 2002, he filed suit against the California Department of Corrections. He asked the federal courts to require the prisons to use sterilized hair-cutting instruments. In a March 2002 article from the *Los Angeles Times*, Stern said that while serving time for bad checks, he'd observed inmates with bleeding scalps after they'd gotten haircuts with unsterilized instrument. He had been placed in solitary confinement for six months for refusing a haircut. He finally submitted, and while he hadn't contracted a disease, he had suffered from a "skin condition."

Further research indicates that Reverend Stern seems to have some type of phobia related to barber shops. He filed a $61 million lawsuit against Reverend Jesse Jackson and Reverend Al Sharpton for having criticized the movie *Barbershop*. Stern headed a group called the National Association for Cosmetologists, Inc. He believed the two civil rights leaders' criticism of the movie would negatively impact African-American barbershops. In addition, along with the help of the NAACP, Stern also sued California banks for using a credit-verification system that he said was tantamount to racial profiling. He argued the practice prevented blacks from establishing bank accounts.

When one takes into consideration the frivolous lawsuits filed by Stern, as well as the other ridiculous allegations he has made, even those against Jackson and Sharpton, would it surprise you that the FBI, in its report to Jim Hood, states the following: "The FBI interviewed and collected documents from both sources. Despite their public claims, neither the individuals nor the information they supplied was credible or substantively useful to our investigation. In short, what was advertised publically—that Killen had made relevant admissions incriminating others—was not what was delivered by these self-promoting witnesses."

It seems unfathomable that the FBI or Hood would not jump at the chance to obtain more evidence against Edgar Killen if there was any to be found.

CHAPTER SEVENTEEN

—◊—

EARLY IN THE BOOK I MADE MENTION of a Colombo Family Mafia hitman who had tortured a confession out of Lawrence Byrd, who ultimately gave up the location of the burial site of the murdered trio. After reading the forty-eight-page report from the FBI to State Attorney General Jim Hood, I'm sure it was evident that no mention was made of the hitman, Gregory Scarpa Sr., also known as the "Grim Reaper." How ironic is it that this was completely left out, yet Edgar Killen, in our visit, provided details to this fact? Is he senile? Is he a "conspiracy theorist"? Is he making excuses for his conviction? The likely answer is no.

On July 17, 2017, while researching information on Edgar Killen and Gregory Scarpa, two vital pieces of information were found. The first piece, which appeared on the website "The Blog" on June 27, 2016, updated on June 28, 2017, provided the following information via the excerpts that pertained to Edgar Ray Killen (It should be noted that Lawrence Byrd, Scarpa's victim, is listed as the person who Scarpa tortured, which ultimately broke the Dahmer case; however, in some instances, Byrd is credited with giving Scarpa the location of the burial site of the murdered trio.):

According to Edgar Killen, it was Byrd whom Scarpa tortured and forced to sign a twenty-two-page confession that detailed the location of the three bodies and included the names of those involved in the murders. However, the following article by Peter Lance, titled "DOJ Report on 'MissBurn' Case Leaves Out a Crucial Detail: The Name of the

Vicious Mafia Killer Who Broke the Case for J. Edgar Hoover's FBI" states the information on the burial site was revealed by the mayor of an unnamed and unknown nearby town. Either way, what is not in dispute, is Scarpa's involvement.

Greg "Grim Reaper" Scarpa, Colombo Family Mafia hitman and top-echelon FBI informant, who tortured a "confession" from alleged Klansman Lawrence Byrd and revealed the location of the bodies of Schwerner, Chaney, and Goodman. Allegedly, Scarpa committed numerous murders while employed as an FBI informant and some were done on behalf of the FBI.

The New York Times reported on Tuesday that a US Justice Department inquiry into the notorious 1964 murders of civil rights workers Goodman, Schwerner, and Chaney has ended with a forty-eight-page report sent to Mississippi Attorney General Jim Hood. Based on the report's findings, Hood has announced that the fifty-two-year-old case is now closed.

The three young voter registration volunteers were kidnapped and tortured by members of the Ku Klux Klan in Neshoba County during what civil rights leaders, including Dr. Martin Luther King, called "Freedom Summer."

After they'd gone missing and their fire-charred station wagon was later found without their bodies, panic set in within the Justice Department of President Lyndon B. Johnson.

The incident inspired the film *Mississippi Burning*, which wrongly concluded that the case was solved after an African-American FBI agent was sent to Mississippi and interrogated a KKK sympathizer.

Although the DOJ report concludes that the "FBI conducted approximately one thousand interviews during the summer and fall of 1964," the truth is that the location of the bodies, buried beneath an earthen dam on the farm of a Klan associate, was not discovered until after FBI Director J. Edgar Hoover sent Colombo crime family capo, Greg "The Grim Reaper" Scarpa Sr., down to Mississippi to break the case.

But there's not a single word of Scarpa's role in that forty-eight-page report, which merely notes that, "In late July 1964, an informant provided accurate information about the location of the bodies." The report otherwise attributes the discovery of the victims to good police work.

In fact, Scarpa Sr.'s mission in what the Bureau dubbed the "MissBurn case," was actually the first of two civil-rights-related interrogations he made at the behest of the FBI director.

The Special Goes South

In the hot summer of 1964, J. Edgar Hoover finally found a way to make some affirmative use of the Brooklyn hitman who had been on his payroll for years. "Whatever else he may have passed along in the way of intelligence," says Fredric Dannen of the *New Yorker*, who wrote a definitive profile of Scarpa in 1996, "we know from the work he did in Mississippi that he became a clandestine asset for Hoover."

The biggest crisis facing the US Justice Department at that

moment was the disappearance of three young civil rights workers, Andrew Goodman, Michael Schwerner, and James Chaney.
Working for the Congress of Racial Equality (CORE), they had
to travel to Philadelphia, Mississippi on June 21 to look into
the Klan's role in burning the Mount Zion United Methodist
Church, and disappeared that same night.

When the empty fire-charred Ford station wagon was recovered a short time later, the FBI was called to work the case. Evidence later presented at trial would prove that the local KKK
kleagle, or recruiter, Edgar Ray Killen, had conspired with a
deputy sheriff to stop the young men for speeding as they left
town.

After a chase, they were forced off the road, driven thirty-
four miles to a remote location, and shot to death in cold blood.
Their bodies were thrown back in the station wagon and driven
to a nearby farm, where they were buried under fifteen feet of
red clay in an earthen dam. The Ford was then set ablaze and
dumped in a swamp.

Mississippi Burning

"Back then, a lot of people feared the FBI as much as the Klan,
and nobody was talking," says Judge W. O. Chet Dillard, who
was state attorney at the time. "Old J. Edgar figured that if he
was gonna break that [case]—and he was hurtin' to break it—he
was gonna have to go to some extreme measures, and he did."

Sometime in early August, the Bureau enlisted Gregory
Scarpa, the FBI's top-echelon informant—who had earlier been
contracted to murder the boss of his own crime family—to go
to Mississippi to accomplish what the agents could not. "Hoover
was getting a lot of pressure about the bodies not being found,"
Scarpa's common-law wife, Linda Schiro, testified in 2007.
"They approached Greg to go down, and found the bodies."
Schiro, who was seventeen when she and Greg were flown to

Mississippi, testified that they went to a hotel and found "eight or nine FBI agents" waiting. Scarpa "winked at the agents," Schiro testified, "then one of them knocked on the door of their room and gave him a gun."

"Greg changed his clothes," she recalled, "and then he . . . left some money on the dresser. He told me that if he didn't come back to . . . go back home." An account of the story by Tom Robbins and Jerry Capeci, which ran in the *New York Daily News* in 1994, alleged that "Scarpa, according to sources, kidnapped [a] Klansman" who had knowledge of the burial site.

A Different Account

But Judge Dillard, who interviewed a number of sources close to the incident, has a different account—one that suggests that Scarpa became even more violent during the interrogations. . . . "The man who knew where Goodman, Schwerner, and Chaney were buried was the mayor of a local town," says Dillard. "After Scarpa grabbed him, they took him to an undisclosed location, and while the agents waited outside, Scarpa started working on the guy." Dillard says that Scarpa first "put a pistol to [the mayor's] head, demanding to know where those boys were," but the mayor told him a phony story.

Interrogation By Razor Blade

It was only after he checked with FBI agents to confirm the lie that he'd "put the barrel of the gun in the man's mouth and cocked it." Then, says Dillard, "Fearing reprisals from the Klan, the mayor lied a second time and the agents outside confirmed it. It was at that point . . . that Scarpa took more drastic steps." Taking out a straight razor, he proceeded to unzip the man's fly. "He was threatenin' to emasculate him," says the judge. And that's when the terrified Klansman "blurted out the location of the dam." . . . Ten years later, a lawyer who represented Scarpa disclosed that Scarpa, the so-called "Mad Hatter," had admitted to interrogation by razor blade. On August 4, 1964, the three bodies were recovered six miles southwest of Philadelphia. Goodman and Schwerner had each been shot once in the head. Chaney, the black man in the group, was shot three times and beaten savagely. . . .

Schiro testified that Scarpa later returned to the hotel and told her they had found the bodies. She said that an FBI agent came by to retrieve the gun and handed Greg an envelope with cash "an inch thick" in a rubber band. After that, Schiro and Scarpa vacationed at the Fontainbleau Hotel in Miami Beach.

Men From Two Secret Societies

At the age of eighty, Killen was sentenced to sixty years in prison. Then, in February 2009, Killen filed suit against the FBI, arguing that his civil rights had been violated—because of the use of Gregory Scarpa Sr, a Mafia killer, in solving the Goodman, Schwerner, and Chaney kidnap-murders. The information that Scarpa obtained by use of torture violates Killen's civil rights . . . right to due process . . . [and] the right to confront witnesses, his lawyer said.

DEA Veteran Mike Levine Comments

One former DEA special agent, Mike Levine, was astonished by Hoover's decision to enlist a known Mafia strongman to further the cause of justice. . . . Here the FBI uses a member of a violent secret society—La Cosa Nostra—to travel down to Mississippi on multiple missions to torture confessions out of two guys who were also members of a violent secret society: the Klan. Since when does the federal government have to stoop to levels like that to make cases? This was during the same era when the CIA was trying to get mob guys to kill Castro. . . .

As Levine notes, such behavior on the fed's part was roundly denounced during congressional hearings in the 1970s, and the popular assumption was that it stopped. "But the fact that the Bureau continued to use a multiple murderer like Scarpa right up to the 1990s," says Levine, "just proves that it didn't."

As to the demise of the "Grim Reaper"—how ironic is it that, in 1986, he refused to accept blood from blood banks after ulcer surgery because he feared the blood may come from African-Americans—whom he despised? He was only willing to accept blood from mobster/bodybuilder Pete Mele, who was abusing steroids and had become infected with HIV after using dirty needles to inject those steroids? On June 4, 1994, Scarpa died in the Federal Medical Center for prisoners in Rochester, Minnesota from AIDS-related complications.

It begs the question, why did Edgar Killen, who was primarily convicted based on forty-year-old testimony, not have Judge Dillard, the unnamed assistant FBI director, and Linda Schiro testify on his behalf in 2005 regarding the events surrounding the torture-induced confession of the Klansman who'd revealed the location of the three bodies. Seemingly, their testimony would at least have been as credible as those of deceased witnesses, defendants who could not even be cross-examined. Maybe Hood and Duncan simply did not want Dillard or Schiro's input, as it may have harmed their agenda.

To further solidify Scarpa's involvement, I contacted his former attorney, Louis Diamond, of New York. Mr. Diamond was gracious enough to speak openly and candidly about "The Grim Reaper." I first became aware of Mr. Diamond's connection to Scarpa while watching the television series *Mobsters*, which aired a segment on Scarpa. His role in the Mississippi Burning case was discussed, and amazingly enough, their coverage coincided with what had been previously reported by the previously mentioned sources.

Mr. Diamond explained that Scarpa was registered as a top-echelon informant with the FBI for more than twenty years, and during that time he'd committed untold numbers of murders. These murders were not only committed with the FBI's knowledge, some of them were committed on *behalf* of the FBI! Need a problem mobster to disappear? No problem, Greg Scarpa could handle it. Apparently, he handled these problems on a regular basis for his "handlers," and took pleasure in doing so. Not only did he enjoy killing, he thrived on torture, and took it to new-and-improved levels.

Louis Diamond, Esq. Mr. Diamond represented Greg "Grim Reaper" Scarpa and numerous other members of the Mafia. Mr. Diamond has verified Scarpa's role in torturing a "confession" out of Lawrence Byrd.

How well did Mr. Diamond know Scarpa? Not only did Diamond represent him in legal matters, he drank and played cards with Scarpa three times a week. According to Mr. Diamond, "There were times when [he] didn't know if [he] would leave there alive when [he] met Greg—anything could set [Scarpa] off."

How violent was Scarpa? According to Mr. Diamond, Scarpa's daughter was regularly driven to school by a private driver. The driver apparently took a liking to Ms. Scarpa, who was fifteen years old, and after taking a detour, made unwelcomed advances toward her. She was afraid she would be raped, and as a defense, she told the driver they could get together at a later time. This pacified the driver, and prevented her from being harmed. When she informed her father of this incident, he disguised himself as an old man, complete with cane, and called the driver to bring him somewhere. The driver was killed. No questions asked.

In another incident, Scarpa left a "sitdown" (Mafia terminology for "meeting") with another made man (officially inducted Mafia member). Upon exiting the building, the other man was shot and killed at point-blank range. Greg Scarpa's response was, "I guess I won the sitdown." There is a difference between being vicious and tough. A coward can be vicious, and not be tough—apparently Scarpa was both.

In one incident, Scarpa had been shot through the eye. He went home, poured scotch into the wound, and drank the remainder of the bottle. At the time, he was on house arrest and had an ankle bracelet to monitor his movements. He did eventually seek medical treatment, but this is a good example of the mindset of the man who broke the Mississippi Burning case. Mr. Diamond shared many more stories of Scarpa, his criminal actions, and just how deeply Scarpa was involved with the FBI and was able to operate with impunity.

Let's review a six-page, typed written letter from Edgar Killen to Cole Thornton, a KKK leader, in which Killen makes references to Scarpa. This letter, written on February 10, 2010, greatly parallels the information in the previous paragraphs.

A true and undeniable message for my hometown, your
Neshoba County and Philadelphia MS. Officials who are so
politically correct. You had all the news media that helped
indicted me for murder on three counts, which you had no legal
evidence yankee All your grand jury heard was slick tongue talk from a
couple of political politicians. Who ordered a number of
testimonies made by F.B.I. agents who in the presence of
Gregory Scarpa Sr. pistol whipped this testimony from low
moral people. That are now deceased. Mr. Scarpa Sr. was a
known mafia who was paid by check thirty thousand dollars of
your tax money. And for the next thirty years was allowed and
protected by the F.B.I. to operate all across America. His
business was murder for hire, drugs and any type of crime. He
was so successful - even male and female prostitution- that his
career ended as godfather of the Colombo crime family in New
York City. Mr. Scarpa Sr. went on to be known in the
underworld as the Grime Reaper. He was never tried and
convicted, but the Grime Riper met the Greatest Judge of all "
the Great God of Heaven". He died of hiv/aids.

I warn you MS. And Neshoba County officials God is still on
his throne and he knows of my every deed, and every speech I
ever made. I am not at peace with you people who promote this
false lie toward me. But I am at peace with GOD. You people
know who you are and you are responsible, who not only to the
tax payers but to Almighty GOD. Who is listening and is every
minute recording your acts, thoughts, and deeds. One by one
you will give account to Him. You took my life from me and my
family but God is our shield and body guard. He is my shield
and I have lived to your joy in a very dangerous and hideous
place. But Almighty God has kept me alive. I do not intend for
this to be my farewell message to you. But only God knows I
see my lives sun setting low as in a few weeks I will be 85 yr
years old. As I stated you took my life from me and my family,

and our hopes of retirement. You never took away our faith in Christ. Nor our love for one another.

Now those who are our friends, GOD bless my friends. Your supervisors voted to fund my trial and that depleted the county treasury. Some of you supervisors told the tax payers that you could not keep your word- Edgar Ray Killen's trial took all the money. Those that told that was defeated and others did not run. I am not trying nor intend to burn any bridges, but I have walked the streets of most major cities in America. I bragged on MS., Phil. MS., and Neshoba County. However I want out of here and retrace my trips, to make apologies to those Americans that I bragged too. Your Mr. Dearman made welcome six yankee communist members to Phil. Is Mr. Dearman your cities greatest? I have no promises to make if I leave here alive and with my mind. I will tell you the complete story, all the above is only an introduction to this part of history. I would like to tell you the real story of how our government played during this time. I never told Neshoba County folks but for some 30 yrs. I had access to the justice dept. files of which there are millions and millions which are hidden, I only read those of interest. I was not hired and not a pimp but I had security clearance so I read and obtained straight evidence. I am not putting names in this newsletter as some are still living and believe it or not I am not a betrayer of no person especially my friends. The justice dept. hid the files on Scarpa the mafia chief but they and Hood are fighting the courts not to give those files to my attorney. For your information I had no real attorney until I left MS. I wrote an attorney in Ohio who practiced law nation wide. He moved to a neighboring state so he can drive to see me. My reading of evidence was not in the justice building, the files were copied and brought to me. These records the F.B.I. has tried for 40 yrs. To find who leaked these records. Your officials kept screaming JUSTICE we demand JUSTICE. I can tell you if

you are serious about justice call your state representatives,
your state senators, your U.S. congressman, your U.S.
Senators, and your governor and ask for justice. Have them
make the files public or give them to courts and then demand
justice. You need not call Hood -your friend- he has the files
and you will never see them. The (FBI) justice dept. not Hood
did not deny Scarpa's pistol whipping. They say they can not release
the files because of National Security reasons. Ask the D.A.
whom you elected why he did not tell you tax payers about the
pistol whipped readings in my trial, and the federal trial in
1967. Ask the D.A. to look you in the eye if he even answers
you. Ask for the truth, not Edgar Ray Killen's word. Above I
wrote that the FBI and Hood says I cannot have those records
pertaining to my case because of National Security. That is true
because if lawyers outside of MS. got hold of them they would
have a National field day. With the way Lyndon Johnson and
the justice dept.- a few hand picked men- tore the U.S.
Constitution to shreds.

In 1776 the founders of the United States of America sent a
Declaration of Independence to the king of England. In that
declaration Thomas Jefferson wrote, that when any form of
government becomes destructive it has the right of the people
to alter or abolish it and to institute new government. We are
invoking this right to rise up and alter the course of our
government, you have had your chance to correct America's
course and you have failed.

To the gentlemen on the board of supervisors lets tell the
public what the salary of your industrial giant is. It is $60,000
Or $80,000 a year plus expenses. Mr. David Vowell could not
stay off the TV for telling the world he could not get industry
into Philadelphia untill I was convicted. Gentlemen where are
the industrial smoke stacks??? Tell me where is the Emerson
motor plant, US motors, where is the glove factory, where is the
two pants factories, where is the pallet factory, the greeting

card factory. Where is La Pacific Lumber Co.??? How many
thousands in Neshoba County is out of jobs today? 1,400 were
fired from the casino in the last year. When I was home the last
figures in Neshoba County of employed people were the lowest
in the state, always number 1 or number 2 in employed people
in the state. Well you locked me up, so please tell me now what
the rate is. Your chamber of commerce has cried their eyes out,
of course Vowell is the cheering sector for them. Oh we are
tired of being last, we are rated last if only we can convict
Edgar Ray Killen then we can be number 1. Well let me
explain "Baby you are getting there" you have me locked up
illegally for almost 5 years and now as of latest figure you are
close to number 1 in the state on unemployment.

Hood said at my trial that my illegal actives caused the civil
rights law to be passed, what he did not tell was in 1964 before
and after a few years MS. Had the very lowest or second lowest
crime rate in the Nation, there you are Baby you were last or
next to last. How about today this year we will come in second
or third place. So stop crying you are headed for the first place
in everything number 2 or number 3 in crime. Highest rate of
unemployment don't cry yet it will go higher. Number 1 in lost
factories, keep crying you will be number 1 in all these. If you
are reading all this will you not please state that at 85 I have
lost my marbles or I am making excuses. You will boil my
Irish German ~~tired~~ blood of which I am overly proud of my blood
line. Please get off your duster and have someone get you these
records and then if its not too late you might join the fight to
clean up our government and the Judicial system. Have you
never read where a great statesman (early American) said all it
takes for this Country to fail is for good men to do nothing.

I realize that this letter I am writing is placing my life in
danger but this 85 year old man thinks no fear and knows no
fear. I have walked with death breathing down my back here
for over four years not the inmates as a whole they are far

better moral people than most of the officers. Don't look at me, I have already told them to their face. I will name one who was pistol whipped- (my attorney said this fed record you can get it. It my do you like me and take all your money, is your freedom not worth it?) Clayton Taylor Lewis was pistol whipped, kidnapped by Scarpa until he went to work with the FBI. A paid informer also a defense attorney for some or all in the 1967 federal trial. Attorneys where are your code of ethics, where is your oath as an officer of the court. If any defense attorney is reading this, you know why John Dear and others knew all, and every defense move that you were going to make in the next days court.

Mitch Moran was a man with a conscious after I lost my legal constitutional bond, I fired Mitch and after a few months Mitch needed to talk with me. He came here (CMCF) and we talked for a period of time. Mitch looked like death he really broke down and confessed all. I felt great sorrow for Mitch he was too sensible a man to have gotten in the bind he was in. the judge Mitch gave me all the money I paid him. As a bribe Mitch told me that he had great regrets that he was unable to defend me as he could and especially that he could not keep my perfectly legal constitutional bond. Mitch did not tell me he was expecting to be murdered, he did have great fear of the illegal actives of two of your elected officials. I never told of Mitch's visit, somehow some official here has a tape of our conversation and before too much could be told, said or done Mitch was facing death. Is it to late to carry Mitch's remains outside MS. and find the cause of death? Don't let Duncan, while looking down tell you, look who's telling this. Yes I'm reminding you of an organization in MS. named Hood, Dickey, Scruggs and Joel Langston (one or two I can't remember) Trent Lott, Bobby Delaughter or Steve Patterson and Edd Peters. One million dollars- call your governor -please call your Rep., Senator., U. S. Congressman and tell them to make

Duncan, Hood and the FBI to show the records. And have the judges rule on showing records of the FBI crimes. I fear that you decent people who read this may think that I am asking you only to help me, NO, NO, NO. I am asking you to WAKE UP if your Federal Government can pay and protect a mafia godfather to kidnap some low grade person and pistol whip him until he signs the statement the FBI presents him. What keeps you from being the next one tried and put away as I was? What about your family, are they safe in a state that is the top ridden crime state of the 50 states. Please for your children's sake call your elected law makers and ask them to help release those federal criminal records. I am not perfect, but I am right! Ask Hood and Duncan where the twisted child rapist was at the time (I understand he was in N.J. during the years in MS. that he claimed he heard me tell I did it). He is not registered SEX OFFENDER! What is the law Hood and Duncan? Why was his sentence cut and he was SET FREE? He is a liar so is Hood.

why is he not registered

Psalms 30:5 For His anger endureth but a moment ; In His favor is life: weeping endure for a night, but joy cometh in the morning.

Edgar Ray Killen

CHAPTER EIGHTEEN

—⁓—

LET'S LOOK AT SOME OTHER NAMES OF people who were still alive in 2005, who were allegedly involved in the murders, yet were not indicted or called as witnesses. Before his death in 2001, Cecil Price reportedly told authorities that on June 21, 1964, he had told Billy Wayne Posey that he had jailed the three civil rights workers, and asked Posey to get in touch with Killen, who allegedly helped plan the murders. Yet James "Pete" Harris, in the FBI report, allegedly made numerous statements to an FBI informant that he and Sam Bowers had plotted this for weeks prior to when it occurred, and never mentioned Killen having been involved in their plot.

Putting this into perspective, does it seem feasible that Edgar Killen, who was undeniably present with various family members all day and was at the funeral home at the time of the murders, would be able to organize this many people on last-minute notice, arrange for a bulldozer and an operator, find a burial site, and coordinate the removal and destruction of the vehicle on such short notice? Please remember that this was well before the days of cellphones, texting, e-mails, and other modern means that allow instant contact. There were only two means of contact during that time, either by phone or in person.

Various family members all testified that Edgar Killen was rarely out of their site that whole day, which eliminates the possibility of in-person visits, as he could not be in two places at one time. It also effectively eliminates contact by phone, as there were no cellphones. This would require the extended use of a landline, which nobody testified as having seen him do.

It has been speculated that twenty or more persons were involved in the planning of the murders. In an interview with Billy Wayne Posey in 2000, he stated, "A lot of persons were involved in the murders [who] did not go to jail"—yet he did not identify any of these persons. Posey was also reportedly the driver of one of the cars that had chased the trio. This act in and of itself puts him on the scene, which should have made him far more culpable than Edgar Killen, yet he was not tried or called as a witness, despite living in Philadelphia, Mississippi at the time of Killen's 2005 trial.

Now let's look at Richard Willis, who died in July of 2011. He was a Philadelphia, Mississippi police officer at the time of the murders. It was established that Willis lied to the FBI about Cecil Price's whereabouts at the time when the three civil rights workers were killed. It seems Price and Willis told the same story to the FBI: Each claimed they'd been patrolling together in Price's car from about 9:30 p.m until about 10:00 p.m., when Price said he had to go release some people from jail—the three civil rights workers.

Left to right; unidentified Meridian (Ms.) police officer, Richard Willis, Deputy Cecil Price, and Sheriff Lawrence Rainey outside of Meridian, Mississippi Federal Courthouse.

When the three workers had been released from jail and were driving away, Price and Willis followed them. Willis told the FBI that he assumed Price was making sure that the three boys left town. He said Price dropped him off at the police station at about 10:40 p.m. After that, Willis was allegedly joined by Constable Clayton Livingston, who rode with him in his patrol car before returning to the police department some time between 11:15 and 11:30 p.m. When they arrived, Willis told the FBI that Price was already there. Supposedly, in a confession by Price before his 2001 death, he admitted he and others had chased the three civil rights workers down Mississippi Highway 19, before they pulled onto another road and stopped. Price arrested the three, put them in his patrol car, and drove them to Rock Cut Road, where Klansmen then shot them to death. Price told Mississippi authorities he did not know the trio would be killed, and never mentioned patrolling with Willis.

A 1964 confession by Horace Doyle Barnette identifies a Philadelphia police officer (Willis was the only officer on patrol) as the one who told the Klansmen the three workers had been released and were traveling on Highway 19. Barnette also said the police officer was present when Klansmen met with Price and Sheriff Rainey about 2:00 a.m. in Philadelphia after the murders and burial of the bodies had taken place. Barnette quoted Rainey as saying, "I'll kill anyone who talks, even if it was my own brother."

Another member of the Philadelphia Police Department, Harold B. Holley, told the FBI a different story, saying Willis was by himself in a patrol car, rather than having ridden with Price. Holley also said he had not seen Willis until about midnight—the same time he saw Price.

It would seem Willis, at a minimum, should have been charged as an accessory, considering he seems to have been covering for Price, who by his own admission was present when the three were killed, and in fact facilitated the killing by stopping the trio. Even if Price had not known they would be killed, his actions still allowed the Klansmen to make contact with the trio, and he had to have known that this would put them in peril. Again, this is assuming that Price in fact made this confession. If he did, it was not introduced into testimony—as opposed to the forty-year-old testimony that *was* used to convict Edgar Killen. Decades-old testimony was perfectly acceptable, naturally, and not too many people were left alive to cross examine, and conveniently, there was no record of Price's testimony to verify that he had in fact confessed anything at all. After looking at these aspects, does it make anyone ponder why Willis, who passed away in July 2011, was not called to testify? Could it be that doing so would not have been beneficial to Hood's quest to target and convict Edgar?

What was the opinion of other court officials mentioned in the FBI report that was submitted to Hood? In the words of the United States Fifth Circuit Court of Appeals, "Ample, in fact overwhelming, evidence against two living suspects exists." What was Hood's reaction? Case closed, not interested. Hood had gotten who he wanted, and exposing anyone else would have possibly undone all the underhanded efforts he'd put toward convicting Killen.

As reported by the Associated Press on Monday, June 20, 2016, the Mississippi Burning civil rights case was closed after fifty-two years. Jim Hood stated, "The evidence has been degraded by memory over time, and so there are no individuals [who] are living now [who] we can make a case on at this point."

Counterpoint and rebuttal: Despite having been degraded by memory and stories that changed, along with witnesses who had admitted to lying under oath (i.e., Mike Hatcher), why wouldn't they have pursued the other persons still alive, and who, beyond all doubt, had active roles in the matter? Why not use them as witnesses? Let's not forget the testimony of the convicted child rapist who, forty years later, had a sudden improvement in memory—that was fine because it was beneficial to Hood's case.

"He [Hood] said, however, that if new information [came] forward because of this announcement that the case [was] closed, prosecutors could reconsider and pursue a case."

Counterpoint and rebuttal: I would think that the FBI report would be a good indicator that there were others alive at the time of Killen's trial who were far more involved in the murders than Killen was—if in fact he was involved at all. If there was testimony from Price implicating others, why was it not introduced, and why hasn't his testimony been released? There was no ongoing investigation it might have compromised, and, releasing it certainly wouldn't have put Price in harm's way.

CHAPTER NINETEEN

—m—

IN THE FOLLOWING CHAPTERS, WE WILL LOOK at the testimony of witnesses who were paid FBI informants. Their testimony was introduced, at least in part, at Edgar Killen's 2005 trial. Please keep in mind that these witnesses were deceased in 2005, and, were therefore unable to be cross-examined. The transcripts of each of these witnesses is provided in full, and the statement/testimony of each witness poses some unique questions.

We will begin with Carlton Wallace Miller. Miller's testimony from the 1967 civil rights trial amounts to twenty-three transcribed pages. On page eight, Miller is asked, "Did you, prior to June 21, 1964, ever hear Preacher Killen discuss methods of controlling Negro citizens of Mississippi?"

After several back-and-forth objections, Wallace Miller stated, "Yes, sir, we were to apply pressure." He then goes on to testify that, "We were to call them up or go see them and threaten them on their jobs and things of that nature." Miller was asked about any other kinds of pressure that were discussed, to which he answered, "whippings and beatings." When asked about the procedure of such action being authorized or approved by the White Knights of the Ku Klux Klan, Miller stated, "After the pressure was applied and they [negroes] didn't respond, then we were to resort to physical pressure. If we wanted to whip someone, the lodge would vote on it and the lodge president or the E. C. would"— [objection entered and overruled]—the lodge would vote on it and then the president or the E.C. [exalted cyclops] of the lodge either had the power to reject it or to okay it; to okay the beating."

It should be noted that Edgar Killen was identified by Miller as having been the kleagle (organizer), and as such, had no power to authorize or reject a motion because he was not the president. When Miller was asked about other actions that had taken place, he testified, "There was elimination." When asked to clarify his statement, he speci-fied that "elimination" meant "murder"—which had to be approved by the imperial wizard. The kleagle could *present* this appeal to the imperial wizard; however, the approval to proceed could only be given by the imperial wizard—no one else.

In the next line of questioning, he was asked if, during the month of May 1964, he had gone to Neshoba County on Klan visits. He answered that he had, but not "for the purpose of going to a Klan meeting." When asked who he had met there, he answered, "Preacher Killen," His response as to why he had gone (if not for the purpose of attending a Klan meeting) was, "To keep some Negroes from playing baseball in Philadelphia." Subsequent questions pertained to the matter of Sheriff Rainey and Deputy Price having been present, and the nature of the discussions had among the White Knights of the Ku Klux Klan in the latter part of April and May of 1964 in Meridian, Mississippi regarding Michael Schwerner.

Miller testified that some members wanted to whip Schwerner, and that Mr. Killen and Mr. Herndon were in charge of these discus-sions. Miller also testified that "prior to . . . this particular meeting, they hadn't been able to see him [Schwerner]. Mr. Killen told us to leave him [Schwerner] alone, that another unit was going to take care of him, that his elimination had been approved." When asked by who it had been approved, Miller answered, "The imperial wizard."

Miller went on to identify Mr. [Sam] Bowers as having been the im-perial wizard. Miller stated that Schwerner was also known as "Goatee," [due to Schwerner's facial hair] and that Killen had told Wallace Miller that Michael Schwerner had been working with the COFO [Council of Federated Organizations] in Philadelphia. Additional statements, by

Miller in regard to Killen's knowledge included, "He told me that he wanted to talk to me, and he and I went to my back room and we sat on the bed . . . we were discussing the civil rights workers. Mr. Killen told me that they had been shot, and that they were dead, and that they were buried in a dam about fifteen feet deep, and he told me that Deputy Price told the FBI the truth about what time he turned them out."

An objection was entered based on that statement having been hearsay, however it was overruled. Miller acknowledged that no one else had been present during this alleged conversation with Edgar Killen; therefore, no one could confirm the conversation had taken place. Take additional note of the fact that Miller was a sergeant with the Meridian Police Department, as well as a paid FBI informant. Does this seem like a possible conflict of interest? If anyone should be so inclined to suggest that things were different then, that this questionable practice was acceptable, then why weren't Edgar Killen's alleged actions and/or knowledge deemed acceptable given the particular time in history?

By "actions" and "knowledge," I'm referring to Edgar Killen's Klan membership—and am not condoning murder, beatings, or whippings. To this day, Killen maintains that he was never a member of the Klan. Even if he had been, this was not a crime—not now, or in 2005. It has been speculated that during the time of the murders, the majority of white Mississippians were either Klan members or Klan supporters, and were opposed to integration; that still does not constitute criminal activity.

It seems obvious that Wallace Miller, like Mike Hatcher, had knowledge of a crime and covered it up—as a law enforcement officer—until it was beneficial for him to no longer do so. In and of itself, those actions should constitute criminal prosecution, yet he benefited financially at taxpayers' expense via payment from the FBI for doing what he should have already been doing as a police officer. As to Miller's testimony concerning Edgar Killen's role in the matter, he never once indicated that Killen was the mastermind or organizer of the murders. At most, according to Miller, Killen had obtained knowledge of it after the fact, and at the very worst, Killen condoned "whippings" or "beatings," which would still be a far cry from murder.

To conclude, let's look at Wallace Miller's possible motivation for having provided this testimony—that no one could later cross-examine in 2005. Miller acknowledged in 1967 that over the course of two years, he was paid "fifteen or sixteen hundred dollars" for his role as an FBI informant. That does not seem like a fortune by today's standards, but, consider the fact that it roughly calculates to around $11,741.37 in our current economy. Being paid that much to stay out of prison, and being in the good graces of the FBI, would be a tempting incentive for most people—especially a discredited and disgraced police officer.

CARLTON WALLACE MILLER, called as a witness for and on behalf of Plaintiff, was sworn and testified as follows:

CARLTON WALLACE MILLER

BY MR. DOAR:

Q   Will you tell the court your full name please?

A   Carlton Wallace Miller.

Q   How old are you?

A   43 years old sir.

Q   Where do you live?

A   Meridian Mississippi.

Q   Are you married?

A   I am sir.

Q   What is your occupation?

A   A policeman with the Meridian Police Department.

Q   How long have you been a policeman with the Police Department in Meridian?

A   Twenty years on April.

Q   What is your present job.

A   I'm a Sergeant.

Q   What responsibilities do you have as a sergeant?

A   I am the shift man there in the absence of the assistant. chief.

Q   Do you hold any other jobs at this time?

A   Yes sir, I worked at a grocery store.

Q   And whose grocery store?

A   Its my wife.

Q   Do you know Preacher Killen?

A   I do, sir.

Q   Can you identify him looking around in the courtroom and see if you can identify him?

A   He's over here sir.

Q   How long have you known him?

A   About all my life.

Q   How do you happen to know him?

A   Well I'm from up in Neshoba County originally and that's where Mr. Killen is from.

Q   What were the circumstances of your acquaintance?

A   Mr. Killen and I were in the same class at school and we lived near each other and we were closely associated and we are distantly related.

Q   Did you and Mr. Killen maintain that relationship after you grew up?

A   Yes sir over the years.

Q   During the period of 1950 did you see him?

A   In 1956, uh, 1955 I had a brother that passed away and Mr. Killen conducted the services. In 1956, I had two children to pass away, also one in 1957 and he conducted the services of those children.

Q   Did you see him during the 1960's?

A   Yes.

Q   Now specifically during the period of 1963 early 1964, did you see Preacher Killen?

A   Yes sir, I saw him several times.

Q   What were the circumstances of you seeing him on those occasions?

A   Mr. Killen has visited in my home several times.

Q   And where were those visits? Here in Meridian?

A   Yes sir.

Q   Have you ever been a member of the White Knights of the Ku Klux Klan?

A   I have sir.

Q   What is the White Knights of the Ku Klux Klan?

A   It's an organization called the Ku Klux Klan.

Q   When you were first contacted to become a member of the White Knights of the Ku Klux Klan?

A   It was in the latter part of March or early April.

Q   Of what year?

A   In 1964.

Q   By whom?

A   Mr. Killen.

Q   Were, uh, where were you contacted?

A   By whom?

Q   Mr. Killen.

Q   Were, uh, where were you contacted?

A   At the police department.

Q   Can you tell us in your own words what was said?

BY MR. BUCKLEY:

Your Honor if it please the Court, we object as to the conversation affecting the other defendants.

BY THE COURT:

I'll let him tell what Killen said and that will not be competent against any other defendants.

BY THE WITNESS:

A   Mr. Killen told me there was a strong organization and asked me if I was interested in joining to help keep the colored people from integrating our schools and I told him I was definitely interested.

Q   Did you see Preacher Killen again that day?

A   Yes sir.

Q   Where did you see him?

A   He came to the police station that night. I was working the three til eleven at night and he came to the police station when I got off and went home with me.

Q   What happened when you got to your home?

A   We discussed this organization and I asked him if it was the Ku Klux Klan and he told me it was, and up until that time the name had never been called. He asked me if I was still interested and I told him that I was.

Q   Then what happened?

A   He joined me.

Q   And where was that?

A   In my dining room in my home.

Q   And how did he join you?

A   He read some papers to me, asked me some questions and gave me the oath.

Q   Now dod you know what Preacher Killen's title was with the Ku Klux Klan?

A   I didn't at that time, I later learned it was Kleagle.

Q   What is Kleagle?

A   Organizer.

Q   And what happened if anything on the next day?

A   I don't believe that I was him the next day.

Q   When did you see him next?

A   Probably the following weekend.

Q   Where did you see him?

A   He either came to my house or to the police station we would usually contact each other at my home or the police department.

Q   What did you do?

A   We went to the Longhorn Drive-Inn.

Q   What is the Longhorn Drive Inn?

A   Its a restaurant located down on Tom Bailey Drive.

Q   And who did you see at the Longhorn Drive-Inn?

A   Mr. Herndon, Frank Herndon.

Q   Now will you look around the courtroom and see if you recognize Mr. Herndon?

A   Yes sir, there on the end there.

Q   Could you identify him for the Court and Jury?

A   He's wearing a robe.

Q   And did you see anyone else there that day?

A   Mr. Jordan.

Q   What is his first name?

A   Jim, James.

Q   Do you see him in the courtroom?

A   I don't see him sir.

Q   Then what happened on that occasion?

A   We went out on the mountain and Mr. Killen swore in Mr. Jordan and Mr. Herndon into the Klan.

Q   Did you have any further meetings with Mr. Killen about the Knights of the Ku Klux Klan?

A   Yes about a week from this date, uh, from this time we met again down on Tom Bailey Drive at a trailer home.

Q   Can you look around here on the inside of the rail and tell me if any of these persons were present at that time?

A   Mr. Harris and Mr. Snowden were present.

Q   Can you identify them?

A   Mr. Harris has on the green sweater and Mr. Snowden has on the suit sitting next to Mr. Harris.

Q   Is Mr. Snowden sitting on the left or the right of Mr. Harris?

A   To his right.

Q   On his right. And what happened at that meeting?

A   That was the time I believe that he swore them in.

Q   Do you, uh, did you attend other meetings of the White Knights of the Ku Klux Klan prior to the 21st day of June, 1964?

A   Yes sir.

Q   And can you tell me whether or not you can recognize any other members of the White Knights of the Ku Klux Klan that are in the court room? You may look around.

A   I know Mr. Atkins.

Q   Just identify him, which one is he?

A   He's this gentleman right her sir, second one from the end.

Q   Sitting next to whom?

A   Mr. Killen.

Q   Do you recognize anyone else?

A   I know Mr. Barnette sir.

Q   And who is Mr. Barnette?

A   He's the ex-sheriff and sheriff-elect of Neshoba County.

BY MR. BUCKLEY:

Your Honor, if it please the Court, as I understand the answer its not responsive to the question---
Counsel mumbling and unable to understand.

BY THE COURT:

I don't believe it was responsive so ask him that question again.

BY MR. DOAR:

Q   Which ones of defendants did you meet at meetings of the White Knights of the Ku Klux Klan between that date that you have heretofore described and of June 21st, 1964.

A   I met Mr. Roberts, Mr. Barnette, and the second Mr. Barnette and Mr. Arledge, Mr. Harris and Mr. Snowden, Mr. Herndon, Mr. Bowers, Mr. Akin, Mr. Killen.

Q   And where were those meetings unusually held?

A   Usually they were held out at Key Field at a warehouse.

Q   Who was head of the White Knights of the Ku Klux Klan?

A   Sam Bowers, do you mean over the State?

Q   Yes sir.

A   Mr. Sam Bowers.

Q   Can you identify Mr. Bowers for us?

A   He's sitting right over there sir.

Q   Do you know where he lives?

A   Laurel.

Q   What discussion were there at these meatiness as to the programs of the White Knights of the Ku Klux Klan?

BY MR. PIGFORD:

We object, Your Honor, there hasn't been any discussion testified to about any specific defendant.

BY THE COURT:

Well, I'll overrule your objection, go along.

BY THE WITNESS:

A   I didn't understand your question.

Q   Was there any discussion about the program of the White Knights of the Ku Klux Klan?

A   Yes sir, we were opposed to integration, we were opposed to the colored going to white schools that was the main thing we were opposed to, and usually that was the topic of our discussions mostly.

Q   What discussion was there with respect to---

BY MR. HENDRICKS:

We object to his leading question, Your Honor.

BY MR. WATKINS:

And we object further to the fact there has been no showing that any particular time the generalized knowledge of this man or what he may have learned by membership in an order without these boys being present would not be admissible at all, your Honor.

BY THE COURT:

I think that's correct, but I'll overrule the first objection, as to the second objection I will sustain that unless and until this witness has tied these defendants or some of them in with those discussions.

BY. MR. DOAR:

Q   Did you prior to June 21st, 1964 ever hear Preacher Killen discuss methods of controlling negro citizens of Mississippi?

BY MR. ALFORD:

Your Honor please, I would like to interpose an object to that question, as a generalized questioned and it goes back prior to June 21, 1964 and we think we are entitled to specific time and place and the names of persons present, therefore, we respectfully object to these generalized questions.

BY THE COURT:

Yes, I think we are interested in and concerned with the time about the 21st or the 22nd of June, 1964 or some date in reasonable proximity to it and you will ask your question in such way to illicit specific answers.

BY MR. DOAR:

All right, Your Honor.

Q   In May, 1964 did you have any discussion with Preacher Killen with respect to methods of controlling negro citizens in the State of Mississippi?

BY THE COURT:

Overruled.

BY MR. ALFORD:

Your Honor, we would raise and objection to the date of May. Your Honor please, that's thirty days or thirty-one days and no specific time or place.

BY THE COURT:

Yes sir, I think that's in reasonable proximity so I'll overrule that objection.

BY MR. DOAR:

Q   You may answer.

A   Yes sir, we were to apply pressure.

BY MR. WEIR:

We object unless he names some place or persons that were present.

BY THE COURT:

Well, he can't tell us everything he knows in one breath, and its hard, and you gentleman are going to have a chance to cross examine and I'm sure you are going to avail yourself of that rather extensively so, I'll overrule your objection.

BY MR. DOAR:

Q   Now then, was there to be various types of pressure.

A   Yes sir, to begin with we were to call them up or go to see them and threaten them on their jobs and things of that nature.

BY THE COURT:

Go to see whom?

BY THE WITNESS:

Their bosses.

BY MR. DOAR:

Q   Was there any other kind of pressure that was discussed?

A   Whippings and beatings.

Q   Was there any kind of procedure whereby such type of action would have to be proved by the Whites Knights of the Ku Klux Klan.

BY MR. ALFORD:

Just a minute Your Honor, we object to that question. Its leading and suggesting, and he's still asking those generalized questions, and we respectfully submit that is not admissible.

BY THE COURT:

I'll overrule the objection.

BY THE WITNESS:

A   After the pressure was applied and they didn't respond then we were to resort to physical pressure if we wanted to whip someone the lodge would vote on it and then the lodge president or the E.C.--- would---

BY MR. WEIR:

Your Honor please, we object to that unless it is referred to the three particular people that is said to have been involved in the indictment, rather than just what was to be done to somebody else.

BY THE COURT:

I'll overrule the objection.

BY THE WITNESS:

either had the power to reject it or to okay it, to okay the beating?

Q   Now, was there any other action?

A   There was elimination.

Q   What does elimination mean?

A   Murder.

Q   Within the Klan structure?

A   That's a term for murdering some, killing them.

Q   And how did that have to be approved if at all?

A   That had to be approved by the Imperial Wizard. If the Klan unit wanted them disposed of would turn that over to the Kleagle in this area or the organizer and then he would carry it to the Imperial Wizard.

Q   Now, can you tell me whether or not there was a unit or Klavern of the White Knights of the Ku Klux Klan in Neshoba?

A   I understand it was.

BY MR. ALFORD, PIGFORD, WEIR: (BASIS NOT RECORDED BY REPORTED AS ALL COUNSEL TALKING AT ONE TIME)

We object.

BY THE COURT:

Sustained.

BY MR. ALFORD:

We request that the Jury be instructed to disregard the answer, Your Honor.

BY THE COURT:

That answer is not competent Members of the Jury, you will not consider it.

BY MR. DOAR:

Q   During the month of May, did you ever go to Neshoba County on Klan visits, during May of 1964?

A   I went up there but I didn't go to a Klan meeting.

Q   Who did you meet, if anyone, up there?

A   Preacher Killen, I met him at a little restaurant just this side of town.

Q   And what was the purpose of your meeting with him?

A   To keep some negroes from playing baseball in Philadelphia.

Q   Did you meet anyone else up there?

A   Preacher Killen called someone and he told me that Sheriff Rainey and Deputy Price were coming out.

BY MR. ALFORD:

We object to that.

BY THE COURT:

Overruled.

BY MR. DOAR:

Q   Did the Sheriff and Cecil Price come out?

A   Yes sir.

Q   And did you meet them?

A   Yes sir.

Q   Do you know if they are members of the White Knights of the Ku Klux Klan?

A   Sir, I don't know.

Q   You don't know that?

A   No sir.

Q   Now, what if any discussion were had at meetings of the White Knights of the Ku Klux Klan during the latter part of April and May, 1964 in Meridian, Mississippi about Michael Schwerner?

A   The meeting that I attended---

BY MR. BUCKLEY:

Your Honor, if it please the Court, I object to the question unless it is shown that one of these defendants was present.

BY THE COURT:

Let me get that question again please?

BY MR. DOAR:

Q   At the meetings in late April, and May of 1964 at the White Knights Klavern, the White Knights of the Meridian Klavern, what if any discussion was had among members about Michael Schwerner?

BY THE COURT:

Now that would not be proper unless and until some of these eighteen defendants were tied in with that, and I'll let you tell if there were and if there weren't I'll sustain the objection.

BY MR. DOAR:

Q   Do you understand the question?

A   Yes sir, I think I do. Some of the members wanted to whip Schwerner.

Q   Let me ask you this, who was in charge of that meeting?

BY MR. BUCKLEY:

Your Honor if it please the Court I think the Jury should be asked to disregard his answer.

BY THE COURT:

Well, I'm not sure, I'll let you develop this a little bit, and I think he understands my ruling, he says he does and I hope he does and I wouldn't think he would answer it like that if he didn't when he says he does understand.

BY MR. DOAR:

Q   Who was in charge of that meeting?

A   Mr. Killen and Mr. Herndon.

Q   And what others of the defendant were present at that meeting if you recall?

A   I don't recall.

Q   What was said in Mr. Killen and Mr. Herndon's presence about Michael Schwerner?

A   Prior to the meeting of this particular one, they wanted to whip Schwerner, at this meeting, they reported that they hadn't been able to see him. Mr. Killen told us to leave him along that another unit was going to take care of him, that his elimination had been approved.

Q   Did he say by whom it had been approved?

Q   Do you know who the Imperial Wizard is?

A   Yes sir, Mr. Bowers.

Q   What if anything did Mr. Killen say about, I'll withdraw that question. Did Mr. Killen or any of the other members of the White Knights of the Ku Klux Klan have any particular name for Michael Schwerner?

A   They called him "Goatee."

Q   What if anything did Mr. Killen say about whether or not Michael Schwerner had visited Neshoba County?

A   He told me they were working with the COFO in Philadelphia.

Q   Did anyone from Meridian go with you up to Philadelphia to meet Preacher Killen, any of these defendants?

A   Mr. Roberts went with me.

Q   Can you identify him?

A   He's sitting right down there.

BY MR. HENDRICKS:

May it please the Court, we don't know what time he's talking about.

BY MR. DOAR:

Q   Can you fix the time of that trip to Philadelphia?

A   I don't remember the date.

Q   Can you fix the month?

A   It was April or May, I believe it was around May.

Q   Of what year?

A   Sixty-four.

Q   Now, have you been paid any money for any information that you have given by the Federal Bureau of Investigation?

A   I have sir.

Q   And when did you start furnishing information to Federal Bureau of Investigation?

A   About the middle of September of sixty-four.

Q   How long did you remain a member of the White Knights of the Ku Klux Klan.

Q   Until December of 1964.

A   And did you have following June 21st a conversation with Frank Herndon about the three COFO workers who were missing in Philadelphia on June 21st?

BY MR. BUCKLEY:

To which I object, Your Honor, this would be after the conspiracy if there was any conspiracy, and it would not be admissible as to these defendants other than Mr. Herndon.

BY THE COURT:

I think that is correct and I'll let him answer and the jury will understand that his answer will only be chargeable to defendant Herndon and will be completely disregarded and removed from your minds insofar as the other defendants are concerned.

BY MR. WATKINS:

Your Honor, on behalf of Mr. Herndon, I object further unless he states time, and place, otherwise Mr. Herndon would not have an opportunity to refute it at all.

BY THE COURT:

Yes, you may be as specific about that as you can.

BY MR. DOAR:

Q   Officer Miller, can you fix the time and place and persons present when that conversation took place?

A   I returned from Summer Camp in the National Guard on June 21st, 1964 and that was on Sunday and I saw Mr. Herndon on Tuesday, that would be about June 23, 1964.

Q   Where were you?

A   We were at his restaurant.

Q   And who was present?

A   Mr. Jordan.

Q   And what, if anything, was said about the missing three civil rights workers?

BY MR. WEIR:

Your Honor please, may we have a continuing objection about this?

BY THE COURT:

With respect to this line of questioning, and with respect to this particular incident you may have a continuing objection and it's overruled.

BY MR. WEIR:

Thank you.

BY MR. ALFORD:

Just a minute, Your Honor, I don't want to belabor the Court, but I wanted to understand the Court's ruling. As I understand it this witness testimony is not to pertain to anybody but Mr. Herndon and anybody that he names, is that correct?

BY THE COURT:

That's correct, insofar as I know understand, I've heard nobody else's name mentioned up to this point. All right.

BY THE WITNESS:

A   Mr. Herndon and I and Mr. Jordan were discussing the civil rights workers being missing, and Mr. Herndon asked me, if anything, the police department was doing about it and I told him we had a missing person report on them was all that we had done that we were looking for them.

Q   Did you have a further conversation with Mr. Herndon about the missing civil rights workers?

A   After that I saw Mr. Herndon practically every day.

Q   Can you tell me whether or not you had further or did he tell you anything further about the missing civil rights workers?

BY MR. WATKINS:

Your Honor please, we respectfully object because every conversation he's asking about is after the day of June 21, 1964.

BY THE COURT:

Yes, I'll overrule your objection as I understand it you are making it on behalf of Mr. Herndon, and I'll overrule it but I think anytime he makes a statement about anything that Mr. Herndon is said to have said to him that he'll give us the time, the place and the date as nearly as he can.

A   The next thing I remember was the date that the car was recovered. Mr. Herndon told me that someone goofed up they were supposed to carry that car to Birmingham.

Q   What car?

A   The civil rights worker's car.

Q   Would you repeat that entire answer, I interrupted you and the reporter may not have gotten all of it.

A   Mr. Herndon told me the day that they recovered the car, the burned car, that they were supposed to carry that car to Birmingham, that somebody had goofed up that it was supposed to be carried to Birmingham and disposed of.

Q   And where did that conversation take place?

A   At the Longhorn.

Q   Do you remember the date of that?

A   I believe it was on the day they recovered the car, probably on a Wednesday or Thursday.

Q   Who was present?

A   I don't recall anyone being present at this time.

Q   Did you have any further conversation with Mr. Herndon about the three missing civil rights workers?

A   He told me one time he figured they had gone to Cuba or some place like that.

Q   What if anything did he say about what happened at the Longhorn restaurant on the night of June 21, 1964?

A   He told me that Mr. Killen came down and they got some boys together and went to Neshoba County.

Q   Did he place the time and place of that happening.

A   You mean where we were?

Q   Yes.

A   We were at the Longhorn Restaurant.

Q   Could you tell me about how long after June 21st that was?

A   About the 23rd or 24th?

Q   Where is the Longhorn Drive-Inn?

A   Down on Tom Bailey Drive, sir.

BY THE COURT:

Is that a restaurant?

BY THE WITNESS:

Yes sir.

BY THE COURT:

Whose restaurant is it?

BY THE WITNESS:

It's Mr. Garrett, Mr. Herndon was the Manager of it.

BY THE COURT:

All right.

BY MR. DOAR:

Q   Now, did you have any conversation with Mr. Killen after June 21 about the three missing civil rights workers?

A   Yes sir. . . .

Q   And as to the first conversation where did that take place?

A   At my home.

Q   And who was present?

A   Just Mr. Killen and I.

Q   When was that?

A   June.

Q   And what did Mr. Killen say?

A   He told me that he wanted to talk to me and he and I went back to my back room and we sat on the bed, and we were discussing the civil rights workers. Mr. Killen told me that they had been shot, that they were dead, and that they were buried in a dam about 15 feet deep, and he told me that Deputy Price told the F.B.I. the truth about what time he turned them out.

BY MR. ALFORD:

We object, this is hearsay.

BY THE COURT:

Overruled.

BY MR. DOAR:

Q   What else did he say?

A   He told me that they got in a chase down Highway 19 at about a hundred miles an hour and he overtaken them and he said he thought that the car tried to turn and go toward Union from House and that's where they overtaken them in that area there.

Q   What if anything didi he say about a church burning.

A   This was later on.

Q   Did you have a conversation with him about the church burning?

A   Yes sir, he told me---

Q   Just a minute. Where was that conversation?

A   At the same time.

Q   Was it that evening?

A   Yes sir.

Q   And who was present?

A   No one.

Q   What did he say?

A   He told me they burned the church to get the civil rights workers up there, referring to Schwerner.

Q   Now, which of the persons in this room do you know of your own knowledge are members of the White Knights of the Ku Klux Klan before June 21st?

BY MR. ALFORD:

Your Honor, we object to this being repetitious he's already asked him that.

BY THE COURT:

I'll let him answer, overruled.

BY THE WITNESS:

A   Mr. Roberts, Mr. Barnette---

BY THE COURT:

Call their first names, so we'll know who you are talking about.

BY THE WITNESS:

Mr. Wayne Roberts, Mr. Travis Barnette, Mr. Doyle Barnette, Jimmy Arledge, Mr. Harris, Pete Harris; Jimmy Snowden, Mr. Herndon, Mr. Bowers, Mr. Akins, and Mr. Killen.

BY MR. DOAR:

After June 21st, did you have any conversation with Mr. B.L. Akin about the three missing civil rights workers?

A   Yes sir.

Q   Can you tell me the time and place of that conversation?

A   I talked to Mr. Akins down at the Longhorn drive-inn and I've talked to Mr. Akins at his place of business, I talked to Mr. Akins in my car, and I also talked to him in his car, we were just riding around.

Q   And what if anything did he say anything on any one of these occasions about---

BY MR. HENDRICKS:

May it please the Court we object to these leading questions, he can ask him what he said but he can't ask him what they talked about.

BY THE COURT:

Well, we are just interested in what he said about a very specific subject matter, and I think his question would have to be limited and I'll overrule your objection.

BY MR. MILLER:

A   Mr. Akins told me---

BY THE COURT:

Yes, just tell us specifically when it was, where it was and who was present and then tell us if one or more of these defendants accused said?

BY THE WITNESS:

A   This was in the latter part of June of '64, Mr. Akins and I were together and he told me---

BY MR. BUCKLEY:

Your Honor, if it please the Court, I would like to interpose an objection the same as before that this is actually a continuation of the conspiracy---

BY THE COURT:

Yes, I make the same ruling.

BY THE WITNESS:

A   Mr. Akins told me that they had went up and burned the Mt. Zion Church for the purpose of getting Michael Schwerner up there.

Q   What if anything else, did he say anything else about the three civil rights workers?

A   Mr. Akins told me that the night it happened that did not go, but that he and Mr. Lyde stayed together and waited until they got back, and he said he gassed up the men's cars that went up there.

BY MR. HENDRICKS:

Your Honor please, we object he didn't name a place or date or who was present, and we object unless he does.

BY MR. DOAR:

Q   Can you give us a time, place and the ones that was present during that conversation?

A   At this conversation no one was with Mr. Akins and myself. We were sitting in the car drinking some coffee?

Q   What time was that?

A   It was the latter part of June.

Q   What year?

A   1964.

Q   What city?

A   Meridian.

Q   Where was your car parked?

A   Down at the Longhorn.

BY THE COURT:

I believe we'll take a fifteen minutes recess at this point.

(whereupon the Court took a recess at 3:31 P.M. for fifteen minutes.

AFTER RECESS:

BY MR. DOAR:

Q   Officer Miller, any conversation that you testified to with Preacher Killen at your home, what, if anything did he say about his activities on the 21st?

A   Preacher Killen told me that he came to Meridian, that he had received a call that the civil rights workers had been arrested and that he came to Meridian and got with Mr. Herndon and they made some calls at the Longhorn at a pay phone on the outside and got some boys together and went to Philadelphia.

Q   How did you happen to leave the White Knights of the Ku Klux Klan?

A   They banished me.

Q   And what does banish mean?

A   Kicked me out.

Q   And during the time, when was that?

A   December of 1964.

Q   Up to that time did you furnish on a regular basis information to the Federal Bureau of Investigation?

A   I did sir, from about the middle of September until then.

Q   About how much were you paid?

A   Over a two year period about from September through the end, approximately how much?

A   Probably fifteen or sixteen hundred dollars.

Q   What did this, what was this for?

A   It was for the work that I was doing, traveling expenses and go all over the communities.

Q   And was that in connection to being a Klan member?

A   Yes sir.

Q   Did you travel around as a Klan member?

A   Yes sir.

Q   And where, for example, did you travel?

A   I went all over the city, Lauderdale County, Jones County, Laurel, Philadelphia, and different places out in the country.

Q   Did you on occasions go down to Laurel to see the Imperial Wizard? Mr. Sam Bowers?

A   Yes sir.

Q   How many times?

A   Probably about three or four times, I went a few times and didn't get to see him because he wasn't there.

Q   You did see him on several occasions?

A   Three or four, yes sir.

Q   Thank you.

CROSS EXAMINATION

BY MR. WATKINS:

May it please the Court.

Q   Wallace, as pertains to Frank Herndon, Jimmy Arledge, James Harris, Travis Burnette, and Jimmy Snowden and Alton Wayne Roberts, now you, yourself personally, never did see or hear either of those defendants make a threat abusive word, intimidation of any kind toward Andrew Goodman, James Chaney, or Michael Schwerner, did you. Did you, yourself personally see that?

A   No sir, I didn't hear any.

Q   Did me first, the date please when you joined the Klan?

A   Later part of March or early April of 1964.

Q   Wallace, what was your purpose or what representation was made to you at that time about the purpose of the Klan, other than the one you stated a while ago. American purposes were stated to you as the purpose of the Klan?

A   Preacher Killen told me that this was a very patriotic, political organization and in order that better men and better business men and better citizens, officers, doctors, lawyers, and peace officers belonged to it.

Q   And did you relate that information to Frank Herndon?

A   I did. . . .

Trial Transcript Page
Mississippi Burning Trial Homepage

CHAPTER TWENTY

—ᴍ—

THE NEXT WITNESS TESTIMONY WE'LL DISCUSS IS that of James Jordan—another paid FBI informant. He testified that he'd joined the White Knights of the Ku Klux Klan in 1964 when he was first approached by Frank Herndon, who told him that the Klan was recruiting members to save the schools and protect the white families. Jordan testified that Wallace Miller had also approached him about joining, and Jordan then decided to do so. When the questioning began about his activities on June 21, 1964, Jordan stated that he had gone to the Longhorn Drive-in to pick up his wife from work around 6:00 p.m. Frank Herndon, who operated the Longhorn Drive-in, was at the Longhorn along with Pete Harris and "Preacher" Killen.

When Jordan was asked about Killen's actions, he testified that Killen spoke with Herndon, came back out, and said he had a job in Neshoba, and needed some men to go with him. Jordan was asked if Killen had specified what kind of job. In Jordan's words, Killen said, "Two or three of those civil rights workers [were] locked up and they need[ed] their rear ends tore up." Jordan stated that the sheriff's deputy had told him he locked the three workers up, and identified Schwerner as "Whiskers" or "Goatee." He was asked if he had ever seen Schwerner, and he said he had seen him once prior to June 21, 1964, when he was with Frank Herndon and they were "down in the colored section of town in Meridian." Herndon had brought Jordan there specifically to let him see Schwerner so that Jordan would know him on sight.

Based on that information, it would seem likely that Herndon knew of a plot to do some type of harm to Schwerner, and was making Jordan aware of it—possibly before Killen knew anything would happen. Even if Killen had had knowledge of what was about to happen to Schwerner before Jordan had known, Jordan still had ample opportunity to warn Schwerner—yet it seems Jordan did not develop a conscience until it benefited him to do so.

Further testimony from Jordan finds that he actively participated in trying to find help—by trying to find men he knew who didn't have telephones. This was supposedly at Killen's request. Jordan went to the home of Alton Wayne Roberts, who agreed to accompany Jordan, and they later stopped Warren's Grocery Store to buy rubber gloves. Again, this was allegedly at Killen's request.

By his own admission, Jordan had opportunity to abandon his role in this plot. He hadn't phoned for assistance; he'd had to leave the group and go to Roberts' home, plus make a stop for rubber gloves. It would seem that within that timeframe, it should have occurred to him that a decision to follow through with that plan, no matter how large or small his role was in it, would not end positively—regardless of who had instructed him to carry it out. Even if it had been "a-heat-of-the-moment" sort of situation, Jordan would have had ample time to cool off. While Jordan alleged Killen had been a planner and had provided instructions, Jordan openly admitted that he had taken an active, physical role in the plot. His allegations against Killen are merely unproven allegations, and even if they were true, they would pale in comparison to the role Jordan himself admitted as having played in the matter.

Jordan goes on to testify that Edgar Killen later provided further instructions that Jordan and the other men were to pick up the civil rights workers "and tear their butts up." To most rational, reasonable people, that phrasing would in no way indicate they should commit murder. How many people tell their children they will get their butts tore up for unacceptable behavior? This is a common phrase used quite often, and as a child, I was often told this same thing by my parents. I frequently got "my butt tore up," but neither of my parents killed me.

After allegedly providing further instructions, Jordan says Killen went to a funeral home to establish an alibi. Prior to this, it was decided that a Highway Patrol car would stop the civil rights workers as they traveled Highway 19 towards Meridian; however, the plans were changed so that it would be Deputy Price who would stop them. If this testimony is true, and a highway patrol officer had initially been in on this plan, who was that first patrol officer? Why did he not intervene? Why did he not testify? His lack of action in preventing this event is certainly more criminal than Killen having had the idea.

The remainder of Jordan's testimony surrounding the murder and burial of the trio is fairly consistent with the other witnesses' versions of the story; however, on page twenty-one of Jordan's transcribed testimony, it says he was asked whether he knew Sam Bowers. Jordan answered yes, and pointed Bowers out to identify him. Jordan testified that he had met Bowers prior to the murders in May, when Jordan and Pete Harris had met with Bowers in Laurel, Mississippi. During the meeting, Jordan stated that Bowers described Schwerner as "a thorn in the side of everyone living, especially white people, and he should be taken care of." If you'll recall, in the forty-eight-page FBI report to Jim Hood, Pete Harris told an informant that he, along with Sam Bowers, were the masterminds of the plan, and neither mentioned Killen as having been involved.

Jordan also said that about a month after the murders, he and Pete Harris met with Bowers again in Laurel, and that "Sam said the best thing to do was to not talk about it, that everything was well done; it was a job to be proud of; if there were any instruments involved, they should be gotten rid of." This is damning testimony, if in fact it's true, having come from the alleged head of the Klan without any mention of Killen. The question of Hood's not charging Bowers or Harris based on this testimony, or at least calling them as witnesses in Killen's 2005 trial, could make one wonder if either of these two would testify in a manner that would not have been favorable to Hood's agenda. Then again, one can only speculate as to why Edgar Killen's defense team did not think of this approach, as they don't need the prosecutor's permission to call witnesses. Something seems rotten in Denmark—or at least in Mississippi.

Jordan was questioned about becoming an informant for the FBI, and acknowledged that he was in fact paid for his information and cooperation. He said the FBI told him they would help him get out of town, as he had lost his job and didn't have anything. His initial payment was "approximately three thousand dollars," which would amount to $22,015 in today's economy. With this money, he bought a car and arranged to rent a trailer and leave Mississippi. He said the FBI agreed to pay him until he got a job and the publicity died down. This arrangement was worth an additional hundred dollars per week for the year it took him to find a job. This would have been another $5,300 he was paid, worth $38,893 today.

Thus far, the current equivalent of what Jordan was paid would be $60,908. He went on to testify that once he obtained employment, the FBI paid him $55 a week, then gave him $25 a week for a while, and they said they would then give him just a hundred dollars a month to bring his salary up to living scale. This payment went on for an unknown time-frame, and, was in addition to the $175 per week he was making while employed at the NASA missile base in Picayune, Mississippi. That amount in 1967, $175, would currently be worth $1,284, yet he needed even more FBI money to be brought "up to a living scale"?

It can be safely assumed that Jordan was paid more than $70,000 in FBI (read, taxpayer) money, essentially as a reward for having actively participated in the murder of three people. Yet his testimony, which could not be challenged or cross examined, was used to convict Killen forty years later. Does that make one think there could have been an underlying conspiracy yet?

JAMES JORDEN [Jordan], called as a witness for and on behalf of Plaintiff, was sworn and testified as follows:

BY MR. OWEN:

Q   Would you state your name please?

A   James Jorden.

Q   How old are you?

A   Forty-one.

Q   In 1964 where did you live?

A   Here in Meridian.

Q   Would you keep your voice up now so that everyone can hear you?

A   Here in Meridian.

Q   How long had you lived here in Meridian?

A   Approximately two years.

Q   What kind of work did you do when you lived her?

A   I worked at a service station for some time, I ran a restaurant here and worked at Akin Mobile Home.

Q   Now, while you lived here in Meridian, were you ever a member of the White Knights of the Ku Klux Klan?

A   Yes sir, I was.

Q   Do you remember about when you joined?

A   No sir, not exactly it was in '64.

Q   What were the circumstances under which you joined?

A   I was approached and asked to join, there were recruiting members to save integration, to save the schools and to protect the white families.

Q   Who asked you to join?

A   I was first approached by Frank Herndon.

Q   And did anybody approach you about it?

A   Wallace Miller did after that.

Q   Did anybody else approach you?

A   No sir, I decided to join.

Q   Now, when you joined, just tell the Court and Jury what the circumstances were?

A   Well, I was to be given an oath and we drove back to the service station where I was working at the time and at that time I met Reverend Killen from Philadelphia. He and Wallace Miller and Frank Herndon took me up there and swore me in.

Q   Now, look around you, all around this room and see if you can identify any of the people that were present when you were sworn in?

A   Frank Herndon.

Q   Frank Herndon is which one. Describe what he's wearing?

A   Pajamas and bathrobe.

Q   Anyone else?

A   No sir.

Q   You don't see anyone else. Now, what happened when you were up there, when you were sworn in?

A   I was told that I was joining, that this oath was to uphold the integration of schools, to keep the colored separated from the white and I was a member of the Klan.

Q   Now, did you, uh, were you given a Klan number?

A   Yes sir.

Q   What number were you?

A   Number three.

Q   Now, did you attend the Klan meetings fairly regularly after you joined the White Knights?

A   Yes sir.

Q   Now, do you recall what you did on June 21, 1964?

A   Yes sir.

Q   Where were you that afternoon?

A   I went to the Longhorn drive-inn to pick up my wife who was working there at the time.

Q   About what time did you go there?

A   Just before six o'clock.

Q   Now, did anyone, uhh, who was there when you were there?

A   Well, there were a lot of people there I didn't know.

Q   Were any of the defendants there?

A   Yes sir. Frank Herndon operated the place at the time.

Q   And were any of the others?

A   Pete Harris was there.

Q   Can you identify Pete Harris?

A   Yes sir, he's sitting right there.

Q   Can you describe him, count down from the right?

A   He's number five.

Q   The fifth man from the right?

A   Right.

Q   Now, did any of these other defendants come to the Longhorn that evening?

A   Yes.

Q   Who?

A   Preacher Killen and two young men.

Q   Can you identify Preacher Killen?

A   Yes sir, he's sitting next to Pete.

Q   Is he the one with the glasses on?

A   Yes sir.

Q   Now, two young men?

A   Yes sir.

Q   Now, can you identify those two young men?

A   This young man right there was one of them.

Q   Which man is he from the left?

A   The second man.

Q   Who was driving the car he came in?

A   He was.

Q   The young man you pointed to over there?

A   Yes.

BY THE COURT:

Do you know the young man's name that you pointed to?

BY THE WITNESS:

I believe it was Sharpe, I found out later.

BY THE COURT:

Do you know the defendants in this case?

BY THE WITNESS:

Yes sir.

BY THE COURT:

All of them?

BY THE WITNESS:

Yes sir.

BY THE COURT:

Do you know them by name?

BY THE WITNESS:

Yes sir.

BY MR. OWEN:

Q   Did you know this man by name at the time?

A   No sir.

Q   Now, what if anything did Preacher Killen do?

A   Well, he went in and talked to Frank Herndon first then he came back out and said he had a job he needed some help on over in Neshoba County and he needed some men to go with him.

Q   Did he say what kind of job it was?

A   He said that two or three of those civil rights workers were locked up and they needed their rear ends tore up.

Q   Did he tell you who locked them up?

A   Yes sir, he said the Sheriff's Deputy locked them up.

Q   And did he indicate to you who any of these people were that were locked up?

A   Just one, Whiskers, Goatee, he had several names for him.

Q   Who was that?

A   Schwerner, I believe was his name.

Q   Now, had you ever seen Schwerner?

A   Yes sir, one time.

Q   Before this date?

A   One time.

Q   Who was with you when you saw him?

A   Frank Herndon.

Q   And Frank Herndon is the man you have identified?

A   Yes sir.

Q   Where did you see him?

A   Down in the colored section of town in Meridian.

Q   What was the occasion, why did you see him?

A   So I would know him if I ever saw him again. He said he was down there and we drove along in front of this restaurant and he told me he wanted me to get a look at him.

Q   Who said this?

A   Frank Herndon.

Q   Did he say anything when you saw him?

A No sir. . . .

Q Now, did you go over to the Longhorn, I mean Akin's place?

A Yes sir, we did.

Q How did you go?

A We went in different cars. I went in the car with the boys over there that came down.

BY MR. HENDRICKS:

We object Your Honor, unless he's more specific about those boys.

BY MR. OWEN:

Q What boys are you talking about?

BY THE COURT:

Speak in the microphone, I didn't get your objection Counsel.

BY MR. HENDRICKS:

He didn't name who he went with, Your Honor.

BY THE COURT:

Yes, ask him that question again, so he can be specific.

BY MR. OWEN:

Q Whose car did you go in?

A I don't remember is I went in Pet Harris' car or in the car that came from Philadelphia with Preacher Killen and Sharpe.

Q Now, after you got over to Akins place, what did you do?

A Well several more calls were made and at that time they said they had two or three men on the way, and asked me if I knew a couple that we might get, that we needed about six or seven men.

Q And who asked you that?

A Reverend Killen.

Q And what did you do?

A I told him I would go and try to find a couple of men that I knew didn't have telephones.

Q   And who did you try to find?

A   I went over to Wayne Roberts' home.

Q   Can you identify Wayne Roberts?

A   Yes sir, he's the first man on the first row.

Q   Now, did you go there directly from Akins place?

A   No sir, we needed some gloves and I asked to stop by and see if I could find any gloves, any rubber gloves, which I couldn't at the time. We stopped at Warren's Grocery Store on the way to Wayne's house.

Q   Who asked you to do that, if you recall?

A   Reverend Killen.

Q   Now, did you see Wayne at his house?

A   Yes sir.

Q   And what did you do?

A   I asked him if he could go, that they needed some help on a case in Neshoba County, and that Reverend Killen was down and could he get away to go?

Q   What did he say?

A   Yes he would.

Q   Then what did he do?

A   We came back to Akins Mobile Home?

Q   And do you remember whose car you went over in to pick up Wayne Roberts?

A   It was Sharpe's car I presume.

Q   He was driving?

A   Yes sir.

Q   And when you got back to Akins who was there?

A   Mr. Akins was there, Pete Harris was, myself, Wayne at that time, then he said there were some more boys on their way which they arrived in just a few minutes.

Q   Who else came?

A   Travis and Doyle Barnett. . . .

Q They came over?

A Yes sir.

Q Whose car did they come in?

A They came in Doyle's car.

Q Did anyone else come over?

A Jimmy Snowden came over with another man.

Q Did anyone else come over?

A Jimmy Arledge, I met at that time, I didn't know him before.

Q Can you identify those for us?

A Jimmy Arledge is the fourth man, and Jimmy Snowden is the last man on the front row.

Q Back over here?

A Yes sir.

Q Now, was Killen still there?

A Yes sir.

Q Now, what conversation was there had after all those people arrived?

A Well at that time Reverend Killen said they had three of the Civil Rights Workers locked up and we had to hurry and get there and we were to pick them up and tear their butts up.

Q Now, did he indicate to you how they were to be stopped?

A He said that a Highway Patrol car would stop them on the outskirts of town.

Q Now, what did you do at Akins Mobil Home after you came back from getting the gloves?

A We gassed up the cars which were Sharpe's and Doyle.

Q Now, did, uhh, was there any conversation about which of this group or wouldn't go?

A Well Pete Harris was not supposed to go, and Mr. Akins couldn't go because he had work to do.

Q Now, what if anything did Preacher Killen say about the time you got ready to leave?

A   He said he would go ahead as he had to get on back there as fast as he could and make the arrangements, there were several cars were coming in and these guys couldn't be held much longer.

Q   And what did he do?

A   He left.

Q   Who left with him?

A   Sharpe and Wayne Roberts.

Q   Then what did you do?

A   I left with Doyle and Travis, Jimmy Arledge and Jimmy Snowden.

Q   Was there any indication at Akins as to where you should go?

A   We were told that as soon as we got to Philadelphia to park on the far side of the courthouse and we would be told where to go and what to do. . . .

Q   Who told you that?

A   Reverend Killen.

Q   Did you go to Philadelphia?

A   Yes sir.

Q   And where did you go?

A   Went to the far side of the court house.

Q   Now, who did you see there?

A   Saw Mr. Barnett standing out beside his pickup truck.

Q   Can you identify Mr. Barnett?

A   Yes sir. Sitting right behind me.

Q   Now, how far is he from the man in the bathrobe?

A   Third man over.

Q   Third man. Are you counting the woman?

A   No sir.

BY THE COURT:

Do you know this gentleman's name that you are identifying?

133

BY THE WITNESS:

Yes sir, he used to be Sheriff over there. I had met him before.

BY THE COURT:

I asked you what his name was.

BY THE WITNESS:

Barnett.

BY THE COURT:

Is that all you know about him?

BY THE WITNESS:

His nickname, Hop Barnett.

BY THE COURT:

All right. Go along.

BY MR. OWENS:

Q   What did he do or say?

A   He told us to wait right there, that he had to leave and he got in his truck and left, said somebody would be, would come tell us what to do.

Q   Then what happened?

A   Reverend Killen came from around the corner, told us that he would take use by and show us the jail and then we would be told where to wait until they were released.

Q   And where did you go then?

A   He got in the car and we drove around the corner by the jail and then he took us to the spot we were supposed to wait behind an old warehouse right at the edge of town.

Q   And where did he go?

A   Reverend Killen?

Q   Yes.

A   We took him back to a funeral home there in Philadelphia.

Q   Why did you take him to a funeral home?

A He said that he had to go there because if anything happened he would be the first one questioned.

Q Just tell the Court and Jury what you did after you left Preacher Killen off.

A We left him off at the spot where we were told to wait, that we would be told when and where to leave town, and we were to follow that they would not be stopped.

Q Now, who was in your car?

A It was Doyle, Travis, Jimmy Snowden and myself.

Q Now, just go right ahead.

A We sat there approximately teen or fifteen minutes. About that time a City Police car came up and said, "they're going on Highway 19 toward Meridian, follow them."

Q And who was in that lead car?

A I didn't know the man at the time.

Q Was he a policeman or was he someone else?

A I presume he was he had on a uniform. . . .

Q Then what happened?

A He turned around and went on back toward town, we turned and went toward highway 19.

BY THE COURT:

Do you know who the policeman was?

BY THE WITNESS:

No sir, at that time I did not.

BY THE COURT:

I didn't ask you when you knew, I asked you if you knew who the policeman was?

BY THE WITNESS:

No sir.

BY THE COURT:

You don't know now?

BY THE WITNESS:

A   No sir, I've been shown pictures of him.

BY THE COURT:

Do you see him in the courtroom?

BY THE WITNESS:

No sir, I don't think I do.

BY THE COURT:

All right, go along.

BY THE MR. OWEN:

Q   Then what did you do?

A   We left and drove our highway 19 back toward Meridian. At that time there was a red car ahead of us and that's what we did, a red Chevrolet. There was some more men in it.

Q   Where did you go?

A   We came back out to the outskirts of Philadelphia. The red car pulled over beside a Highway Patrol car and we pulled up behind it.

Q   And what happened then?

A   The man driving the red car got out and said something to the Patrol car and he walked back to our car and said, "never mind, they will stopped by the Deputy Sheriff, these men are not going to stop them."

BY MR. OWENS:

Q   Can you identify the man?

BY THE COURT:

Just a minute Counsel. I'll overrule the objection.

BY MR. OWEN:

Q   Can you identify the man that got out of the red car?

BY THE COURT:

Just a minute Counsel. I'll overrule the objection.

BY MR. OWEN:

Q   Can you identify the man that got out of the red car?

A   Yes sir.

Q   Who was he?

A   Posey. Sitting right next to Reverend Killen.

Q   How many men from the right?

BY THE COURT:

What was his name?

BY THE WITNESS:

Seven.

BY MR. OWEN:

Q   The Court asked you what his name was?

A   Posey.

Q   Who else was in that car?

A   There was Sharpe, another young man and Wayne Roberts.

Q   Then what happened?

A   About that time the Deputy's car came by, said something to the man in the red car, and the Deputy's car, and we took off to follow them.

Q   What deputy are you talking about?

A   Cecil Price.

Q   Can you identify him?

A   Yes sir, the gentleman sitting right there.

Q   How many from the left?

A   Four, no, five.

Q   Now, just tell the Court and Jury what happened after you took off?

A   Well, we were following the red car as we were told to do, we got on down the highways a good ways, the car broke down. Evidently it broke down, it stopped beside the road. We stopped behind it. Posey told us to come on and go ahead that it would be stopped anyway by the Sheriff, the Deputy Sheriff, and we were to follow them. He got in the car with us and left this young man there to try and fix his car.

Q   Then what did you do?

A We went on back toward Meridian from Philadelphia to a cut-off highway, I don't know which number it is, toward Union, and we were traveling at a pretty high rate of speed and about that time we caught the tail end of the Deputy's car ahead of us.

Q Then what did you see?

A We saw a little wagon in front of him which he had pulled over to the side of the road.

Q What kind of wagon?

A I don't know sir, I didn't get that close to him at that time.

Q How did he pull it over?

A He turned on his red light.

Q Then what happened?

A We pulled up behind him, he got out and went up and told the three men that were in the car to get out.

Q And did they get out?

A Yes sir, they got out and he told them to get in his car.

Q Now, who told them that?

A The Deputy Sheriff. They got in the back of his car and Posey told Arledge to get in their car and follow them and we turned and went back.

Q And did you see anything happen when these three boys got in this car?

A They got in the car?

Q What, if anything, did you see or hear when they got in?

A Well I heard a thump like the Deputy was rushing them up to get in there or where he hit one of them or the car or what, but I did hear a thump.

Q And were these people who got in the car, were they white people or negroes?

A Two white men, one negro.

Q Then what did you do?

A Turned the cars around come back toward highway 19.

Q Then where did you go?

A   Turned left on highway 19 all the way to, oh about 34 miles to this other cut-off road which wasn't a paved highway and then they said somebody had better stay here and watch in case anything happens, 'til the other car comes.

Q   How about the people, uhh, did you pass the red car going?

A   Yes sir.

Q   You were going toward Philadelphia?

A   Yes sir.

Q   And was anyone in the red car when you passed it?

A   This young man and Sharpe were still there.

Q   Now, did any of these people, uhh did they both stay there?

A   No sir, Sharpe got in the, I believe he got in the wagon or the other car that was ahead of us, I don't know where he got in the police car or not.

Q   Then you drove toward Philadelphia?

A   Yes sir.

Q   Which way did you turn off?

A   We turned left off the highway.

Q   On to what kind of road?

A   Just a graded clay road. I got out of the car to watch and see if anything was happening, and the other cars proceeded on up the road.

Q   Will you tell the Court and Jury what you heard and what you did?

A   Well, I hear a car door slamming, and some loud talking, I couldn't understand or distinguish anybody's voice or anything, and then I heard several shots.

Q   Then what did you do?

A   Walked up the road toward where the noise came from.

Q   And what did you see when you walked up the road?

A   Just a bunch of men milling and standing around that had been in the two cars ahead of us and someone said, "better pick up these shells." I hollered, "what do you want me to do?"

Q   Then what did you do?

A   Then ---

Q Excuse me, did you see these three boys?

A Yes sir, beside the road.

Q How were they?

A They were lying down.

Q Were they dead?

A I presume so, yes sir.

BY MR. HENDRICKS:

We object to what he presumes.

BY THE COURT:

Sustained.

BY MR. OWEN:

Q What did you do then?

A We put them through the back window of the truck lid of their wagon.

Q Is that the station wagon?

A Yes sir. At that time the Highway Deputy, or the Deputy Sheriff's car turned around and went back toward Highway 19, Posey said, "just follow me, I know where we're going."

Q So what did you do?

A Got back in all the cars, Posey and some of the boys were in the wagon, got back in the cars to follow Posey 'cause he said he knew where we were going.

Q At the time you left, who was up there at that spot?

A We were all up there.

Q Who are we?

A Travis and Doyle Barnett, Jimmy Snowden, Arledge, Sharpe, Posey.

Q How about the Sheriff?

A The Deputy Sheriff was there. . . .

Q And after you got these boys loaded up where did you go?

A   I don't know sir. We went the same road we were on, we kept on veering back toward Philadelphia. I thought on the road we were on at the time, come to the edge of Philadelphia, turned back to the left out of town until we came to the edge where the lights were and then down several more dirt roads.

Then I found out later to the dam site, I found out later, I did not know at the time where it was. I thought it was construction. We went through a barbwire fence and was there.

Q   And what did you do then?

A   Opened the back of the station wagon, took the boys out and took them down in this hollow.

Q   Was there any equipment there?

A   Two bulldozers.

Q   Then what happened?

A   Posey told us to go back up the road and listen out that the operator was not there yet so Jim Snowden and I walked back up the road to wait.

Q   Then what happened.

A   Then at that time we thought we heard something coming through the woods but it was nothing but a cow and about that time he said Doyle and Raymond Sharpe were going to find the bulldozer operator because he wasn't there when we got there so they left to go and get him.

Q   Then what happened?

A   Well they came back in a different way they did not come back in by us at that time and we heard someone whistle across the way and Snowden said, "I'll go see who it is" and he walked down the road just a little ways, came back and said it must be the operator and about that time we heard the bulldozer crank up.

Q   And how long did it operate.

A   I don't know, twenty minutes, at that time I wasn't counting the time.

Q   And what did you do then?

A   We got back in the car and then we were going to put the license plate back on it which had been taken off of Doyle Barnett's car.

Q   Did you have any conversation with Posey at that sight?

BY MR. ALFORD:

We object to his leading and suggesting.

BY THE COURT:

Overruled.

BY THE WITNESS:

A   Posey told us we could go back to this place and put the license plate back on the car and Sharpe knew the was to come round the road and that he would wait there and take the operator back.

Q   Then what if anything did he indicate about the station wagon?

A   He said the station wagon, don't worry about it it would be taken to Alabama and be burned.

Q   By whom?

A   He said by the operator.

Q   Did he indicate to you the name of the operator?

A   He said, "Herman will take it to Alabama" is all I know.

Q   Then where did you go?

A   We went back to a warehouse and office building and gas pump on the outside of Philadelphia.

Q   And who did you see there?

A   Well it was Travis and Doyle and I, Wayne and some other man that I had never seen before, as well as Posey and Sharpe.

Q   Can you identify the man that you had never seen before?

A   I couldn't at that time, but since that time I've seen his picture.

Q   Is he in this courtroom?

A   The gentleman sitting right next to Mr. Price.

Q   Which side of Mr. Price?

A   Mr. Price's left.

Q   Was he up there?

A   Yes sir.

Q   What did you do then?

A   We got out of the cars, Doyle put the license plate back on his car at that time, they handed me all the gloves, told me to get rid of them when we got back to town or on the way and I said I'll take care of them.

Q   Now, where did you go at that town?

A   We came back toward of Philadelphia and right in the main section of town right to the outskirts by a big brown grocery store we pulled into a parking lot behind Sharpe's lot.

Q   And who did you see at that time, if anybody?

A   There was a police car sitting there with two other men sitting that I don't know at that time who they were.

Q   You don't know any of the men in the police car?

A   I knew the Deputy Sheriff sitting on the opposite side of the car.

BY THE COURT:

I didn't understand the witness identification of the man sitting left to Deputy Price?

BY THE WITNESS:

He was the same City Policeman that pulled up and told us which way he was headed out, Your Honor.

BY THE COURT:

What was his name?

BY THE WITNESS:

I didn't know his name at that time.

BY THE COURT:

Do you know it now?

BY THE WITNESS:

I've been told what his name was.

BY THE COURT:

What is it?

BY MR. HENDRICKS:

We object to what he's been told.

BY THE COURT:

I ask you what is his name now?

BY THE WITNESS:

Willis.

BY MR. OWEN:

Q   Who are you pointing to now, who are you talking to now?

A   The policeman sitting next to the Deputy right here.

Q   Which side of Price?

A   The Deputy is sitting right there.

Q   Oh. Can you identify the City Policeman?

A   It looks like the gentleman sitting right next to the Deputy.

BY MR. HENDRICKS:

We object to what he looks like.

BY THE COURT:

Yes, I sustain the objection.

BY MR. OWEN:

Q   Then what happened after you got to this parking lot?

A   We stopped there, Posey got out and talked to the men in the car then he came back and told us to go on home that everything would be taken care of.

Q   Then where did you go?

A   We came back toward Meridian.

Q   And do you remember about what time you left the City of Philadelphia?

A   A quarter of twelve.

Q   And what did you do after you got back to Meridian?

A   I went home.

Q   Do you remember about what time you arrived in Meridian?

A   Close to one o'clock, yes sir.

Q   Now, do you know Sam Bowers?

A   Yes sir.

Q   Can you identify him in the courtroom?.

A   Sitting right behind, next to the lady nurse.

Q   Now had you seen him prior to this that happened?

BY MR. BUCKLEY:

We object, Your Honor, after this happened, this is immaterial to this case?

BY THE COURT:

Overruled.

BY THE WITNESS:

Yes sir I saw him before.

Q   And what were he circumstances under which you met him?

A   I first met him at a meeting somewhere on the outside of Raleigh, Mississippi.

Q   Did you see him at any time other than that?

A   Yes sir, we went down to Laurel to see him one time, there was some discrepancy about some finances in our Klan.

BY THE COURT:

I think he ought to give us some time or some place to see if it has any relationship with this case so let your questions be accordingly.

BY MR. OWEN:

Q   This particular time that you saw him where was he?

A   At a church somewhere out near Raleigh, I don't know the route.

Q   Now, subsequent to that time where had you seen him?

A   We went to Laurel, Mississippi and went to a restaurant and he was called and we went to a restaurant and he was called and we went on the outskirts of town and sat there and talked.

Q   Who was with you?

A   Well there was Pete Harris, Mr. Akins' son.

Q   Do you remember when that was?

A   It was about May of that year. . . .

Q   On that occasion what if anything did this man say about Schwerner?

A   He said he was a thorn in the side of everyone living, especially white people and that he should be taken care of.

Q   Now, after the 21st of June, 1964, did you have an occasion to see this man again?

A   Yes sir.

Q   When did you see him?

A   It was about a month after all of this had happened we saw him in Laurel again.

Q   Do you remember who went with you?

A   Pete and uhh, Harris, Pete Harris and I.

Q   Was there any conversation at that time about what happened?

A   Sam said the best thing to do was not to talk about it, that everything was well done, it was a job to be proud of, if there were any instruments involved they should be gotten rid of.

BY THE COURT:

Let me ask you this. You say you picked up some cartridges at the scene of this dam where there were, uh, was some shooting?

BY THE WITNESS:

No sir, I heard someone say "let's get up all of the cartridges" as I walked up.

BY THE COURT:

Were the cartridges got up?

BY THE WITNESS:

I don't know.

BY THE COURT:

How many shots did you hear?

BY THE WITNESS:

About four.

BY MR. OWEN:

Q   Now, were any of these people or how many of these people were armed if any? On June 21, 1964.

A   I think we all were.

BY THE COURT:

Let me ask you this, you say you heard four shots. Do you know what these shots were directed at or to?

BY THE WITNESS:

No sir.

BY THE COURT:

Do you know where either one of these individuals that you had taken out of that truck was hit by those shots?

BY THE WITNESS:

I don't know if they were hit by those shots, I understand though they were shot.

BY MR. WEIR:

We object to that Your Honor, what he understands.

BY THE COURT:

Yes, I sustain the objection. I want you to understand this is real important. Do you know whether or not that either one of these boys, Schwerner, Goodman and Chaney were living at the time of these shots.

BY THE WITNESS:

I don't know sir.

BY MR. OWEN:

Q   When had you last seen them?

A   When had I last saw them? When they were put in the Deputy Sheriff's car on that highway going to Union.

Q   And how long before you heard those shots yourself?

A   Well driving back on highway 19 up there was approximately thirty minutes, twenty minutes.

Q   And were they living at the last time you last saw them?

A   When they were put in the Deputy Sheriff's car.

BY THE COURT:

Was that the last time you saw them?

BY THE WITNESS:

Til' I got up there where their bodies were, sir.

BY THE COURT:

That wasn't what Counsel asked you and what I asked you. Do you know whether they were living or dead when you saw them last?

BY THE WITNESS:

They were living when they got in his car ---

BY THE COURT:

I didn't ask you that either. I said were those boys, Schwerner, Goodman and Chaney living the last time you saw them?

BY THE WITNESS:

Yes sir.

BY THE COURT:

They were?

BY THE WITNESS:

Yes sir.

BY MR. OWEN:

Q   When was the last time you saw these three individuals?

A   When we got to this dam site.

Q   Now, at that time were they living?

A   No sir. I don't believe, I'm not a doctor but they weren't checked to be.

Q   But this was the same three boys that you had seen?

BY MR. ALFORD:

We object to his leading.

BY THE COURT:

Yes, I sustain the objection.

BY MR. ALFORD:

And we would move the Court to instruct the jury to disregard the answer.

BY THE COURT:

Yes, don't consider his answer. You tell Counsel one thing and tell me something else. Go along. . . .

BY MR. OWEN:

Q   Now, when Price put these boys in his car, just describe the direction that you took?

A   We turned right around ---

BY MR. ALFORD:

Your Honor please, we object. This is repetitious.

BY THE COURT:

I'll let him go along.

BY THE WITNESS:

We turned down the highway and came back to highway 19.

BY MR. OWEN:

Q   Then which way did you go?

A   We turned left on highway 19.

Q   And then which way did you turn the left time that you turned?

A   To the left again.

Q   Is that the place where you loaded these bodies?

A   Yes sir.

Q   Now, in connection with the information that you told the F.B.I. did you give this information to the F.B.I.?

A   Yes sir.

Q   Now, did you give this information, uhh, did you receive money from the F.B.I.?

A   Yes sir, I was told that they would help me. I told them when they first came, I told them if I tell you anything now when I was first approached on this, they came to the job several times and everything else, they knew all about the case, it was just a matter of tying it up---

BY MR. PIGFORD:

If the Court please, we object to any conversation between this man and the F.B.I. Agent, it would be an impossibility to cross examine him.

BY THE COURT:

I don't understand him to be narrating a conversation go along.

BY MR. OWEN:

Go ahead.

Q   Yes sir, they told me they would help me get out of town, I told them I didn't have anything, I had lost my job---

BY MR. ALFORD:

We object, Your Honor, this is hearsay.

BY THE COURT:

I don't think that's hearsay, he's telling what the officers promised him.

BY MR. OWN:

Q   Go ahead.

A   They would help me get out of town which they did.

Q   Do you know how much money they paid you?

A   At that time?

Q   Yes.

A   Approximately three thousand dollars.

Q   And what did you do with that money?

A   I bought a car so I could leave town and made arrangements to rent a trailer and take my family away from Mississippi.

Q   And did you do that?

A   Yes sir.

Q   And subsequent to that time, did you receive any money from the F.B.I.?

A   They told me they would help me and see that I didn't starve 'til I was situated and got a job and after the publicity of all of this died down.

Q   And about how long was it before you were able to get a permanent job?

A   A year.

Q   And during that year, if you recall, about how much money did they furnish you?

A   A hundred dollars a month. Per week, I'm sorry.

Q   A week?

A   Yes sir.

Q   And after you got a permanent job about how much money did they furnish you?

A   After I went to work, $55.00 a week, then they give me $25.00 a week for just a while and they said they would then give me just a hundred dollars a month to bring my salary up to a living scale.

Q   Now, where were you working at the time you gave the F.B.I. the information?

A   In the NASA Missile Base out of Picayune.

Q   And how much were you making at that time?

A $175 a week was about what I was taking.

Q   That's all, Your Honor.

Trial Transcript Page
Mississippi Burning Trial Homepage

CHAPTER TWENTY-ONE

—⟋⟍—

OUR FINAL FBI INFORMANT IS DELMAR DENNIS. During his initial testimony, he identified his occupation as being a minister. He was twenty-seven years old, and had been a minister since he was fourteen years old. He had ministered churches in Leake, Jasper, Neshoba, and Lauderdale Counties, however at that current time, he was not pastoring a church. When asked if he was a member of the White Knights of the Ku Klux Klan, his response was, "I have been up to the present time, yes sir." He said he joined the Klan at the Cash Salvage Store on 65th Avenue in Meridian, in March of 1964. Those present at the time he had joined were Edgar Ray Killen, Wayne Roberts, Frank Herndon, and Pete Harris, and Delmar Dennis credits Killen as having been in charge of the meeting.

When asked about the purpose of the meeting, Dennis testified that Killen explained to him "what a fine organization that it [the Klan] was, that it stood for Christianity and American constitution, and that it was for the purpose of segregation and preservation of the white race." Killen then administered the oath to those who wished to join. Killen allegedly told the new recruits that the "Klan was an organization of action, no Boy Scout group, that we were here to do business." Allegedly, Killen said the Klan would "need to do, and would do burning crosses; people would need to be beaten, and occasionally there would have to be elimination [murder]."

Multiple objections were entered, and they were ultimately overruled.

Dennis proceeded to testify that Killen "explained that any project that was carried out by the Klan had to be approved by the Klan, that no person was to do anything on their own, and if they did, they would not receive any money or any help whatsoever from the Klan." Dennis was asked if he could explain approval for the types of actions regarding Klan procedure that he'd discussed. His answer was, "Yes, a person would report to the local klavern, [local Klan lodge] and the next meeting after he decided that certain things should be done, it would be voted on by the group, and if approved, it would be carried out by those who volunteered to carry out. This included cross burnings and occasional beatings, but elimination was reserved by the ruling of the state organization, and after approval of a local klavern, it had to be approved by the state."

Please note that according to Mr. Dennis, the klavern, in its entirety—not one person in particular—had to approve an elimination before it could be presented to the state organization. At no point did Dennis specify who had made the suggestion, just that it had been approved through the klavern for proposal to the state organization. If Killen was in fact a Klan member, why would a unanimous vote by the klavern make him more criminally accountable than any of the other members? Why not implicate *all members* who were present?

The next question asked of Dennis was, "Did you attend any subsequent meetings of the Klan prior to June 21, 1964?" He acknowledged that he had attended regularly scheduled weekly meetings, although the meeting locations often varied. He said that Killen, as kleagle, was the leader for the first few weeks, as they were still organizing as a klavern, and after that, the officers of the klavern were in charge. He was asked about his knowledge of Schwerner, of whom he initially knew nothing, but acknowledged having been present at subsequent meetings where Schwerner was discussed. When asked of his if he had been present at meetings in which Schwerner's "elimination" was discussed, Dennis replied, "sometimes in early April of 1964 at Cash Salvage Store. After Mr. Killen explained the approval of elimination process after it was suggested by someone in the meeting."

Now, according to this statement, *someone*—not Killen—suggested the elimination. Killen explained the rules regarding elimination, allegedly, but had not suggested a plot or plan, or masterminded the murders. Exactly how does explaining a procedure make one guilty? Just as an example, if I explained to you how to process methamphetamine, and you elect to create a lab to produce methamphetamine, does it make me criminally responsible for the action you elected to engage in?

It was asked of Dennis if he could identify who was present at the meeting. His response was, "Wayne Roberts, Pete Harris, Edgar Ray Killen, Frank Herndon, [and] B. L. Akin." When asked what was said at the meeting, his answer was, "It was explained that it was necessary for a project to be approved, at which time somebody in the group—I do not remember who it was or if it was one of the defendants—said that he believed we should vote on the elimination of Goatee."

To the reader, please remember that Dennis was an FBI informant, and according to his statement, he could not remember who had suggested that Schwerner be eliminated. However, forty years later, this statement was over-looked, and Edgar Killen was, in part, convicted by this statement, or at the very least, its lack of introduction. Dennis was asked if Schwerner had been discussed at a subsequent meeting prior to June 21, 1964. He acknowledged that Schwerner had been discussed at a meeting behind the Longhorn Drive-in in Frank Herndon's trailer. He further testified that Herndon and Pete Harris were present at the meeting. Please take note of Pete Harris's constant presence. Dennis testified that Harris and Herndon said "even though the state had approved the elimination of Schwerner, that nothing had been done about it, and they were wondering if anything was going to be done about it or who had volunteered to take care of the job."

Dennis alleges that, on what was believed to have been June 16, Schwerner was in Neshoba County and would possibly have been present in the Mount Zion Church. This was allegedly discussed at a meeting in a vacant gym in Neshoba County. Among the defendants present was Herndon, B. L. Akins, and Wayne Roberts, and the meeting had allegedly been called to order by Mr. Killen. This meeting was supposedly attended by more than "seventy-five people"; in addition to those previously listed, "Hop" Barnette was also present, and . . . absolutely nobody else he could apparently recall out of more than seventy-five people? Selective memory? Dennis said Barnette interrupted the meeting by saying that on the way over to the meeting, he had passed the Mount Zion Church and seen that there was a meeting being held. He thought that at the time that it must have been an important meeting, because the church was heavily guarded. He wanted to present what he had found to the group and see what they wanted to do about it.

In response, Killen allegedly asked "if the group thought that anything should be done about it, and some person in the group suggested that there probably were civil rights workers in the church, or it would not have been so heavily guarded, and it was agreed that something would be done."

Following more objections, Dennis said, "They asked for volunteers to go out to the church. . . ." Wayne Roberts, according to Dennis, was "the only one of the defendants that [he] definitely [knew had] left the place." He then added that in addition to those in the Neshoba County group, "Mr. Barnette and Billy Wayne Posey from Philadelphia" also went along. It is alleged by Dennis that Billy Birdsong, from the Meridian group, later reported that "all of the Negroes who came out of the church and left by way of exit guarded by the Meridian group, were beaten, and that it was his understanding that those who left by way of exit guarded by Neshoba County men. . . . "

At that point, an objection was entered by Mr. Hendricks, who stated, "This is the worst kind of hearsay." The objection was overruled. Dennis continued his answer by saying, "And he, Billy Birdsong, who was making the report, objected to the fact that those guarding the exits from Neshoba County had not beaten anyone who came out that way, and he stated very heatedly that he disapproved of this, that he didn't like it all; he thought they should have been beaten."

Dennis was asked if anybody else had said anything, to which he answered, "Billy Wayne Posey said it was his understanding when they left the gym to go to the church, they were to get anybody there [who] was white, and that no white person came out the exit he was guarding, and therefore, no one was beaten." He was then asked, "Did you observe anything about any of the defendants that night they came back from the church to the meeting?" Again, an objection was entered, and the court directed Dennis, "Yes, I think you had better be a *little* more specific."

The question was posed as, "Did you notice anything, or what, if anything, did you notice about any of the defendants who came back who had gone there with you from Meridian?" Dennis stated, "Wayne Roberts had blood on his hands, or knuckles, and he told me he got this when he was beating a nigger." Dennis was asked what he did then, and he answered, "Well, shortly after the report, it was agreed that we had better leave the building, so the meeting broke up."

Dennis left the meeting in the same car as B. C. Lyles, Wayne Roberts, Dick Warner, and Billy Birdsong. He added, "Birdsong went back through the speech again he had made in the gym, and expressed his disapproval of the way it [had been] handled at the other exit, and told those of us [who] were in the car, that they had certainly taken care of the ones [who] came out the exit where they were, that they had taken care of theirs." Dennis was then asked, "What did Wayne Roberts say?" He answered, "He agreed that they were well beaten and well stomped. He said there was one exception to what Birdsong had said, that one old negro woman wasn't beaten."

Next, he was asked whether he knew Sheriff Rainey, and stated that he did; he had first come to know of him early in the summer of 1963. He also confirmed that he knew Cecil Price, and identified both by pointing out their seating arrangements in the courtroom. He also was asked if knew whether or not the Rainey and Price were members of the White Knights of the Ku Klux Klan. His response was, "I knew them as members." He also testified that he knew them to have been members prior to June 21, 1964. The next line of questioning was in regard to his role as an informant for the FBI. He was asked, "Now, have you furnished information to the Federal Bureau of Investigation about the activities of the White Knights of the Ku Klux Klan?" His response was, "I have." Dennis went on to testify that he had begun furnishing the information in November of 1964, and that he had been paid for it for almost three years.

He said he was paid on the basis of expenses incurred and information obtained, and, was paid approximately five thousand dollars a year. There was an attempt to ask him questions about Sam Bowers, which were followed with a series of objections. Eventually it was established that he did in fact know Bowers, and had had a conversation with him on December 24, 1964 in Philadelphia at a southern Methodist church. He was then asked, "What, if anything, was said by Cecil Price about the three civil rights workers being killed?" Dennis's answer was, "He said the government knew more about the case than he thought they did, and he had concluded that Jordan was the man [who] was giving the information to the Bureau." When asked why Price had thought it was Jordan providing information, Dennis stated, "Yes, he said it was Jordan, because Jordan was the only person who could have seen him hit Chaney the night the three men were killed." An objection was entered, and a motion was made to grant a mistrial. These were overruled.

He was asked if he had had any conversations with Frank Herndon after the civil rights workers had gone missing. Dennis indicated that he had, and that the conversations had taken place at the restaurant Herndon operated. According to Dennis, "Frank said he was being accused of being for that, but that he was not. He said he had witnesses who would say he was at work the night the men were killed." The questioning was again directed toward Dennis's conversations with Sam Bowers that had taken place after June 21. When asked what Bowers had said, Dennis stated, "He said Judge Cox would probably make them take those bodies back and put them where they got them, that they found the bodies on an illegal search warrant." After more questions concerning Bowers and he and Dennis's method of communication, Dennis's testimony concluded.

Now let's take a moment to review some of Delmar Dennis's testimony. To start, Dennis, if he was being totally honest and accurate with his testimony, had, at the very most, placed Killen at Klan meetings.

Killen maintains to this day that he had never been a member of the Klan. Even if he had been a member, however, it was not then, nor is it now, a crime. So, Killen's presence, or lack thereof, at Klan meetings would be irrelevant, as it seemingly was for others whom Dennis identified as having been present at meetings. Killen had allegedly explained procedures for obtaining approval on Klan actions. Again, that would not be a crime. Anyone can explain how to commit a crime or provide a theory for it, but providing theories or explanation does not indicate participation in criminal conduct.

Beyond these allegations, Dennis did not implicate Edgar Killen in any criminal action, and he was ultimately acquitted in the 1967 trial. Let's not overlook the fact that Dennis, much like Jordan and Miller, had nothing to corroborate their testimonies, such as recordings, witnesses, etc. This could have very well been by design, as it would have allowed the FBI to coach them on their testimonies with no way for it to be contradicted. And, like Jordan and Miller, Dennis was a paid informant, if you'll recall. He testified to receiving $5,000 per year, for three years, of taxpayer money. The current equivalent worth of that would be $39,066 per year, or roughly a grand total of $117,198 used to convict what very well could be an innocent man, sacrificed for actions in which he took no part.

Would these informants have lied for their money? Would money have been their motivations? Please look at what each man received in compensation from the FBI, and then take into consideration that the median

Book cover of Delmar Dennis' book "Klandestine" written after 1967 trial. Dennis was a paid FBI informant.

household income in 1964 was $6,676.00. That should certainly answer the question as to whether money may have been their potential motives. Ultimately, Delmar Dennis wrote a book about his role in the investigation—which provided him with an additional source of income.

DELMAR DENNIS, called as a witness for and on behalf of Plaintiff, was sworn and testified as follows:

DIRECT EXAMINATION

BY MR. DOAR:

Q   Would you tell the Court and jury your full name?

A   Delmar Dennis.

Q   Where do you live?

A   3228-46th Street, Meridian.

Q   What is your occupation?

A   I'm a minister. . . .

Q   How long have you lived in Mississippi?

A   All of my life.

Q   Where were you raised?

A   I was raised in Scott County, Mississippi.

Q   How long have you been, excuse me, how old are you?

A   27.

Q   How long have you been a minister?

A   Since I was 14. 13 years sir.

Q   What churches have you held or had in State of Mississippi?

A   I have served churches in the Southern Baptist Denomination, the Methodist and the Southern Methodist.

Q   And where did you have those churches?

A   In Scott County, Leake County, Jasper County, Neshoba County and Lauderdale County.

Q   When were you a minister in Neshoba County?

A   I was there for about 6 months in 1960.

Q   What is your present church?

A   I'm not pastoring a church at the present time.

Q   What was the last church that you were pastor of?

A   The First Southern Methodist Church in Meridian.

Q   When were you pastor of that church?

A   I was pastor of that church on October 7 of 64 so it has been a little less than 3 years.

Q   Do you any writing?

A   Yes, some.

Q   And this is in connection with your work?

A   Yes.

Q   Are you a member of the White Knights of the Ku Klux Klan?

A   I have been up to the present time, yes sir.

Q   When did you join the White Knights of the Ku Klux Klan?

A   In March of 1964.

Q   And where did you join?

A   Joined at the Cash Salvage Store on 65th Avenue in Meridian.

Q   And can you look around the courtroom on the inside of the rail and tell me whether anyone sitting there was present at that meeting of the White Knights of the Ku Klux Klan when you joined?

A   Edgar Ray Killen was present, Wayne Roberts, Frank Herndon.

Q   Anyone else?

A   Pete Harris.

Q   Can you identify those for the Court by counting down.

THE COURT:

Who was the last one?

THE WITNESS:

Pete Harris.

THE COURT:

Thank you.

THE WITNESS:

A   The first person on the end Wayne Roberts, the fifth is Pete Harris, the seventh is Edgar Ray Killen and Frank Herndon is over here in his pajamas.

Q   Who had charge of the meeting?

A   Edgar Ray Killen.

BY THE COURT:

Who is Pete Harris?

BY THE WITNESS:

James Harris, I believe.

BY MR. DOAR:

Q   Can you tell me the purpose of that first meeting of the White Knights of the Ku Klux Klan?

A   Yes, Mr. Killen explained, first of all what a fine organization that it was that it stood for christianity and American constitution and that it was for the purpose of segregation and preservation of the white race.

Q   Was anything else said by Mr. Killen at that meeting?

A   Quite a bit was said by Mr. Killen at that meeting and at other meetings.

Q   I'm just asking you about this meeting?

A   Mr. Killen administered the oath to those that wished to join and explained other things.

Q   Did you join?

A   I did.

Q   Did you get a number?

A   I did.

Q   What was your number?

A   Number thirty-two.

Q   Did Mr. Killen explain the Klan action?

A   After the swearing in ceremony he explained that it was an organization of action no Boy Scout group, that we were here to do business.

Q   Did he explain what he meant by that?

A   He said there would be things that the Klan would need to do and would do and among those would be the burning crosses, people would need to be beaten and occasionally there would have to be elimination.

Q   What did he mean by elimination?

A   He meant killing a person.

BY MR. BUCKLEY:

Your Honor may it please the Court I'm going to object to this testimony, telling what someone had mentioned.

BY THE COURT:

He said he said it so I'll overrule your objection.

BY MR. DOAR:

Q   Did he explain how various types of action would be approved?

BY MR. WEIR:

Now if Your Honor please we object to various actions and ask the Court to ask him to define it just as to the action in this case.

BY THE COURT:

Well I assume that's what his question calls for.

BY MR. DOAR:

Q   Did he say how the action was described in your answer to my last question?

BY MR. WEIR:

And I object again if Your Honor please.

BY THE COURT:

Overruled.

BY MR. WEIR:

May I have a continuing objection.

BY THE COURT:

Yes and it stands overruled.

BY THE WITNESS:

A   He explained that any project that was carried out by the Klan had to be approved by the Klan, that no person was to do anything on their own and if they did, they would not receive any money or any help whatsoever from the Klan.

Q   Did he say who would approve these projects?

BY MR. BUCKLEY:

Your Honor please the Court I would object to the testimony of this witness will be used against anyone until and unless it is shown to be a part of this, uh, as they are alleged, a conspiracy or a plot.

BY THE COURT:

I understand that's what he's trying to prove so I'll overrule your objection Counsel.

BY MR. HENDRICKS:

If it please the Court we object to his leading type questions.

BY THE COURT:

Overruled. Let's get along gentlemen, let's don't give rise to so many frivolous type objections.

BY MR. DOAR:

Q   Would you answer?

A   Could you repeat the question please?

Q   Can you explain the type of approval for the various types of action of the Klan procedure which you have discussed?

A   Yes, a person would report to the local Klavern and the next meeting after he decided that certain things should be done it would be voted on by the group and if approved then it would be carried out by those who volunteered to carry out and this included cross burnings and occasional beatings, but the elimination was reserved by the ruling of the State Organization and after approval a local Klavern it had to be approved by the state.

Q   Now after the approval, I'll withdraw that. Did you attend any subsequent meetings of the Klan prior to June 21, 1964?

A   I did.

Q   Where did yo attend those meetings.

A   Some of them were held at the cash salvage store, some of them were held at Harrison Box House, some of them were in the trailer at Frank Herndon. . . .

Q   When were the meetings ordinarily held?

A   The first meetings were usually held on a Tuesday or Thursday night, but they rotated the night as well as the place of meetings.?

Q   Were they regular weekly meetings?

A   They were weekly meetings, yes sir..

BY MR. HENDRICKS:

If it please the Court he stated one or more meetings in April and we would like for him to testify as to the date.

BY THE COURT:

I would expect that you would find that out on cross examination Counsel.

BY MR. DOAR:

Q   Who was the leader of the meetings during the April date 1964 at Meridian?

A   Edgar Ray Killen was the leader of the Kleagle for the first few weeks as we were still organizing and after that the officers of the local Klavern were in charge.

Q   Now, did you know a man named Mickey Schwerner?

A   I did not know him.

Q   Did you know of him?

A   Yes sir.

Q   Did you ever hear any discussion of Mickey Schwerner at Klan meetings prior to June 21, 1964?

A   Yes sir there were several discussions about him.

Q   Now could you fix the time and the place of those several meetings and tell us who was present at the meetings, the dates of the first meeting and if there were others?

A   Sometimes in early April 1964 at Cash Salvage Store. After Mr. Killen had explained the approval of elimination process it was suggested by someone in the meeting.

Q   Let me ask you if you could tell us those who were in the meeting?

A   Those that I have already identified. Would you name those again for us?

A   Wayne Roberts, Pete Harris, Edgar Ray Killen, Frank Herndon, B.L. Akin.

Q   Now what was said?

A   It was explain that it was necessary for a project to be approved at which time somebody in the group, I do not remember who it was or if it was one of the defendants, said that he believed we should vote on the elimination of "Goatee."

Q   And who was Goatee?

A   Goatee was Michael Schwerner. . . .

Q   What if anything was said by Preacher Killen.

A   He said that we were not yet organized in a Klavern and it would not be necessary for a local Klavern to approve that project that it had already been approved by the State Officers of the Klan and had been made a part of their program and it would be taken care of.

Q   Now was Mickey Schwerner discussed at a subsequent meeting prior to June 21, 1964?

A   He was.

Q   And where was that meeting held?

A   There was a meeting in early May held at Frank Herndon's trailer, at that time parked behind the Longhorn.

Q   What is the Longhorn?

A   The Longhorn is a drive in restaurant.

Q   And did any of the defendants work there?

A   Frank Herndon was running the Longhorn at that time.

Q   And who was present at this meeting?

A   Frank Herndon was running the Longhorn at that time.

Q   And who was present at this meeting?

A   Frank Herndon and Pete Harris.

Q   And what was said?

A   It was said that even though the State had approved the elimination of Schwerner that nothing had been done about it and they were wondering if anything was going to be done about it or who had volunteered to take care of the job.

Q   Now when was the third time or was there another time that Mickey Schwerner was discussed?

A   This is prior to June 21st.

Q   June 21st

A   It was believed on June 16th that he was in Neshoba County. It was mentioned there that he might be present in the Mount Zion Church.

Q   And where was that meeting?

A   That meeting was held in an abandoned or vacant gym in Neshoba County.

Q   Now, referring to, strike that. On the 16th of June tell us about that meeting at the Bloom School?

BY MR. HENDRICKS:

We object. He didn't name the school, Your Honor. He's putting words in his mouth.

BY THE COURT:

Rephrase your question.

BY MR. DOAR:

Q   Tell us about this meeting that was held in Neshoba County, just tell us how you got there, who you went with among the defendants, who you saw them you got there among the defendants.

A   Frank Herndon called and told me that we had been invited to a visit in a meeting of the Neshoba Klavern and for us to meet at the Longhorn early that afternoon and go in as few a cars as possible and so we started to meet there oh before sundown that day and I went in a car, there were five of us in that car, was Wayne Roberts is the only one who is a defendant in this case.

Q   There were other people in the car?

A   There were.

Q   And did another car go?

A   Mr. B.L. Akin took a car in which there were other people.

Q   And were any other of the defendants in Mr. Akin's car if you know?

A   I don't ow that they went in this car.

Q   And when you got to, will you just tell in your own words what happened that night?

A   The meeting was called to order by Mr. Killen.

Q   Let me ask you where did you go first?

A   We went first to the H& H Restaurant which in on Highway 19 just as we are going into Philadelphia.

Q   And what happened there?

A   We met with some people from Neshoba County. Edgar Ray Killen is the only one that I recall that I knew and we had a cup of coffee and then drove out to the gym.

Q   And where was the gym.

A   It was out Highway 16 east for a few miles and then turned south.

Q   And how far did you go south, if you recall?

A   I don't recall but it was only a little ways after we turned off of Highway 16.

Q   Do you know the name of the place you went to?

A   No sir.

Q   Can you describe it?

A   It was a gym that had once been part of a school system there was consolidated, no longer in use, it was not lighted except by the lights that were provided at the meeting.

Q   And what time of day or night was it?

A   Well, by this time it was between eight and nine o'clock and dark.

Q   Did you go inside the gym?

A   Yes sir.

Q   About how many people were present?

A   I would say more than 75.

Q   And can you tell me if any of the other defendants were present?

A   Mr. Akin was there and Pete Harris and Frank Herndon.

Q   I don't recall anybody else. Uh, let's see. Mr. Killen of course was there and Hop Barnette was there.

Q   Anybody else from Meridian?

A   I don't recall anybody else from Meridian that's a defendant.

A He's sitting by Mr. Akin. He's the fourth one down from the left over here.

Q Who is he sitting next to on the other side?

A Sam Bowers.

Q Now, what did Mr. Killen say at that meeting?

A Well, they called the meeting to order and started to make some routine announcements and was interrupted shortly after the meeting?

Q And who interrupted him?

A Hop Barnette.

Q And what did Hop Barnette Say?

A He said that on the way over to the meeting that he had passed the Mount Zion Church and there was a meeting being held and there must be an important meeting because the church wa heavily guarded and he wanted to present what he had found to the group and see what they wanted to do about it.

Q And what was said then?

A Edgar Ray Killen asked if the group thought that anything should be done about it and some person in the group suggested that there probably were civil rights workers in the church or it would not have been so heavily guarded and it was agreed that something would be done---

BY MR. HENDRICKS:

We object to what someone said unless he's a member of one of these defendants.

BY THE COURT:

Yes. I sustain the objection.

BY MR. DOAR:

Q What was said in the presence of the defendants that you have named?

A Yes sir.

BY MR. HENDRICKS:

Move to exclude that, Your Honor, and ask the jury to disregard it.

BY THE COURT:

I will overrule it as to those persons who are defendants in this case who were present. Otherwise I will sustain.

By Mr. DOAR:

Q   Then what happened?

A   They asked for volunteers top go out to the church. . . .

Q   Who left the church among the defendants?

A   Wayne Roberts is the only one of the defendants that I definitely know left the place.

Q   Any of the people from Neshoba County?

A   Mr. Barnette left with the group and Billy Wayne Posey from Philadelphia also went with the group.

Q   And do you see Billy Wayne Posey in the court room?

A   Yes, he's the one, two, three, the fifth person from my left in the row.

Q   Can you tell me whether the men that left were armed?

A   They were armed.

Q   How long were they gone?

A   Sir, I wouldn't know exactly but I would say between 45 minutes and an hour.

Q   Did they come back?

A   They did.

Q   And did they again assemble in the abandoned, uh, gym?

A   Yes sir. . . .

Q   And what, if anything, was said then in the presence of the defendants that you have named?

A   A report was given to what took place at the church.

Q   And who gave the report?

A   Billy Birdsong from Meridian.

Q   And what did he say?. . . .

A   He said that the group from Meridian was guarding one of the exits from the church and that all of the negroes who came out of the church and left by way of exit guarded by the Meridian group were beaten and that it was his understanding that those who left by way of the exit guarded by Neshoba County men---

BY MR. HENDRICKS:

We object, Your Honor, to his understanding. This is the worst of hearsay.

BY THE COURT:

He is making a report and I am saying that that report is not evidence or proof of anything that the report said happened, but I am letting it in for the purpose of showing the report and what it was. Go ahead.

BY THE WITNESS:

And he, Billy Birdsong who was making the report, object to the fact that those guarding the exits from Neshoba County had not beaten anyone who came out that way and he stated very heatedly that he disapproved of this, that he didn't like it at all, he thought that they should have been beaten.

BY MR. DOAR:

Q   What, if anything, was said by anyone else?

A   Billy Wayne Posey said it was his understanding when they left the gym to go to the church they were to get anybody there that was white and that no white person came out the exit he was guarding, and therefore, no one was beaten.

Q   Did you observe anything about any of the defendants that night that they came back from the church to the meeting?

BY MR. BUCKLEY:

We object Your Honor, he's just asking him for anything.

BY THE COURT:

Yes, I think you had better be a LITTLE more specific.

BY MR. DOAR:

Q   Did you notice anything, or what if anything did you notice about any of the defendants that came back that went up there with you from Meridian?

A   Wayne Roberts had blood on his hands, or knuckles and he told me he got this when he was beating a nigger.

Q   What did you do then?

A   Well, shortly after the report it was agreed that we had better leave the building so the meeting broke up.

Q   What did you do then?

A   Well, shortly after the report it was agreed that we had better leave the building so the meeting broke up.

Q   What did you do then?

A   I got in the car in Birdsong and came back to Meridian and--

Q   Who else was in the car?

A   B.C. Lyles, Wayne Roberts and Dick Warner.

Q   Was anything said about what happened out at the church in Mr. Robert's presence on the way home?

A   Yes.

Q   What was that?

A   Birdsong went back through the speech again he had made in the gym and expressed his disapproval of the way it was handled at the other exit and told those of us that were in the car that they had certainly taken care of the ones that came out the exit where they were, that they had taken care of theirs.

Q   What did Wayne Roberts say?

A   He agreed that they were well beaten and well stomped. He said there was one exception to what Birdsong had said that one old negro woman wasn't beaten.

Q   Now do you know Sheriff Rainey?

A   I do.

Q   When did you first know him?

A   I first knew him early in the summer of 1963.

Q   And do you know Cecil Price?

A   I do.

Q   Can you pick them out here in the courtroom and tell me where they are sitting?

A   Mr. Rainey is second from the left, and Mr. Price is sixth from the right, right there.

Q   And do you know whether or not they are members of the White Knights of the Ku Klux Klan?

A   I knew then as members.

Q   Can you tell me where they were members prior to June 21, 1964?

A   Yes sir, they were.

Q   Can you tell me how you know they were members?

A   I first was told that they were members and then I talked with them about Klan business, in Philadelphia. . . .

Q   Can you tell us when you talked to either Deputy Price or Sheriff Rainey?

A   My brother was living in Philadelphia at the time and I was there to visit him and this is where I first met Mr. Rainey and I dropped by and visited with him several times while I was in Philadelphia.

Q   Was this prior to June 21st?

A   A few times prior to June 21st, yes sir.

Q   Now, have you furnished information to the Federal Bureau of Investigation about activities of the White Knights of the Ku Klux Klan?

A   I have.

Q   And when did you first start furnishing this information to the F.B.I.

A   In November of 1964.

Q   And have you been paid anything for this information?

A   I have.

Q   And how long a period of time have you furnished information?

A   Its almost three years, since November, 1964.

Q   And how were you paid?

A   I was paid on the basis of expenses incurred and information obtained.

Q   Do you know about how much you've been paid?

A   Approximately five thousand dollars a year.

Q   And have you continued to furnish information to the Bureau up to the present time?

A   I have.

Q   Do you know any of the other defendants as members of the White Knights of the Ku Klux Klan?

A   Sir, I believe I've named those that I know are members of the White Knights.

Q   Now after the June 21st, 1964, did you have any I'll withdraw that question. Did you ever hod any office of the White Knights of the Ku Klux Klan?

A   Yes sir.

Q   And what office did you hold?

A   I was first Chaplain of the local Klavern and later Province Titan.

BY THE COURT:

Province what?

BY THE WITNESS:

Titan. T I T A N.

BY MR. DOAR:

Q   What is the Province Titan.

A   It's the Administrative Office that represents the Imperial Wizard.

Q   And who is the Imperial Wizard?

A   Sam Holloway Bowers.

Q   And when did you become the Titan of a province.

A   The latter part of November in 1964.

Q   And what province was that?

A   It included Lauderdale County, Clarke County, Newton, Leake, Neshoba and Kemper Counties.

Q   And did you, what were your functions as the Titan?

A   I represented the Imperial Wizard in Administrative matters.

Q   Did you see the Imperial Wizard from time to time?

BY MR. BUCKLEY:

Your Honor it it please the Court I object to this as having to do with anything about this alleged conspiracy as it happened after June 21st, 1964.

BY THE COURT:

I'll overrule your objection. I'm not sure you and I heard the same question. Go along.

BY MR. DOAR:

Q You may answer.

A What was the question, sir?

Q The question was did you see the Imperial Wizard Sam Bowers frequently?

A I did. I saw him many times.

Q Now, did you have any conversation with Cecil Price about the civil rights workers----

BY MR. WEIR:

We object.

BY THE COURT:

Counsel, let him finish his question. You don't even know what he's fixing to say.

BY MR. DOAR:

Q ---after June 21st, 1964.

BY THE COURT:

Now, do you wish to be heard on your objection?

BY MR. WEIR:

Yes sir, Your Honor please, we object to the question as being irrelevant.

BY THE COURT:

Overruled.

BY THE WITNESS:

A Yes sir.

Q Can you tell me where that conversation took place?

A I stopped by the courthouse on one occasion and mentioned it briefly to him and I stopped by on the 24th of December of 64 and met with him in this Southern Methodist Church.

Q In what city?

A   In Philadelphia.

Q   Was anyone else present?

A   Not when I was talking to him, my brother was present and we asked him to step outside while we talked.

Q   What if anything was said about Cecil Price about the three civil rights workers being killed.

A   He said the government know more about the case than he thought they did and he had concluded that Jorden was the man that was giving the information to the Bureau.

Q   Did he say why?

A   Yes, he said it was Jorden because Jorden was the only person who could have seen him hit Chaney the night the three men were killed.

BY MR. WEIR:

We object and move the Court to grant us a mistrial.

BY THE COURT:

Overruled.

BY MR. DOAR:

Q   Now did you have any conversations with Frank Herndon after the civil rights workers were missing?

A   Yes.

Q   Can you tell me where the conversation or the conversations took place?

A   They took place in the restaurant he was operating.

Q   Can you tell me when they took place?

A   Not exactly sir, it was shortly after the bodies were found, that he discussed the case with me.

Q   What did he say, was anyone else present?

A   No sir.

Q   What did Frank Herndon say?

A   Frank said he was being accused of being for that but that he was not. He said he had witnesses who would say he was at work the night the men were killed.

Q   Now, did you have any conversation with Sam Bowers about the missing civil rights workers?

A   Yes.

Q   And, uh, did you, can you tell us where those conversations took place?

A   They took place in or near Pachuta, Mississippi.

Q   And when did they take place, when did the first conversation take place?

A   The first conversation was very shortly after the bodies were found.

Q   Was anyone else present?

A   No.

Q   What did Sam Bowers say?

A   He said that Judge Cox would probably make them take those bodies back and put them where they got them, that they had found the bodies on an illegal search warrant.

Q   Did you have any other conversation with him?

A   I did. On another occasion shortly after that meeting he said that he was pleased with that job that it was the first time that Christians had planned and carried the execution of Jews.

Q   Did you ever have any kind of a code method of communication with Sam Bowers?

A   We used the code name "Aunt Mary's" for our meeting place and he would call my home and identify himself by an alias, usually a Ralph Simmons or a Ralph Phillips or Mr. Sinclair and ask me to meet him at Aunt Mary's and Aunt Mary was between our two cities at Pachuta, Mississippi.

Q   Did you have any other kind of code between you and Sam Bowers?

A   We talked in terms of the logging operation as regarding the Klan itself.

Q   Did you have any code word that referred to the missing civil rights case.

A   This was the big logging operation.

Q   And did you have any kind of a code for---

BY MR. HENDRICKS:

We object, Your Honor, this is leading. He can ask him something but he can't tell him.

BY THE COURT:

I think that's what he's asking him, overruled.

BY MR. DOAR:

Just tell me---

BY THE COURT:

Excuse me, Mr. Doar, what did you say the last code for the last operation was called?

BY THE WITNESS:

The big logging operation.

BY MR. DOAR:

Q   What other code words did you have?

A   Truck drivers represented local officers in the Klan, the local Klavern, our own scalers, we referred to our scalers as our investigators, those that were gathering information for the KBI, the Klan Bureau of Investigation.

Q   Did you have any other words? Did you have any words for the defendants involved in this case?

A   The, I don't recall, no sir, I don't remember any specific names that were given to those.

Q   I am handing you a one page document, do you recognize that?

A   Yes sir.

Q   What is that document?

A   It's a letter from Sam Bowers?

Q   How is it signed?

A   It's signed, Yours truly, Willoughby Snead.

Q   What is, who does that refer to?

A   Sam Bowers.

Q   And who is the letter addressed to?

A   Mr. Dennis.

Q   And what is the date of the letter?

A   January 6th, 1965. . . .

Trial Transcript Page
Mississippi Burning Trial Homepage

CHAPTER TWENTY-TWO

—⁓—

THERE HAS BEEN A LOT WRITTEN AND a lot said about Cecil Price. In most writings and documentaries, his complete story is not told. If you remember, when I asked Edgar Killen about Price during our visit, he simply stated, "[Cecil] Price was no Lawrence Rainey. He [Rainey] was the best sheriff Neshoba County ever had." The exact role each alleged participant played will probably never be known. What is *not* up for debate, however, is that Edgar Ray Killen was not there (and his alleged instructions to "tear their butts up" is a far cry from "kill them").

Cecil Ray Price outside of Meridian (Ms.) Federal Courthouse.

It had been said that Price had turned state's witness [testify for the prosecution] against the other participants, but it was never explained why he turned witness. Is the reason important? What did he tell them? Why did it take four years after Price's death to bring Killen to trial? Everything put forth by the prosecution was readily available to Hood and Duncan prior to Price's death. My curiosity made me wonder why a man who had been sentenced to prison in 1967, who had served his time and returned home, then, by all accounts, led a peaceful and uneventful life, would suddenly turn informant?

The only answer or alleged explanation I have found was within the forty-eight-page FBI report to Jim Hood. On page twenty-two, in five condensed paragraphs, appears the only explanation I have been able to locate. How accurate and honest it is, would be anybody's guess. Are you doubting the FBI and its methods? Please remember their use of Greg "Grim Reaper" Scarpa. Don't forget the information that was bought and paid for with your tax money—and can *never be verified*. But it *can* possibly cause an innocent man to die in prison.

The explanation as to why Cecil Price turned informant: In the 1990s, Price began working as an independent, third-party examiner, conducting road driving tests for persons attempting to obtain their commercial driver's license (CDL). Price was caught selling passing test results for personal profit without ever having performed the actual road test. Because this scheme involved filing false federal government forms with the Mississippi Department of Public Safety (CDLs fall under the jurisdiction of US Department of Transportation), he was charged with violating Title 18, United States Code 1001: false statements.

He plead guilty on December 6, 1999, and was sentenced to three years of probation, supposedly in return for his agreement to cooperate with the Mississippi attorney general's office by providing information about the 1964 murders of the three civil rights workers. According to the FBI report, in the summer of 2000, Price provided information during interviews with the Mississippi attorney general investigators and attorneys. Cecil Price allegedly said he had advised Edgar Killen of the arrest through Wayne Posey. Later, Killen called Price after dark and told him to come to Jolly's Car Lot in Philadelphia, where Price later heard Killen tell a group of Meridian Klansmen that Price would release the victims, who would first be stopped by highway patrol officers while the group was on their way back to Meridian, and then turn them over to the Meridian Klansmen.

Supposedly, Price admitted that he later agreed to stop the victims after releasing them from jail, and did so. He insisted that he'd thought they would only be beaten. He confirmed that a car had broken down while they were pursuing the victims, and Price speculated that it was Wayne Posey's car. He said Roberts, Jordan, Posey, Arledge, Snowden, and H. D. Barnette were present at the murder scene, and corroborated Barnette's contention that Roberts and Jordan were the shooters, adding that most of the individuals present had had guns. Please note that Jordan, the same Jordan who had been an informant for the FBI, was one of the shooters—yet was paid to testify against people far less responsible than he was for the crime.

Cecil Price said Edgar Killen gave the order to release the "boys" from custody, organized the group, set up the meeting at a car lot, then attended the wake for his uncle at a funeral home to create an alibi. Price said he later learned from Killen that Killen knew the victims were buried in a dam at a pond. In May of 2001, Price died after a fall from a piece of machinery while working in Neshoba County.

In the documentary *Neshoba*, it is speculated whether Price's death was an accident, a murder, or a suicide. What is not open to speculation, and was confirmed by Price, was that Edgar Killen was not present at the murder scene, nor did he order the victims to be murdered. By his own supposed admission, Price was far more culpable than Killen could ever have been, as it applies to murder charges. Why was Price not prosecuted? This seems to be a repetitive cycle: let persons far more criminally responsible go free, and target Edgar Ray Killen instead. Is anyone seeing a pattern here, or doubting that Edgar Killen, who was probably the least responsible of the participants, if he was involved at all, was the intended target simply because of his outspoken views? As one Neshoba County resident seen in the documentary put it, "The only thing Edgar is guilty of is talking too much."

It still begs the question, why weren't Price's interviews recorded and transcribed? If they were, why were they not put forth as evidence in 2005? It would seem they would be at least as credible as forty-year-old testimony—and we know beyond a doubt that said recording technology was available in 2000, especially to an attorney as sharp as Jim Hood. Further still, none of Hood's attorneys or investigators were called to testify as to the statements made by Price: that Killen had later told him that he knew the victims were buried in a dam.

Price left out an important detail. If in fact Killen had made this statement, Price did not specify when Killen gained that knowledge. Had it been before or after the murders and burial? In the absolute worst-case scenario, if Killen had known about it before it was common knowledge, does that make him solely responsible? Or responsible at all for events that occurred outside of his presence? An additional question regarding the validity of Price's admission needs further consideration.

Price was sentenced to three years of probation in February 2000 in return for cooperation, yet he did not give his first statement until the summer of 2000. That seems like quite a while to wait (three to four months) to take a statement from a cooperating witness on one of the most famous cases in Mississippi's history. No need to hurry when you have already selected your target.

In closing this chapter, the reader should know that prior to having written it, I called Mr. Max Kilpatrick, attorney at law, to ask for his input, as he represented Mr. Price during his 2000 trial. The call went unreturned, and he is seemingly the only person who would be in a position to verify or deny that Mr. Price had turned state's witness. Considering the lack of proof that would verify whether Price had ever said anything to anyone about the murders, and the fact that it took an additional four years after his death to bring the case to trial, it can be speculated that Mr. Price was used as a very convenient scapegoat following his death.

SOUTHERN DISTRICT OF MISSISSIPPI
FILED

FEB 24 2000

BY _____ DEPUTY

UNITED STATES DISTRICT COURT
Southern District of Mississippi
Eastern Division

UNITED STATES OF AMERICA

v.

CECIL RAY PRICE

JUDGMENT IN A CRIMINAL CASE
(For Offenses Committed After November 1, 1987)

Case Number: 4:98cr20LN

Defendant's Attorney: Max Kilpatrick
                           P.O. Box 520
                           Philadelphia, MS 39350

THE DEFENDANT:

■ pleaded guilty to count(s) _____1_____
☐ was found guilty on count(s) _____ after a plea of not guilty.

Accordingly, the defendant is adjudged guilty of such count(s), which involve the following offenses:

Title & Section	Nature of Offense	Date Offense Concluded	Count Number(s)
18 U.S.C. §1001	False Statements	May 4, 1998	1

The defendant is sentenced as provided in page 2 of this judgment. The sentence is imposed pursuant to the Sentencing Reform Act of 1984.

☐ The defendant has been found not guilty on count(s) _____
and is discharged as to such count(s).
■ Count _____2_____ is dismissed on the motion of the United States.
■ It is ordered that the defendant shall pay a special assessment of $ __100.00__, for count(s) __1__, which shall be
due ■ immediately ☐ as follows:

IT IS FURTHER ORDERED that the defendant shall notify the United States Attorney for this district within 30 days of any change of name, residence, or mailing address until all fines, restitution, costs, and special assessments imposed by this judgment are fully paid.

Defendant's Soc. Sec. No.: _____-5731

Defendant's Date of Birth: __04/15/38__

Defendant's USM No.: __05241-043__

Defendant's Mailing Address:

__444 Center Avenue__

__Philadelphia, MS 39350__

Defendant's Residence Address:

__Same__

_____
February 17, 2000
Date of Imposition of Sentence

_____
Signature of Judicial Officer

__Tom S. Lee, Chief United States District Judge__
Name & Title of Judicial Officer

__2/23/00__
Date

134

Defendant: PRICE, Cecil Ray
Case Number: 4:98cr20LN

PROBATION

The defendant is hereby placed on probation for a term of __three (3) years__

While on probation, the defendant shall not commit another federal, state, or local crime, shall not illegally possess a controlled substance. Also, a person with a felony conviction shall not possess a firearm or destructive device. If this judgment imposes a fine or restitution obligation, it shall be a condition of probation that the defendant pay any such fine or restitution. The defendant also shall comply with the standard conditions that have been adopted by this court (set forth below). The defendant shall comply with the following additional conditions:

For offenses committed on or after September 13, 1994: The defendant shall refrain from any unlawful use of a controlled substance. The defendant shall submit to one drug test within 15 days of release from imprisonment and at least two periodic drug tests thereafter, as directed by the probation officer.

◻ The above drug testing condition is suspended based on the court's determination that the defendant poses a low risk of future substance abuse. (Check, if applicable.)

■ The defendant shall not possess a firearm or destructive device.

SPECIAL CONDITIONS

The defendant shall perform 100 hours of community service work at the direction of the supervising U.S. Probation Officer within the first full year of supervision.

STANDARD CONDITIONS OF SUPERVISION

1) The defendant shall not leave the judicial district without permission of the court or probation officer;

2) The defendant shall report to the probation officer as directed by the Court or probation officer, and shall submit a truthful and complete written report within the first five days of each month;

3) The defendant shall answer truthfully all inquiries by the probation officer and follow the instructions of the probation officer;

4) The defendant shall support his or her dependents and meet other family responsibilities;

5) The defendant shall work regularly at a lawful occupation unless excused by the probation officer for schooling, training or other acceptable reasons;

6) The defendant shall notify the probation officer ten days prior to a change of residence or employment;

7) The defendant shall refrain from excessive use of alcohol and shall not purchase, possess, use, distribute, or administer any narcotic or other controlled substance, or any paraphernalia related to such substances, except as prescribed by a physician;

8) The defendant shall not frequent places where controlled substances are illegally sold, used, distributed, or administered;

9) The defendant shall not associate with any persons engaged in criminal activity, and shall not associate with any person convicted of a felony unless granted permission to do so by the probation officer;

10) The defendant shall permit a probation officer to visit him or her at any time at home or elsewhere and shall permit confiscation of any contraband observed in plain view by the probation officer;

11) The defendant shall notify the probation officer within seventy-two hours of being arrested or questioned by a law enforcement officer;

12) The defendant shall not enter into any agreement to act as an informer or a special agent of a law enforcement agency without the permission of the Court;

13) As directed by the probation officer, the defendant shall notify third parties of risks that may be occasioned by the defendant's criminal record or personal history or characteristics, and shall permit the probation officer to make such notifications and to confirm the defendant's compliance with such notification requirement.

135

CHAPTER TWENTY-THREE

—⚊—

On August 15, 2017, I received a letter from Edgar Killen, who was adamant that some information in this book be dedicated to Richard Barrett. I had read about Barrett in previous research for this book, but Barrett had honestly not seemed too worthy of much attention in the greater scheme of this story. Much like other things, however, there was more to it than meets the eye.

A simple internet search for Barrett reveals the following generic information: He was born in 1943 and died April 22, 2010. He was an American lawyer, white nationalist, and self-proclaimed leader in the National Skinheadz movement. He was a speaker and editor of the monthly newsletter, *All The Way*. He was also general counsel of the Nationalist movement, which he founded in Mississippi.

He was born in New York City and his family moved due to the influx of Jewish and Puerto Rican immigrants. He graduated from Rutgers University, but later returned his diploma to a then-Marxist professor, Eugene Genovese, following service in the infantry in the Vietnam War. He graduated from Memphis State University Law School in 1974. In 1969, he served as executive director of the South Carolina branch of the American Independent Party on behalf of George Wallace's presidential bid. He organized and chaired the National Youth Alliance. In 1976, he was chairman of Democrats for Reagan, and in 1977 he was judge-advocate of the Veterans of Foreign Wars.

In 1982, he published *The Commission*, which advocated for the resettlement of "those who were once citizens to Puerto Rico, Mexico, Israel, the Orient, and Africa." His position was that "non-whites, especially blacks, were inferior: The Negro race . . . possess[es] no creativity of its own [and] pulls the vitality away from civilization." He also promoted sterilization and abortions of the "unfit." In 2004, he organized a booth at the Neshoba County Fair for the purpose of allowing the public to shake hands with Edgar Killen and sign a petition of support for him. Killen did not appear at the event.

Barrett was killed on April 22, 2010 at his residence. Neighbors reported having seen smoke come from his house, and when firefighters arrived, they found Barrett's body near the back door of his home. He had been beaten to death by twenty-three-year-old Vincent J. McGee, who had stolen Barrett's wallet and a gun before setting fire to Barrett's corpse. McGee later claimed that Barrett had dropped his pants and asked him to perform a sexual act on him, which caused McGee to panic. An autopsy later revealed that Barrett had been stabbed thirty-five times and had suffered blunt force trauma to the head. After being arrested, McGee provided information that led to the arrest of accomplices Michael Dent, Vicky Dent, and Albert Lewis. McGee was ultimately sentenced to sixty-five years in Parchman Prison.

It is somewhat ironic that McGee—who was black, had a history of violent offenses, and had been recently released from Parchman was sentenced to sixty-five years for manslaughter (stabbed thirty-five times, blunt force trauma to the head, and the victim's body set on fire, seemingly to cover up evidence, is more serious than manslaughter, especially if it's in the commission of another felony, i.e. burglary) and his accomplices, only received sixty-five years at twenty-two years of age. Yet Edgar Killen received sixty years at eighty years old, forty years after his alleged crimes had been committed, as opposed to McGee who was quickly apprehended, confessed, and linked to the crime.

This claim concerning Killen having attended the Neshoba County Fair is totally inaccurate, as is quite a lot of information about him. The county fair in question was not the Neshoba County Fair; it was the Mississippi State Fair, which was held in Jackson. The reason that piece of information is important is because of the involvement of two other people: Jerry Mitchell of the *Clarion Ledger* newspaper in Jackson, and Malcolm McMillin, who was sheriff of Hinds County at the time.

Information according to Killen's letters, albeit somewhat condensed, provides some insight on the matter.

Richard Barrett, the white supremacist who collaborated with "that red-bearded ultra-liberal" Jerry Mitchell to set up Edgar Ray Killen.

[Barrett] was born and reared in the Bronx, New York City. After high school, he came south to law school, where he earned his degree and license to practice law. Richard had more pure hatred for blacks than any other Yankee I ever knew. Somehow Richard drove people from him. He lived in Hinds County (Jackson, Mississippi), where the sheriff, Malcolm McMillin, pure hated Richard, and made life so unbearable he drove Richard out of Jackson. Richard had a home in Learned, Mississippi, about forty-five minutes out of Jackson, where he lived the balance of his life.

Richard was a Baptist by faith. He was voted out of his church for always telling of his hate. He helped organize a small group of National Socialist Members and printed a small newsletter out of Learned, Mississippi. He really was a white supremacist. I was not a follower of Mr. Barrett; also not a hater of him. We seldom saw each other. I knew him mostly by the media. Richard would do anything to get his name in the news. About a year and a half before I was indicted in 2005, Richard, for the first time, called me.

He asked if he could visit me in my home. I not once thought of Richard letting Jerry Mitchell and McMillin paying him to set me up. He came to see me as a friend. Yeah, a wolf in a lamb's coat. I must admit, he was nice to me. We went to church and I fed him Sunday dinner. We did not discuss much of Richard's business, but everything went nice. He did say in the future we might put together a business. We had no agreement of any type or fashion. Just friends.

Some weeks later Richard called me again. He told me he had something going where we could make some money. The state fair was coming up, and Richard said he was getting a booth at the fair for him and myself, where we could greet fair-goers. He claimed a picture [would be] ten dollars and an autograph, five dollars. I kindly informed Richard I had no intentions of being at the fair. Richard could not get media attention; only [by] including my name and Mitchell's helped him . . . and Mitchell controlled the publicity. He could quote Barrett, whom he hated.

Barrett informed me the fair had refused [the] booth [idea], so Barrett sued, and Hood ruled the law [and] let Barrett have the booth.

I have never sought publicity in my life, yet the communists were always after me. I truly have no respect for the media. The chief of security hired hundreds of security people to come to the fair. They exhausted their budget. All this time, I went to work every day and ignored Mitchell, Barrett, and McMillin, and of course, all media. Finally, the chief of security had a brain storm. He called my house and kindly explained his condition. He was worried and concerned about safety. He needed to know how many days I expected to spend at the fair so he would know how much money to borrow to pay his security.

Chief fully intended to provide security at the fair. Upon being told I never had any plans to make that year's fair, the man almost shouted. He assured my family, on our next visit, we would be given a VIP-stay at the fair, and thanked for the millions of dollars saved. He then realized he had been listening to Barrett, Mitchell, McMillin, and their gang members. When the fair's chief of security told the media he had been informed that I had no plans for the fair, well, the news media subdued Mitchell. McMillin lost his hopes of becoming a hero in winning the riot at the fair, regardless of the deaths.

Well, Barrett was not surprised; he had no promise. He closed the booth and went to Learned, his home. Of course, Barrett kept all the money he was given and never told he had no promise from ERK [Edgar Ray Killen] I heard nothing more from Barrett. I do remember he was at my trial and walked in front of the World Court TV camera, again seeking publicity. Of course, Barrett nor I spoke at my trial. While I was in Rankin County lockdown—I did not belong to their group, but the NSM [National Socialist Movement] world-wide accepted me as a friend, and sent me volumes of accurate information.

So, thanks to them. Many members did not support Barrett due to his dictator attitude. The blacks started threatening Barrett, and he made a very touching plea to the NSM for protection, which as far as I know went unheeded. So Barrett's body was found behind his Learned, Mississippi home, partly burned. Of course, Barrett could not expect no protection from the Hinds County Sheriff Department, nor from the State of Mississippi. So Barrett paid for his beliefs with his blood. Some members wrote me [in jail] after Barrett's death that Barrett had his faults, but he also had some good.

I cannot remember how many terms McMillin served as sheriff of Hinds County. He finished his term during the fair setup. Here, he told the world I did not need to come to the fair, I should be in jail. He thought that statement would get the black vote. He was that far off from good judgment. Jackson went a number closer to being murder [crime] capital of America. During McMillin's terms in office, [it] finally reached number two in murder and number one in crime.

I am not blaming McMillin with all crimes increase, but lack of control in Jackson is out of control. The present governor, Phil Bryant, felt he owed McMillin much, as Bryant's first job was deputy sheriff under McMillin. So, when McMillin was defeated [was out of a job], Bryant appointed McMillin as chairman of the Mississippi Parole Board. Here, no consideration of qualifications. He completely failed here. In some six months, forced to leave board. McMillin died in his seventies.

Let's digress on part of the author. Please ponder that Hood—yes, the same Jim Hood who hounded Edgar Killen, and most certainly would have known of Barrett's intentions to have Killen as a fair attraction—ruled in favor of Barrett having a booth at the fair. Is it too far-fetched that Hood was counting on this to set up Edgar Killen? Hood certainly doesn't have a history of concern in regard to upholding Edgar Killen's civil rights and liberties.

Killen previously said that he had never accepted fees for his public speaking and preaching. Additionally, there is documented proof that Sheriff McMillin did in fact oppose Edgar Killen's presence at the fair, and openly said that Killen should be in jail. So, we have an elected public official expressing nothing more than an opinion that Killen should have been in jail, when Killen, at that time, had not been accused of or had been on trial for a crime. Could that have possibly been prejudicial in his subsequent trial?

If that hadn't been the intent, it certainly worked out well for Hood. Also, while Barrett was voted out of his church for his hate-filled rants,

Edgar Killen maintained his role as a preacher for various churches for more than sixty years.

CHAPTER TWENTY-FOUR

—✕—

Wʀɪᴛɪɴɢ ᴛʜɪs ʙᴏᴏᴋ ʜᴀs ʙᴇᴇɴ ᴀ ʀᴀᴛʜᴇʀ ғʟᴜɪᴅ endeavor. New information has surfaced almost constantly, which is not necessarily a bad thing, but has made it difficult to keep the story in a chronological order to make it easier to follow. Recently, three additional names were discovered in relation to the 1967 civil rights trial: Mrs. Minnie Herring, who, along with her husband, ran the Neshoba County Jail; Mr. Clayton Lewis, who, among other things, later became the mayor of Philadelphia, Mississippi and was associated with Highway Patrolman Maynard King, a.k.a., "Mr. X."

Let's first review Mrs. Herring's role. In the 1967 trial, she was called as a witness by the plantiff (the federal government). The gist of her testimony was her verification that the three civil rights workers had been booked into the jail by Deputy Price on June 21, 1964 at about 4:00 p.m., and released at about 10:30 p.m. She also clarified the process of how persons were booked into the jail, items they were allowed to keep, booking ledgers, and the procedures for posting bonds.

Of relevance to her testimony, was that when Price brought the three to jail, two other men were present who did not come inside. She identified them as having been Mr. Poe and Mr. Hughes, both highway patrolmen assigned to Neshoba County. This could be entirely coincidental, but the question remains: Are these two men the highway patrolmen who were initially supposed to stop the three workers upon their release, and were they [Poe and Hughes] there simply to visually identify

Schwerner, Chaney, and Goodman? If they had business at the jail, why did they not enter the building? Beyond that, wouldn't their presence in a case of this magnitude justify having called them as witnesses? They could have verified they had seen Price bring the three workers in, and testify as to what, if anything, they heard.

While not very informative as far as how it relates to Edgar Killen's role, please recall that others have placed Killen near the jail at some point directing the participants. Yet Mrs. Herring made no mention of having seen him, nor did the plantiff's other witnesses, Reverend Charles Johnson, Ernest Kirkland, and Officer E. R. Poe. None of these witnesses mentioned Edgar Killen in *any capacity* in their testimonies.

Next, let's review the role of Clayton Lewis, who is somewhat more interesting in the greater scheme of things, mostly due to his actions. According to Edgar Killen's arch enemy, Jerry Mitchell, in a story dated February 16, 2010, Mitchell reported that the FBI paid $30,000 (current equivalent, $200,000) to Lewis after an FBI agent told Lewis that two agents had brought the money to Mississippi and delivered it to Highway Patrolman Maynard King, who was to then pass on the reward money. Maynard King was the infamous "Mr. X," who met with FBI Inspector Joseph Sullivan and told Sullivan that the bodies of the three civil rights workers were buried in a dam on Olen Burrage's property.

Now the question is, who told King where the bodies were buried? Someone suggested to Mitchell that Olen Burrage was the informant. The roving reporter and I share the same thought on this, that this can't be true. My reason for thinking that Olen Burrage was not the informant is simple: Burrage had more money than he knew what to do with, and he had to live in that area. If Edgar Killen and his "Klan" was as violent as they have been reported to be, would Burrage have risked his safety, and possibly his life, for what would have been a paltry sum of money?

Mitchell's opinion is that Burrage could possibly have been the one who released the information, and Burrage was the one who the Mississippi Sovereignty Commission guessed at the time had tipped off the FBI. However, Mitchell has a different take on that matter. His conclusion is that King would have had to have gotten the information from someone who: a) was close to King; and b) had access to inside information from the killers or from the Klan.

Maynard King was close with Clayton Lewis, who served as defense attorney in the 1967 trial. If Lewis was the one who told King, it could have been an arrangement where Lewis would collect the money and then give it to his client. According to FBI records, assuming they are not fabricated, Lewis shared with agents what the defense strategy would be. If this is truthful, it would certainly be improper.

It should be noted that Lewis was friendly with the Klan, and after agents asked Lewis about his Klan activities, according to a 1965 FBI report, Lewis "voluntarily advised bureau agents that the defense plan for the case 'was to muddy the waters' and attack the credibility of James Jordan and other government witnesses. Remember James Jordan? He, according to Cecil Price, was one of the shooters. Rather than attacking Jordan's credibility, shouldn't the focus have been on prosecuting him rather than convicting someone who wasn't present?

James McIntyre, now disbarred, was one of Edgar Killen's attorneys in 2005, and he also played a part in 1967: McIntyre represented Sheriff Lawrence Rainey in the 1967 trial, and Rainey was who confirmed the suspicions about Lewis, who later died in 1983. Allegedly McIntyre remembered one hearing where the defense planned to spring an issue on the prosecution, only to see that prosecutors were prepared for it. Yet McIntyre is the same man who, in 2005, was supposedly "defending" Edgar Killen?

Lewis, who began serving as mayor of Philadelphia in 1965, initially represented Sheriff Rainey before Lewis went on to later represent Herman Tucker, identified by prosecutors as the dozer operator who had buried the trio's bodies. Tucker was acquitted in 1967. According to FBI documents, Lewis was a Klan member, and told an informant he had attended three meetings, two of which were held in his pasture. When he spoke with the FBI, Lewis told agents the defense planned to discredit key witness James Jordan by introducing evidence that proved Jordan had been on drugs and that Jordan's wife was a prostitute—for whatever that may have proven.

William B. Huie, who wrote about the case in his 1965 book, *Three Lives for Mississippi*, told the FBI that he had received information from Lewis, who had been a partner in a car business with Pete Jordan. Huie told the FBI he offered Lewis $25,000, which he received from the *New York Herald Tribune* to locate the trio's bodies, according to the November 14, 1964 report. "Lewis did not discourage this offer; however, bodies were shortly thereafter located by the FBI."

In 1989, when *People* magazine did a story in advance of the twenty-fifth anniversary of the killings, the magazine named Lewis as the one who had told the FBI where the bodies were buried, yet the magazine offered no proof, nor did they tell how they knew this to be true.

Presumably, Lewis could have been a source of information that had come from somebody else, but who would Lewis have gotten said information from? Sheriff Rainey and Tucker? Possible, but not likely. The Klan believed Jordan was the one who told the FBI where the three bodies were buried. Jordan died in 1988, and his son, Terry, wished his dad had been alive to defend himself. Stanley Dearman, the retired editor of the *Neshoba Democrat*, is convinced that Jordan shared the location of the bodies with Clayton Lewis, who in turn, told Maynard King.

"Pete told me on a number of occasions that Clayton Lewis was like a daddy to him," Dearman said. "And Clayton Lewis was very close to Maynard King." Interestingly, Jordan later became close friends with FBI Agent John Proctor, who worked closely with Sullivan on the "Mr. X" matter. Please keep the names Proctor and Sullivan in mind, as we will see more about them soon. It should also be noted that Stanley Dearman is by no means a fan of Edgar Killen. The *Neshoba* documentary shows former Philadelphia Mayor Harlan Majure testifying that he knew of a lot of good that had been done by the Ku Klux Klan, and that as far as he knew, Killen enjoyed a good reputation within the community. Mr. Dearman and Mr. Majure are brothers-in law, yet Mr. Majure's testimony apparently caused Mr. Dearman quite a bit of discomfort, to say the least.

Maynard King died of a heart attack in 1966 and, as mentioned previously, Clayton Lewis is also deceased. Taking all testimonies into consideration, along with the information provided by Edgar Killen, Linda Schiro's testimony (Scarpa's girlfriend), as well as confirmation of Scarpa's attorney, Louis Diamond, the most likely scenario for how it seems the FBI broke the case: having Scarpa beat the living hell out of Lawrence Byrd, and threaten to castrate him (as so many people reported and agreed as having happened, including both a prosecutor and judge). It's unfortunate, but Mr. King and Mr. Lewis are not here to either confirm or deny the accusations against them, or the credit given to them.

CHAPTER TWENTY-FIVE

—∿∿—

SAM BOWERS, AS MENTIONED IN PREVIOUS CHAPTERS, stated information that will later be *very relevant* to Edgar Killen's story, and should further indicate coverups, suppression of evidence that could vindicate Killen; that he was obviously targeted for prosecution, not because of his guilt, but because others who were deemed untouchable or weren't sought after for political reasons, were deceased by 2005, and that fact could only help the prosecution because they couldn't be questioned in front of Killen's jury.

This could and should also explain why Bowers, who was still alive in Parchman Prison, was not brought in to testify in 2005 instead of Winstead, a convicted child rapist—despite the fact that, at that time, both men were serving time in the same facility. It was previously established that Jerry Mitchell, of the *Clarion-Ledger*, and Edgar Ray Killen are not exactly fans of each other. Yet on December 27, 1998, Mitchell wrote an article that revealed the following information; taped interviews from October 1983 made by Debra Spencer, an oral historian for the Mississippi State Department of Archives and History, and of additional interviews conducted in January and November of 1984. Please pay special attention to these dates.

According to Mitchell's article, Sam Bowers gave his interview on the agreement that it would be sealed until his death. For the record, Bowers died on November 5, 2006 in Parchman Prison. Now, review the last paragraph and look at the dates. Bowers specified that his interview should be "sealed until his death," which occurred in 2006—yet Mitchell reported this in his article from 1998. This is a difference of eight years, give or take a few months, yet Mitchell reported this *eight years prior* to Bowers' death. Mitchell must have had a crystal ball hidden under his desk at the *Clarion-Ledger*.

According to the taped interviews, Bowers revealed the following: He admitted that he "thwarted justice in the 1964 killings of the three civil rights workers," and said that he "didn't mind going to prison because a fellow Klansman got away with murder." Bowers stated, he was "quite delighted to be convicted and have the main instigator of the entire affair walk out of the courtroom a free man. Everybody—including the trial judge, the prosecutors, and everyone else—knows that that happened. This hurts the imperial authority when they have to stoop to conquer, and I think that I did make them stoop to conquer."

In the US District Court trial in Meridian in 1967, witnesses testified that Bowers ordered the killings of the trio. Klansman James Jordan pleaded guilty to conspiracy (Since when does shooting someone amount to "conspiracy"?) and testified against fellow Klansmen. Please remember, Jordan was also paid by your tax dollars to testify against fellow Klansmen. Bowers, Price, and five others were convicted of federal charges of conspiracy to violate the civil rights of the trio by killing them, seven others were acquitted, and three others had mistrials. The most any Klansman served in prison was six years. What was Jordan's prison sentence? Four years. That's all, even after witness Doyle Barnette testified that Jordan was the one that removed Chaney from Price's car, shot him, and made the following statement; "Well, you didn't leave me nothing but a nigger, but at least I killed me a nigger."

Allegedly, the *Clarion-Ledger* and super-sleuth Jerry Mitchell obtained FBI confessions from Jordan and Klansman Horace Barnette. Jordan testified in the case, but the jury in the 1967 trial never heard his confession, or that of Barnette, both of whom implicated Killen as having helped plan the killings. At this point it should also be noted that, according to Killen, Mitchell has a copy of his motion of discovery for the 2005 trial, which Killen himself does not have, that neither Hood nor

Mitchell will provide.

Barnette claimed, as did others, that Killen stated, "Three civil rights workers were going to be released from jail and we were going to catch them and give them a whipping." As previously stated, and for the record again, "give them a whipping" is a long way from murder. Later, when the group of Klansmen arrived in Philadelphia, Barnette alleged that Killen said, "We have a place to bury them, and a man to run the dozer to cover them up." This, Barnette said, "was the first time I realized the three civil rights workers were to be killed."

Let's look at a few counterpoints to the previous paragraphs. Jordan and Barnette testified in the 1967 revealing these confessions; however, the jury never heard these confessions. Why not? Surely, they would have helped in securing a conviction against Killen, and maybe others. Were these confessions ruled inadmissible for some reason? Maybe they had been obtained illegally, perhaps as a result of having used a mob hitman—who also happened to be on the FBI's payroll—to torture a confession out of them? The answer to this question will probably never be known. Next, as reported many times previously, the general instructions Killen allegedly gave, was for them to give the trio a whipping, or "tear their butts up." Generally speaking, giving somebody a whipping does not require them being buried by means of a bulldozer.

Thus far, Barnette is the only member of this group that alleges Killen specifically indicated murder. Is it possible Barnette forgot the script, or fabricated an even-more-compelling story to take attention away from himself, or gain favor with the FBI and the prosecution? In the opinion of Joe Sullivan, who headed the FBI investigation into the murders, Killen "was the moving force," but since Killen had an alibi for the night of the murders, a mistrial was declared. Killen claims that Jordan "fabricated more than 90 percent of what he told. He was not a close associate of mine." The harsh reality remains that Jordan shot at least one person [Chaney] that night, and afterwards, according to witness was paid for information by the FBI, and, walked away a richer man after a mere four-year sentence. Would he have embellished the role of others and minimized his own to achieve this? I would guess that he most certainly would have; he had a lot to gain.

Back to the subject of Sam Bowers: Killen said he didn't know that he himself was the "main instigator" Bowers was referring to, and that he didn't know Bowers until they met at the trial. According to the media, Killen was Bowers' boss. Sheriff Rainey also said of Barnette, that his confession was a lie, and that he never knew Barnette prior to the trial, that "Barnette was never in the Klan. The damn FBI was paying all those witnesses to lie. I attended some of the Klan meetings. They had open meetings, but that was all." When Rainey was asked about the "main instigator" having gotten away with murder, he said, "I thought Bowers was the head man on all of that. I never heard of anybody else."

Both Sullivan and Public Safety Commissioner Jim Ingram, who headed the civil rights desk for the FBI, said the actual, "main instigator" in the killings was Bowers. "He was the one man responsible," Ingram said. It begs the question that if Hood and Duncan had introduced Mr. Ingram's statement to the jury in Edgar Killen's 2005 trial, would the outcome for Killen have been different?

To further establish this—that Edgar Killen took the fall for Bowers and others—let us look at what Bowers himself said during his taped interview: He denied direct-involvement, but said that if authorities "had wanted to put a charge on [him], they could have gotten [him] for obstruction of justice." Bowers said he did "everything [he] could to frustrate the investigation." [He] was "up there doing everything [he] could to keep those people from talking and everything else."

Rita Bender, Schwerner's widow, said of Bowers' interview, that it "raises the question of what did he do? Who got away with it? And *what did he do to make it happen?*" Excellent point, and it also raises other questions. If Bowers made this admission and essentially took all responsibility, why was Edgar Killen prosecuted for that role, and not Bowers—or at least justify the need to bring Bowers to testify in Edgar Killen's 2005 trial? If Duncan and Hood were truly seeking the mastermind, and not targeting a man for his beliefs and opinions, they had the culprit at their feet. Would this have been too easy? Would it have not garnered enough press attention, quenching their thirst for future political offices?

The reclusive Bowers, who never talks to the media, referred to himself as a "criminal and a lunatic," and justifies lynchings and killings as ways to preserve the southern way of life. "Citizens not only have a right, but a duty, to preserve their culture," he said. "By taking someone's life, though?" Bowers was asked on tape. "If that person wants to put his life on the line in order to destroy that culture, yes," he replied.

The FBI blamed the Klan for not only the killings of the trio, but for seven others in Mississippi, plus dozens of bombings of churches, homes, and businesses. Bowers, the Klan leader, was convicted in only one murder, that of NAACP leader Vernon Dahmer. Bowers said he had nothing to with the deaths, but expressed pride that most of the killings remained unsolved. "Every stone in the Watergate conspiracy has been uncovered, exposed to the light of day. Yet in the Philadelphia case and dozens of other cases in Mississippi, very, very little is known, much of what they think they know is inaccurate. The case has never really been solved, in the sense that Watergate has been solved. So, here is a bunch of semi-literate rednecks in the state of Mississippi really putting up a better show against the imperial authority than Richard Nixon and the Republican Party did in Watergate."

Bowers confirmed in the interview that a mob of Klansmen had killed the civil rights workers, but maintained that he and two others who were convicted of conspiracy weren't involved. He did not name those men.

Still, the question remains: How did Jerry Mitchell get these sealed records eight years prior to Bowers' death when they were to be sealed until Bowers' death? If Mitchell had this information as a reporter, surely Hood and Duncan, in their legal capacities, could have also gotten it. However, Duncan and Hood aren't the only ones responsible.

How about that person who allowed Mitchell access to the sealed records? What was that person threatened and or bribed with? Why hasn't Mitchell been questioned about this? If he had this information, and he obviously did, shouldn't he have let the prosecution and Edgar's defense know that, which would have possibly allowed an innocent man to escape what is essentially a death sentence? Do the words "journalistic integrity" mean anything to Mitchell? My guess would be, absolutely not.

Reflecting upon the visit the Bohannons and I had with Edgar Ray Killen, I recall asking him specifically about Mitchell's role in Killen's trial. His response was, "Mitchell is a communist, a communist supporter, and those three civil rights workers were all communists trained at a communist training school to come to Mississippi to create trouble between blacks and whites. If Jesus was being lead to the cross today, Mitchell would be the one throwing rocks at him."

While this may sound harsh, if Mitchell helped Hood and Duncan secure his conviction, or knowingly withheld evidence that could have kept him out of prison, who can blame Killen for his animosity? As he said about Mitchell, "I wish him no harm unless I'm the one bringing it to him."

EPILOGUE

THIS PROJECT BEGAN IN JANUARY OF 2017. It is now February of 2018, and it is hoped that the reader has an accurate understanding of Edgar Ray Killen and the circumstances surrounding his first and second trials, as well as his conviction and incarceration. The 1960s was a turbulent time in American history, and unless you were there and witnessed the events as they unfolded, it is probably next to impossible to grasp the events that happened during this decade.

Edgar Killen has been nothing less than forthright and open in his correspondence with me, and everything he has told me has been verified. While there may be some slight discrepancies in his version of the events, I have found nothing that indicates he intentionally misled me. This has been in the form of wrong dates, slight differences in time frames, and sometimes forgetting names of some people in certain events. Considering these events are more than fifty years old, his age, and prior brain trauma, his memory has proven to be rather good. If these same excuses were valid enough to allow Jim Hood to not prosecute others who were obviously more involved, it should be valid enough reasons for Edgar Killen.

He has also remarked on his opinion of law enforcement and is generally supportive of police officers. What he absolutely does have a problem with are "crooked politicians, and specifically Jim Hood, Marcus Duncan, and Marcus Gordon, as well as the liberal media, in particular, Jerry Mitchell of the *Clarion-Ledger*." More than any others, he credits these four individuals for his 2005 trial and conviction. After reviewing the trial transcripts and testimonies, as well as the statements of the FBI informants, along with the evidence regarding the use of a mafia hitman to torture a confession out of a Klansman, I can't say that I blame Killen for his animosity.

If nothing else comes of telling Edgar Killen's story, it is hoped that new light can be shed on his case by revealing the facts that have been written about in this book, and that it will allow his name to be cleared and provide some peace and comfort to his family and friends. While Edgar Killen has been painted as the ultimate villain by those who promote their agendas at his expense, be that reason to sale newspapers or for political gain and public appeasement, the one thing that can't be argued is that the four people he mentioned could never have been the survivor Edgar Killen proved himself to be.

These "men" would have never survived growing up in the Great Depression, working from dawn to dark, six days a week, and most certainly would have never stuck to their beliefs, regardless of that cost. It would be a fair bet to say that Edgar Killen could have out-worked these four even at eighty years old, and even at that age, he entered prison and survived another twelve years while confined to a wheelchair.

If it was their effort to silence him, it failed. If they hoped he would die off before his story could be told, it didn't work. He was tougher than anyone could imagine. Most importantly, he maintained a strong faith in God and believed in the power of prayer. To Mr. Hood, Mr. Duncan, and Mr. Mitchell, I hope each of you have a clear conscience when your days on earth come to an end. I know Edgar Ray Killen did.

Edgar Ray "Preacher" Killen passed away in Parchman Prison on January 11, 2018. He was six days short of his 93rd birthday. I was honored to attend his funeral on January 18, in Union, Mississippi. I met several family members and friends of Edgar Killen and they shared stories of Edgar's kindness and concern for all people. Although my contact with Edgar had been limited, I sensed that these stories were all true and that Edgar truly had been a good man. I found comfort in knowing that he was in a far better place now and that his family and friends would no longer have to constantly hear or read negative media opinions of him.

I had no idea how wrong I was in that thought. After the services were over, I stopped at a local store and while in line, I noticed the front page of the local newspaper, "The Neshoba Democrat." There was an article that contained quotes by the mayor of Philadelphia, Mississippi, James A. Young, and the editor / publisher of the newspaper, James Prince, III. Their comments were blatantly disrespectful to Edgar's family and friends and I thought these comments should not be allowed to go unchallenged.

The next day I spoke with J.D. Killen and he told me that the article had bothered him, his family, and several people who knew Edgar. With the blessing of J.D. Killen, I sent a letter to Mayor Young and Mr. Prince. The letter is included in full and as of this writing, neither of these men responded, which is exactly what was expected of them.

In Loving Memory

of

Edgar Ray Killen

Age: 92

Entered this Life: January 17, 1925
Departed this Life: January 11, 2018

Funeral announcement photo of Edgar Ray Killen.

Jan. 19, 2018

Mayor James A. Young
City of Philadelphia, Ms.
525 Main St.
Philadelphia, Ms. 39350

Mayor Young,

I am writing this letter to you due to some quotes you made in the January 17, 2018 edition of "The Neshoba Democrat." The quotes I refer to are as follows; "A legacy of hatred and prejudice died last week with Edgar Ray Killen, the 92- year old man convicted in the 1964 murders here of three young men registering blacks to vote", Philadelphia Mayor James A. Young declared on Monday.

"He represented everything that was wrong in our state and nation", said Young, the city's first black mayor now in his second term. "That embodiment that he carried has died." You were further quoted on page 5-A as saying; "A representation of hatred has died, and I think we are better off to say that and tell the story. Not to let things linger or hinder our walk to make things better."

I would like to ask some questions regarding some of the comments and I will also explain to you my interest and concern in this matter as I am clearly not a citizen of your city or state. I will also address comments made by Mr. Leroy Clemons, Alderman-at-Large, and James E. Prince III, editor and publisher of "The Neshoba Democrat."

My questions to you, sir, is this. Did you personally know Mr. Edgar Ray Killen? Did you know his true character? Did you know his propensity toward Christian kindness and virtues? I was honored to attend Mr. Killen's funeral service. This was with the consent and blessing of his wife, Mrs. Betty Jo Killen, and his younger brother, Mr. J.D. Killen. Prior to the service beginning, I was able to meet with several of Mr. Killen's family members and friends and they shared stories with me of his numerous acts of kindness and Christian practices they witnessed over the years prior to his incarceration.

They spoke of Mr. Killen growing crops of mustard greens, collard greens, turnip greens, and other crops that he could produce in abundance to share with whomever needed them within his community. The people he provided for were both blacks and whites and he happily provided this service for people that were unable to physically maintain their own gardens or did not have the financial means to grow their own food or purchase it. If they were unable to come pick what they needed, he would spend his Saturday's picking it and bringing it to those who needed him to do so.

Mr. Killen also pastored to over 18 churches during his 60-plus years as a Baptist Preacher. He presided over an untold number of weddings and funerals and did not receive compensation as he thought it was his duty as a minister to provide these services. His friends and family members spoke with great fondness of Edgar returning from funerals he presided over with his suit wet and stained with mud from assisting with the burial of the deceased after the services were complete. They recalled stories of Edgar having a radio show in which he delivered sermons. Ironically, most of the donations that supported this show was sent in by black families. One of the most touching stories was of a black man who had enough money to pay for his relative's funeral service, but not enough to cover the transportation to the Delta region where the man was to be buried. Not only did Edgar pay for the transportation, he accompanied the family to the Delta and helped to dig the grave and bury their deceased relative.

Mr. Killen, by his own admission, was a staunch segregationist. He believed this to be the teaching and will of God as He made the races different and therefore each race was meant to be with its own kind. Does this make Edgar a criminal? Does this make him a man that was filled with hate toward other races? One of the pastors that conducted his eulogy, of which there were three, spoke of having visited Edgar in prison in December of 2017. He spoke fondly of Edgar's profound religious belief and faith in God as well as his sense of humor and kindness. For the record, it was the first, and unfortunately, the last time he met with Mr. Killen.

It seems that a common phrase when speaking of race relations in today's society is "cultural diversity." Let us take a moment to look at the true meaning of this phrase. By definition, "cultural diversity", is the existence of a variety of cultural or ethnic groups within a society. With that definition in mind, was Mr. Killen truly wrong in his belief of keeping the races separate? Sir, if the races mix and become one, how can a society remain diverse? If the races become one race, does that not eradicate and devalue the culture and heritage of each race?

Was Mr. Killen truly wrong in wanting each race to promote and preserve their own race, keep their own identity, and promote their own culture in a peaceful and Christian manner? Mr. Young, Edgar was not a hate filled, murderous individual. Let us not forget that two of the three young men that were murdered were white. Yes, they were of the Jewish faith, but Jewish is a religion, not a race.

Further, sir, your comments did not harm Edgar. He is now in a place where he is beyond harm by you or any other mortal person. However, it is shameful that you would place these comments in a public forum where they can harm Mr. Killen's family and friends in their time of grief. Your one- sided allegations against a man that you clearly did not know was shameful and nothing less than a political ploy to gain favors with the voters of your town for your own agenda.

I would be willing to bet, that if given the opportunity, you would never voice these allegations in person to Mr. J.D. Killen, Edgar's younger brother, or Mrs. Dorothy Dearing, his younger sister, in a face to face setting. Mr. Killen and Mrs. Dearing are both God fearing people and would not shirk from a meeting with you, should you ever be willing to face them. For that matter, I too would be willing to meet with you personally for further discussion if it could be conducted in a civil manner and fairly reported by Mr. Prince, who is clearly one-sided and prejudicial toward Edgar and lacks the couth to respect the Killen family.

Let me now address Mr. Prince who was quoted as saying the following; "Edgar Rays death is a book end for our community, the end of an era in which for a season we were ravaged and stained by evil, but nothing to compare with the unmerciful suffering of the families of the three dead young men."

"What was intended for evil, this community has used for the good so that all may possess a sense of dignity and hope regardless of the color of their skin", Prince said. Mayor, again I wonder, just how well did Mr. Prince know Edgar? Did he know his virtues, values, and beliefs? I feel very safe in saying that he, like you, absolutely did not. The agenda of Mr. Prince is clearly to promote sales of his third- rate newspaper that is only fit to wrap fish in or line bird cages, by appealing to those who are too ignorant to think for themselves.

I know I can speak for Mr. J.D. Killen and myself as well when I say that we welcome a face to face meeting with Mr. Prince and he will be given ample opportunity to speak his opinion of Edgar and back that opinion with facts. After all, if Mr. Prince has any "journalistic integrity", he should have a foundation for his opinion and be willing to stand behind it IN PERSON and not just express it within the safe confines of his office where it goes unchallenged. In fact, I offer an open challenge to Mr. Prince: To start, please publish this letter in your "newspaper" and have an in person meeting to voice your opinions of hate and rhetoric to those who have opposing views.

Mayor Young, you too sir, are welcome to participate. If you have the means to verify and justify your openly negative and uneducated opinions of Edgar, then let us openly and civilly debate this in a public forum. After all, wouldn't that be the democratic way to settle an issue? Just remember, "civilly" is the key word. Is this possible? If so, please contact me with a date and time that we can do this.

As to Mr. Clemons, it is well known that he advocated, promoted, and endorsed Edgar's trial and conviction. To his credit, he did not blatantly and openly vilify Edgar in the article I am referencing. While his comments were generic, at least he showed the couth and respect Mr. Killen's family deserved by not personally attacking Edgar in this article. Thank you, Mr. Clemons.

Now to my interest in Mr. Killen and his trial and ultimate conviction. I contacted Edgar by letter in December of 2016. I did not know him or his family personally prior to this and I was in search for a story to write a book about. I was not a "professional writer", yet one of my goals was to become a published author. Until that time, and as of this current time, my livelihood has been in law enforcement. In fact, my entire adult life has been spent in law enforcement and this has covered nearly thirty years.

I also read old cases as a hobby. Quite by chance I read Mr. Killen's story and was intrigued and convinced that he had been railroaded simply for his racial and political views. I wrote a letter to Mr. Killen and this began a steady correspondence that lasted until days before his passing. I also secured a visit with him in May of 2017, and, with the assistance of an attorney, secured a contract to turn his story into a book. I have researched FBI reports, witness testimony, reviewed video documentaries, and obtained quite a bit of insight from a well-respected attorney from New York City, who by means of a former client, had crucial information regarding this case.

I have concluded the following. An accused person, when "reasonable doubt" exists, shall not be found guilty. Was there "reasonable doubt" in Edgar's case? Yes, by leaps and bounds, and this reasonable doubt shall be pointed out in abundance in my forthcoming book. Was there a collaboration between the prosecution, judge, defense, and jury? Sadly, it seems there was. Did the late Judge Marcus Gordon have a personal vendetta against Edgar? Yes, he most certainly did. Will this be addressed? Count on it.

Is Jim Hood and Marcus Duncan complicit in this case? Yes. Did they stoop to new lows, even by Mississippi standards, to secure a conviction? Yes sir, they did. Proof? Read the book. Improprieties on the part of the jury? Plenty, sir. Was Edgar's attorneys more criminally inclined than he ever could have been? The facts speak for themselves.

Mayor Young, let us now skip 50 years ahead from what Edgar was accused of and look at the current conditions of your city. According to the latest available census reports, I have found the following facts:

According to NeighborhoodScout>ms>crime, the following is true; "The chance of becoming a victim of either violent or property crime in Philadelphia is 1 in 26. Based on the FBI crime data, Philadelphia is not one of the safest communities in America. Relative to Mississippi, Philadelphia has a crime rate that is higher than 85% of the state's cities and towns of all sizes." Mayor Young, I ask you this, is this the fault of Mr. Edgar Ray Killen? Did Mr. Killen's "racism" many years after the fact contribute to this extraordinary crime rate? If you recall, he was incarcerated and therefore had no influence on a crime rate that occurred under YOUR WATCH!!!

Further, the demographics show that the racial make- up in your city of blacks and whites is roughly 50 / 50. However, there is seemingly more crimes perpetrated by blacks than whites. Sir, what do you suppose is the reason for this phenomenon? Did Edgar influence this from within the walls of Parchman Prison? Is he masterminding this from beyond the grave? Quite possibly, could it be that blacks, for whatever reason, are just more prone to criminal activity than whites? The statistics are inclined to say that is the case. You may take solace in the fact that this seems to be the case nation-wide and not just in your city. Mr. Killen certainly gets around, doesn't he? It is also reported that your unemployment rate exceeds 28%. Is it Mr. Killen and his "racism" and "hatred" keeping these poor souls from getting jobs, or is it their own laziness and free access to money provided by tax-payers who bother to go to work every day, and as a reward become crime victims and still get labeled as "racists" and "haters"?

Mayor, does it concern you in the least that according to the latest data on demographics, blacks are responsible for the majority of crime committed within your city? What are you doing about this? Please know that this includes crimes in which blacks are victims as well as offenders. By comparison, white on black crimes pale. This applies nation-wide and is not limited to your city. Please don't throw out that well-worn and antiquated accusation of "racism" toward me for merely repeating what the FBI reports. You don't know me, so please don't jump to conclusions about me. Hell, maybe the FBI is "racist" for reporting this. Taking into consideration Edgar was incarcerated the last 12 ½ years of his life, which far exceeded your time as mayor, is he really the villain? By contrast, in 1964 the state of Mississippi was listed as the most integrated state in the nation and boasted the lowest crime rate. Sir, what exactly was wrong with those statistics? What have you done to improve upon that? To the best of my knowledge, the correct answer is "nothing."

Do you assume any responsibility or just "pass the buck" to the ultimate "white devil" of Neshoba County? Mayor, you should really be ashamed of yourself for your comments that were made in a public forum. The only thing that you accomplished was hurting the survivors of Mr. Killen. Do you care? Was the political gain worth it? Is your conscience clear? Mr. Prince, the same question applies to you.

Mayor, if your conscience permits you, you should offer condolences to Mr. Killen's family. Mr. Prince, you too should use your "newspaper" to express Christian consolation to Edgar's friends and family. I pray that I am wrong, but somehow, I do not see either of you being man enough to do this. For this reason, I hope my forthcoming book exposes those responsible for railroading Edgar as the criminals and self-serving lowlifes they truly are. This applies to all that were complicit in this travesty and mockery of justice.

On a final note, Mr. Prince, I challenge you to print this in your poor excuse for a newspaper. Mayor Young, I challenge you to prove me wrong and give your blessing to Mr. Prince to print this. Further, please solicit the input and opinions of those that truly knew Rev. Edgar Ray Killen. Don't speak ill of the dead and cause further pain and grief to his survivors without giving them a chance to tell their side of the story. That is an act of true hatred and cowardice, but that sadly seems to be the manner in which you choose to conduct yourselves. It does not take a brave man to enter an arena of battle if there is no one to do battle with. I pray that my book helps to clear the name and legacy of a truly great man and provide peace to his surviving family and friends. It was my honor to write his story, consider him a friend, and more importantly, for him to consider me a friend. R.I.P. Mr. Killen.

Brian Boney, Author
'A Race Against the Clock:
The Authorized Biography of
Edgar Ray "Preacher" Killen'

c.c. Alderman-at-Large Leroy Clemons
    James Prince III, c/o Neshoba Democrat
    Mr. J.D. Killen
    Mrs. Betty Jo Killen

U.S. DEPARTMENT OF JUSTICE REPORT TO THE ATTORNY GENERAL OF THE STATE OF MISSISSIPPI

INVESTIGATION OF THE 1964 MURDERS OF MICHEAL SCHWERNER, JAMES CHANEY, AND ANDREW GOODMAN

U.S. Department of Justice, Civil Rights Division
United States Attorney's Office, Southern District of Mississippi
Federal Bureau of Investigation

Table of Contents

I. Introduction 3

II. Factual Summary: 1964 Murders 5

III. Initial Federal Investigation: 1964 8

    A. Initiation of Federal Investigation 8

    B. Discovery of Bodies 10

    C. Further Confidential Source Information 11

    D. Jordan and Barnette 11

    E. Charging the 1967 Federal Prosecution 13

IV. *United States v. Price* Evidence Summary 13

    A. Overview 13

    B. Carlton Wallace Miller (deceased) 14

    C. Delmar Dennis (deceased) 15

    D. Joseph Michael Hatcher 16

    E. James Jordan (deceased) 16

    F. H.D. Barnette (deceased) 20

    G. Defense Witnesses 21

    H. *Price* Trial Conclusion 21

V. 2000 Price/Posey Proffers and State Murder Investigation 22

VI. *Mississippi v. Killen* Evidence Summary 24

VII. Federal "Emmett Till Act" Investigation Summary: 2010 through 2016 ... 25

    A. Emmett Till Act Investigation Overview 25

    B. Legal Authority, Issues, and Limitations 26

    C. Emmet Till Act Investigation Witnesses 28

    D. Emmet Till Act Investigation / Subjects 41

    E. Potential Forensic Evidence 42

VIII. Analysis of Evidence Regarding Surviving Subjects 42

    A. Jimmy Lee Townsend 43

    B. James Thomas "Pete" Harris 43

IX. Conclusion 45

ATTACHMENT A 47

I.   Introduction

The Civil Rights Division of the United States Department of Justice (Division) and the Federal Bureau of Investigations (FBI), assisted by the United States Attorney's Office for the Southern District of Mississippi (USAO), have completed their investigation into the June 21, 1964 murders of Michael Schwerner, James Chaney and Andrew Goodman, three volunteers in the civil rights movement working in Neshoba and Lauderdale Counties, Mississippi. The investigation and this report are authorized by the Emmett Till Unsolved Civil Rights Crime Act, 28 United States Code § 509 (Pub.L.110-344, 122 Stat. 3934) (Emmett Till Act). This Emmett Till Act investigation focused on (1) whether sufficient admissible evidence currently exists to support further state prosecution against any surviving person for involvement in the murders; and (2) whether certain witnesses made recent federally prosecutable false statements to FBI agents. We closely coordinated with Jim Hood, the Attorney General for the State of Mississippi, because of his prosecutive authority in this case.[1]

After considering all credible leads and exhausting all viable investigative tools, we have determined that no further federal investigation is warranted at this time. Additionally, we have concluded that there is insufficient evidence to support a prosecutable federal violation of any person under Title 18 United States Code § 1001, for willfully making material false statements to federal investigators. In this report, we also convey our investigative findings to the Mississippi Attorney General for his consideration of whether there is sufficient evidence to support state criminal charges.

At the outset, it should be acknowledged that nine individuals have been successfully prosecuted for these heinous crimes. In the 1967 case of *United States v. Price* (*Price*), the Department's Assistant Attorney General for Civil Rights John Doar and his team of federal prosecutors convicted eight defendants – James Edward Jordan, Cecil Ray Price, Alton Wayne Roberts, Horace Doyle "H.D." Barnette, Billy Wayne Posey, Jimmy Arledge, Jimmy Snowden,

---

[1] Federal charges related to the 1964 killings – even if supported by sufficient evidence – cannot be legally brought against anyone because the-then-existing statute of limitations bars the United States from prosecuting anyone for federal criminal civil rights charges related to these murders. Prior to 1994, these charges were not capital offenses and were thus subject to a five-year statute of limitations. See 18 U.S.C. § 3282(a). In 1994, some of these civil rights statutes were amended to provide the death penalty for violations resulting in death, thereby eliminating the statute of limitations. See 18 U.S.C. § 3281 ("An indictment for any offense punishable by death may be found at any time without limitation."). However, the *Ex Post Facto* Clause prohibits the retroactive application of the 1994 increase in penalties and the resultant change in the statute of limitations to the detriment of criminal defendants. *Stogner v. California*, 539 U.S. 607, 611 (2003). The Civil Rights Division has used non-civil rights statutes to overcome the statute of limitations challenge in certain cases, such as those occurring on federal land or involving kidnapping across state lines with death resulting. The facts of the present case do not support the elements necessary for prosecution under any other federal statutes. Thus, the state of Mississippi is the only forum available for any prosecution related to the murders.

and Sam Holloway Bowers[2] – for violating the federal criminal civil rights conspiracy statute.[3] In 2005, Mississippi Attorney General Hood and Neshoba County District Attorney Mark Duncan convicted Edgar Ray Killen of state manslaughter charges in *Mississippi v. Killen* (*Killen*).

Federal efforts over the past three years have been extensive and exhaustive. When we began our Emmett Till Act investigation, five of the individuals believed to have been involved were still alive: Killen (prosecuted in 2005), Richard Andrew Willis (died in July 2011), Olen Lovell Burrage (died in March 2013), James Thomas "Pete" Harris, and Jimmy Lee Townsend. Harris and Townsend are still potentially culpable for state offenses related to the murders. Department attorneys and FBI agents have (1) reviewed a massive number of relevant documents assembled over nearly fifty years (including elaborate FBI confidential source files and transcripts from two 1960s grand jury sessions); (2) examined voluminous records from the Mississippi investigation that led to the 2005 *Killen* prosecution; (3) interviewed all surviving, willing and competent, potential witnesses, often on multiple occasions; (4) sought voluntary information from subjects of the investigation; (5) evaluated and assessed several tangential allegations; (6) met with the victims' families to seek their input; and, most significantly; (7) made extensive use of the full panoply of law enforcement investigative tools – non-prosecution agreements, covert activities, and other confidential investigative undertakings authorized by law but proscribed from public reporting, to include a federal § 1001 grand jury investigation.

With the passage of fifty years, few persons with any direct knowledge of the facts relevant to the June 21, 1964 murders remain alive. Most of the original cooperators and confidential sources are deceased. Many of these elderly witnesses have understandably imperfect recollections. Other witnesses are reluctant to provide information. Some witnesses, despite comprehensive efforts – including pursuit of evidence to support federal prosecution for false statement (see discussion in Section VII.B.2) – to evoke truthful information from them, appeared to continue to conceal crucial relevant information. These realities impacted the results of our investigation and current prospects of uncovering any further information useful for prosecutive purposes.

Additionally, we provide in this report our analysis of the currently available evidence relevant to a state murder charge to assist the Mississippi Attorney General's prosecutive

---

[2] Attachment A lists the individuals who are referenced throughout this report and provides a brief summary of their relevance to events.

[3] A total of twenty-two individuals were charged as being involved in the murder conspiracy. The above eight were convicted. Eight others – Richard Andrew Willis, Olen Lowell Burrage, James Thomas "Pete" Harris, Bernard L. Akin, Travis Maryn Barnette, Frank J. Herndon, Lawrence Andrew Rainey, and Herman Tucker – were acquitted. Mistrials were granted as to three defendants – Edgar Ray Killen, Jerry McGrew Sharpe, and Ethal Glenn "Hop" Barnette. Finally, Otha Neal Burkes, Jimmy Lee Townsend and Oliver Richard Warner were charged in preliminary charging documents, but they were not included in the final indictment and were not trial defendants.

- 4 -

decision. We make no recommendation as to whether there is a prosecutable state murder charge. Such decision is properly the exclusive province of state prosecuting authorities.

This report summarizes the information learned during this investigation, as well as relevant information from prior investigative and prosecutive work conducted by both federal and Mississippi authorities during the intervening fifty years since the murders. We trust that our work will allow for state authorities to make a fully informed decision. And, under the mandate of the Emmett Till Act, the Department and the FBI would continue to assist the state if it decides that the evidence is sufficient to support a state murder or other criminal prosecution.

II. Factual Summary: 1964 Murders

The following summary of facts is provided to assist in understanding the remainder of the report. It relies heavily, but not exclusively, upon the public records of the *Price* and *Killen* trials, particularly the detailed confessions of convicted defendants Jordan and H.D. Barnette, and Jordan's subsequent testimony in *Price*. It should be noted that certain information related in this summary and elsewhere in this report, while instructive and illuminating, would be inadmissible in a future criminal trial, such as when a witness is deceased or is a protected confidential source,[4] and therefore unavailable to testify. Additionally, where necessary in this report, certain facts are presented in a manner so as not to reveal the identity of a protected confidential source.

In the summer of 1964, promoted as "The Freedom Summer," the Congress of Federated Organizations (COFO), one of the most active civil rights groups in Mississippi, planned a concentrated effort to register African Americans to vote. Michael Schwerner, a twenty-four-year-old former New York social worker, was an established civil rights organizer with COFO working in and around Meridian and Philadelphia. In 1964, Schwerner teamed up with James Chaney, a twenty-one-year-old African-American COFO volunteer from Meridian. Together with Schwerner's wife, Rita, they established a community center and organizing headquarters in Meridian.

A Mississippi white supremacist organization, the White Knights of the Ku Klux Klan (Klan), was fiercely opposed to all forms of desegregation, especially voter registration efforts. The Klan adopted violence to achieve its ends.

Schwerner was particularly reviled by the Klan for his work. Indeed, the killing of Schwerner was a routine topic discussed at Klan meetings attended by both Meridian and Philadelphia Klansmen, but Klan orthodoxy prevented such action unless authorized by the state Klan leader. Several weeks before the murders, state Klan leader Sam Bowers gave that authorization.

---

[4] While the identity of certain FBI protected confidential sources cannot publicly be released to protect against possible harm to these elderly individuals, the information that each witness provided to a past or to the current investigation has been shared with the Mississippi Attorney General for his assessment of its prosecutive value.

On the evening of June 16, 1964, a large group of Meridian and Philadelphia Klansmen, including Klansmen later involved in the June 21 murders, attended a Klan meeting.[5] The Klansmen discussed a reported gathering, thought to include civil rights workers, at the African-American Mount Zion Methodist Church in Neshoba County just outside of Philadelphia. Schwerner and Chaney had visited that church and worked with its parishioners. Several armed Klansmen left the Klan meeting and drove to the church looking for white civil rights workers. Although no civil rights volunteers were present at the church, the Klansmen beat the African-American parishioners whom they encountered and returned later to burn down the church. Afterwards, it was speculated by some Klansmen that the attack on the church might lure Schwerner back to Neshoba County.

Schwerner and Chaney were in a COFO training program in Ohio when they learned about the assaults and arson. Andrew Goodman, a twenty-year-old college student and new volunteer from New York, joined Schwerner and Chaney in leaving Ohio for Mississippi. They arrived in Meridian by June 20, 1964.

On Sunday morning, June 21, 1964, the three civil rights volunteers left Meridian to visit with the victims of the Klan church attack near Philadelphia. They drove a 1963 Ford station wagon with Mississippi tags registered to COFO. The men spent the early afternoon in Longdale, an African-American community outside of Philadelphia where the church's parishioners lived. They spoke with various victims of the Klan attack and other members of the community.

At about 3 p.m., Neshoba County Deputy and Klan member Cecil Ray Price, who shared the Klan's antipathy for COFO, pulled the three men over during their return to Meridian through Philadelphia. Deputy Price recognized Schwerner and identified the station wagon as belonging to COFO. He arrested the three men and took them to the Philadelphia jail. He booked Chaney for speeding and held Schwerner and Goodman for investigation, ostensibly in connection with the church arson. Price contacted Edgar Ray Killen, a Philadelphia minister and Klan leader, and advised him that Schwerner and the two other civil rights volunteers were in custody.

Killen saw an opportunity to punish the COFO workers. Joined by two other men, he set out to Meridian to meet with Meridian Klan members.[6] Killen sought help from Meridian

---

[5] Meridian, Mississippi, and Philadelphia, Mississippi are approximately forty miles apart. In 1964, Meridian was a thriving, mid-sized municipality, and Philadelphia was a much smaller, rural town. Klansmen from the two communities often attended the same Klan meetings and had previously acted in concert. Thus, some members of the Meridian Klan chapter knew members of the Philadelphia Klan chapter, but others from the two groups were not acquainted.

[6] A now-deceased cooperating government witness, James Jordan, identified the two accomplices by name as Jimmy Lee Townsend and Jerry McGrew Sharpe, both from Philadelphia. The information related to Townsend (still living) and Sharpe (deceased) is discussed in more detail later in the report.

- 6 -

because the Klan preferred to use non-local Klansmen to conduct acts of violence, minimizing the chance that a participant would be recognized by a victim or a witness.

Killen and his Philadelphia accomplices arrived at Meridian's Longhorn Restaurant, a Klan gathering place, at about 6 p.m. Killen delivered the news to the Meridian Klan that Deputy Price was holding the arrestees in jail but could not detain them for long. Killen appealed for Meridian Klansmen to come to Philadelphia to abduct and assault the arrestees when they were released from jail. Killen announced that the civil rights workers "needed their asses tore up," and instructed the Klansmen to get gloves and to bring guns to Philadelphia.

To assist Killen, Meridian Klan leaders, including James Thomas "Pete" Harris, made calls to recruit other Meridian Klansmen. As their numbers grew, the Klansmen relocated from The Longhorn to the Akin's Mobile Homes property, a Meridian business owned by a now deceased Klan leader. Eventually, five recruited Meridian Klansmen – James Jordan, H.D. Barnette, Travis Maryn Barnette,[7] Jimmy Arledge, and Jimmy Snowden – armed with handguns and equipped with gloves, drove to Philadelphia in one car. The three Philadelphia Klansmen, joined by Meridian Klansman Alton Wayne Roberts, drove separately to Philadelphia. They reunited in downtown Philadelphia. Harris and the other Meridian Klan leaders remained in Meridian and did not travel with the group to Philadelphia. Significant to our later investigation, no evidence suggests that Harris went along with the other Klansmen to Philadelphia or ever joined their group later that night.

Arriving in downtown Philadelphia after dark, the recruited Meridian Klansmen reconnected with Killen and the Philadelphia Klansmen, and they were joined by Philadelphia Klansman Billy Wayne Posey. The Meridian Klan contingent parked on a street near the jail and the Philadelphia group assembled nearby waiting for notification that the civil rights workers had been released from jail. Killen left the group, asking to be driven to a funeral home in Philadelphia to establish his alibi.

At about 10:30 p.m., Deputy Price told Chaney to pay a $20 fine and released the three men from the jail. He told them to "see how quickly they could get out of Neshoba County," and escorted them to their station wagon impounded near the jail. The young men immediately drove from Philadelphia south on Highway 19 toward Meridian, the direct route home. The waiting Klansmen were alerted when the three civil rights workers were released. They immediately drove off in two separate cars following the victims' station wagon. Posey drove the Philadelphia Klansmen in his 1958 Chevrolet, and H.D. Barnette drove the Meridian Klansmen in his Ford.

Price, driving his official patrol car, joined the two carloads of Klansmen at the outskirts of Philadelphia, and they all sped after the victims' station wagon. After a high-speed chase, Price caught up to the victims when they turned onto a roadway from Highway 19, in an apparent attempt to elude their pursuers. Pulled over by Price, the three civil rights workers were forced into his patrol car. The Klan convoy, with a Klansman now driving the victims' station

---

[7] As discussed in the summary of the *Price* trial at Section IV.E., the testimony was conflicting as to whether Travis Barnette was present at the killings.

- 7 -

wagon, reversed direction on Route 19 and drove to an isolated location just off the highway on Rock Cut Road about ten miles south of Philadelphia.

Significantly, before the Klansmen overtook and abducted the victims, Posey's Chevrolet had mechanical troubles. Ultimately one man was left alone with Posey's disabled car while the other Klansmen completed the murder plot.[8]

The three victims were quickly shot and killed alongside Rock Cut Road and their bodies were loaded into their own station wagon. At least seven of the eight defendants convicted in *Price* (all now deceased) - Price, and Klansmen Roberts, H.D. Barnette, Arledge, Snowden, Jordan, and Posey - were at the murder scene.[9] After loading the three bodies into the station wagon, Price returned to Philadelphia on Highway 19, while the rest of the group headed away from the highway on Rock Cut Road.

Posey immediately instructed the remaining Klansmen to follow him. Posey drove the victim's station wagon with the bodies in it, leading the other Klansmen in Barnette's Ford along back roads to the Old Jolly Farm. The farm was a property outside of Philadelphia owned by Olen Lovell Burrage. The three bodies were buried by a bulldozer at Burrage's Old Jolly Farm in an earthen dam then under construction at the farm. Burrage was seen in a car with two other never-identified men near the dam site shortly before the bodies were buried. He was later seen at Burrage's "truck garage," a trucking business office and warehouse that were across the street from Burrage's home. Burrage supplied gasoline from his gas pump for use to incinerate the victims' station wagon later that night and Burrage also offered the use of one of his trucks for the mission.

The Klansmen left the Burrage property between about 1:00 a.m. to 1:30 a.m. on June 22, 1964. Someone drove the civil rights workers' station wagon to a location on Highway 21 near Philadelphia and set it ablaze in a swampy area alongside the highway. The rest of the group returned to Philadelphia. Then, the Meridian Klansmen returned to Meridian.

III. Initial Federal Investigation: 1964

A. Initiation of Federal Investigation

Department of Justice attorneys were active during the summer of 1964 investigating and litigating voter registration cases throughout rural Mississippi and were thus working closely with COFO organizers. When the three COFO volunteers failed to return as scheduled from

---

[8] This individual was specifically identified by Jordan, the government's cooperating witness in the *Price* trial, as Townsend, a then 17-year-old who worked at Posey's gas station outside of Philadelphia (see discussion about testimony in *Price* trial in Section IV).

[9] There are conflicting accounts as to whether Travis Barnette and/or Sharpe (both now deceased) were also present. In the 1967 federal trial, Travis Barnette was acquitted and Sharpe was granted a mistrial.

their June 21 visit to Neshoba County to investigate the Mount Zion Church arson, a COFO representative called a Department attorney to report that the men were missing. Local law enforcement officials in Lauderdale and Neshoba Counties had advised COFO that no persons of the victims' description were being held. The Department attorney alerted the FBI, which promptly sent a Meridian-based Special Agent to Philadelphia and opened a federal investigation into the victims' disappearance.

Price was confronted by the FBI on June 22, 1964. He admitted that the previous day he had arrested and jailed the three victims. Price maintained, however, that after releasing the men that evening, he last saw them driving from downtown Philadelphia toward Meridian. Price became a prime suspect after a review of records and the interviews of local law enforcement personnel and administrative staff could not account for Price's whereabouts between 10:40 p.m. and 11:30 p.m. on June 21. Additionally, six days after the disappearance, a Knoxville reporter recorded an interview with a local Philadelphia man who claimed that Sherriff Rainey and others were bragging that the Klan had killed the young men and that Deputy Price had been involved. This significant information was conveyed to the Goodman family attorney and the FBI.

The charred station wagon registered to COFO and driven by the victims was recovered in the swamp on June 23, 1964. The discovery of the torched station wagon two days later suggested the victims were deceased rather than missing, and the investigative activity increased accordingly. Quickly, the FBI moved massive FBI resources into Mississippi. It established a new Jackson Field Office which coordinated a vast manhunt and investigation termed the "MIBURN" (Mississippi Burning) investigation.

The federal investigation faced daunting challenges. At best, persons with relevant information were reluctant to cooperate. Many potential witnesses, including law enforcement officers, were deceitful and obstructionist. False leads were deliberately planted, requiring unnecessary investigative attention. Federal authorities were required to conduct the investigation independent of local and state law enforcement.

The FBI conducted approximately 1000 interviews during the summer and fall of 1964. The record demonstrates an enormous federal effort to locate the missing men and to identify those responsible for their disappearance. Most importantly, the FBI developed a relatively complex internal security-type intelligence operation, utilizing local confidential sources and cooperators. This effort depended upon infiltration, surveillance, and deception of the Klan. Initially, only hearsay information was provided by already trusted state law enforcement officers or local civil rights advocates. In time, rumors led to sources with personal knowledge of what had occurred and who was involved. FBI special agents gained the trust and assistance of often begrudgingly cooperative Klansmen and local law enforcement officers (some of whom were also Klansmen) to act as confidential sources. The FBI also skillfully instilled distrust among the Meridian/Philadelphia Klansmen.

Meanwhile, local law enforcement officials ostensibly conducted a parallel investigation. Local spokespersons brazenly speculated that the three COFO volunteers had purposely disappeared in order to attract attention to their cause. A local Coroner's Jury was initiated. Eventually, the local county prosecutor unsuccessfully subpoenaed FBI agents to a Neshoba

- 9 -

County grand jury and expressed an intention to prosecute only those persons who were cooperating with federal authorities, but never initiated any such prosecutions. More important, no state or local criminal charges were brought in the 1960s for the murders of the three civil rights workers.

B. Discovery of Bodies

Initially, the federal investigative effort concentrated on a search for the bodies of the victims. Enlisting the assistance of a large number of Navy personnel from the Meridian Naval Air Station, FBI agents first focused on the swampy area surrounding the charred station wagon. The FBI conducted other searches for the bodies in other Neshoba County locations throughout the summer without success, until, in late July 1964, an informant provided accurate information about the location of the bodies. That informant, who to this day remains anonymous, related that he knew from personal knowledge that the bodies had been buried in a dam on the Neshoba County farm owned by Olen Burrage and that the bodies were still buried there.[10] Based on that disclosure, the FBI obtained a federal search warrant on August 3, 1964, to search the Old Jolly Farm outside of Philadelphia.

Burrage, a native of Neshoba County, was well known in his community. He owned several properties in Neshoba County, including the over 250 acre Old Jolly Farm, located about two miles from his home. Burrage operated an interstate trucking business, located across the street from his home, which had over a dozen vehicles and employed a number of local men as drivers.

The next day on August 4, 1964, the FBI executed the search warrant. When the FBI arrived on August 4, Burrage was compliant, insisting that he wished to cooperate fully. Later that day, after several hours of excavation with heavy equipment and digging by hand at the newly completed dam, FBI agents discovered the three bodies. When told of this discovery, Burrage claimed to have no knowledge of how they came to be buried on his land.

The FBI learned that Burrage had contracted in May 1964 to build the dam on the Old Jolly Farm. He had hired several local men with bulldozers to construct an earthen dam structure to form a pond. Two of the bulldozer operators, including now-deceased *Price* defendant Herman Tucker, maintained that they worked to build the dam until late afternoon on June 21, the day the civil rights workers disappeared.[11] They claimed that they observed nothing unusual when returning to the job site the next Monday morning and that they had no further relevant information. Neighbors who lived near the Old Jolly Farm also denied seeing or hearing anything unusual the evening of June 21.

---

[10] There is no written record of the identity of this source. The only FBI agent who knew the source's identity is now deceased.

[11] One now-deceased witness identified the bulldozer operator who buried the bodies as "Herman," and Herman Tucker, a deceased acquitted defendant in *Price*, was a bulldozer operator who was working on Burrage's dam.

- 10 -

C. Further Confidential Source Information

The FBI's discovery of the bodies sent a clear message to the Klansmen involved in the murder and to their supporters that someone with direct knowledge of the events had revealed information to law enforcement. A few days after the bodies were discovered, H.D. Barnette, abruptly moved his family back to his home state of Louisiana. Meanwhile, the FBI continued its infiltration activities.

Sources identified other Meridian and Philadelphia Klansmen, the Klan leaders, the locations of Klan meetings, and what had been discussed at those meetings. The FBI learned of pre-existing plans to conduct surveillance on Schwerner and other COFO workers, discussions about killing Schwerner, and additional facts about the events of June 21. The FBI also conducted 24-hour surveillance of certain Klansmen.

Klan confidential source information accelerated in volume and improved in quality. One early important FBI source, for example, Sergeant Carlton Wallace Miller (deceased), a Meridian police officer who later testified in *Price*, was first paid by the FBI beginning in September 1964. He continued his relationship with the Klan while supplying information to the FBI. Miller advised the FBI that he had helped establish the Meridian Klan group and related important hearsay and lead information. This source and other sources proffered the names of Meridian and Philadelphia Klansmen likely involved in the murders. Miller and a number of confidential sources received significant financial incentives and additional necessary financial support commiserate with their cooperation.

In mid-October, James Jordan was interviewed by the FBI. At that time, he denied having any relevant information or being a member of the Klan. Jordan admitted knowing the specific Klansmen about whom he was questioned, but he claimed not to know whether the men were in the Klan. Meanwhile, other confidential sources advised that the Meridian Klan had begun to suspect that Jordan was cooperating with the FBI and that he was furnishing the information that was actually being provided by other sources. Later in October, Jordan disappeared from Meridian and FBI sources advised that suspicious, angry Klansmen were looking for him. H.D. Barnette was still out of the state.

D. Jordan and Barnette

The FBI located Jordan in Gulfport, Mississippi, and H.D. Barnette in Louisiana. With limited options and resources, Jordan and H.D. Barnette elected to work with the federal authorities and, after successive interviews, provided detailed confessions discussed in depth in Section IV.

When first approached by the FBI in Gulfport in late October, Jordan continued to deny that he was a Klansman, but, contrary to his previous interviews, he did offer the names of others who were in the Klan and suggested that those Klansmen might provide information to the FBI regarding Klan activities and the murders. Later, Jordan claimed that he had heard about the details of the murders but he continued to deny any personal involvement. Finally, on November 5, 1964, Jordan signed a lengthy statement detailing his personal account of the murders and the

- 11 -

burial of the civil rights workers. In subsequent interviews, Jordan furnished the FBI and Department prosecutors with more detail and clarification.

Days after Jordan's November 5 disclosure, an important detail of his account was corroborated by two highway patrolmen (both now deceased), providing greater confidence in Jordan's overall account.[12] When the FBI next approached H.D. Barnette in Louisiana, they were equipped with detailed information about the murders, and H.D. Barnette almost certainly realized that someone had already implicated him. H.D. Barnette subsequently signed his own detailed confession on November 20, 1964. Like Jordan, in subsequent interviews, H.D. Barnette expanded upon his signed confession, and clarified some of the details. Jordan later pled guilty to federal charges and testified for the government, but H.D. Barnette stood trial in *Price*, despite his confession.

The confessions of Jordan and H.D. Barnette generally corroborated each other's account of the events of June 21, 1964, and the events that led to the murders. Most specifically, both Klansmen agreed on the details related to seven defendants who were ultimately convicted in *Price* for pursuing, abducting and killing the victims. Both men also related consistent information about Killen's involvement in the planning of the murders. Both provided inculpatory information related to Harris and Burrage. Jordan also specifically identified Townsend as being present until he was left behind with Posey's disabled car, which was consistent with H.D. Barnette's recollection of "someone else from Philadelphia" being present and then left with Posey's vehicle.

Jordan additionally provided inculpatory information against state Klan leader Sam Bowers, the eighth defendant adjudged guilty in *Price,* who authorized the killings, but was not present at the murders.

But, it should be noted that there were several significant differences in the accounts provided by Jordan and H.D. Barnette. Most significantly, Jordan claimed to be acting as a look-out at the time of the shootings, but H.D. Barnette stated that Jordan was the person who shot Chaney. Further, although Jordan identified Townsend by his full name, Sharpe by his last name, and Tucker by his first name; H.D. Barnette, who was from Meridian, did not identify any of these three Philadelphia men by name.

---

[12] These two officers confirmed that they had encountered Posey and Deputy Price in their vehicles on Highway 19 just outside of Philadelphia shortly after the civil rights workers had been released. During previous interviews, the highway patrolmen admitted only that they helped Deputy Price transport the three men from the site of their arrest to the jail. After Jordan reported their night-time encounter with Price and Posey on Highway 19 just before the chase of the victims began, the FBI used that information to persuade the officers to admit this significant fact (see *Price* trial summary in Section IV).

- 12 -

E. Charging the 1967 Federal Prosecution

In December 1964, federal criminal civil rights charges were filed in a criminal complaint in the Southern District of Mississippi and the charged defendants were arrested. Thereafter, eighteen defendants were indicted by a federal grand jury in the Southern District of Mississippi on January 15, 1965, for violating Title 18 United States Code §§ 241 (Conspiracy Against Rights) and 242 (Deprivation of Rights Under Color of Law). The applicable federal criminal statutes were the two criminal civil rights statutes of the time. In 1964, a § 241 conspiracy had a ten-year maximum sentence while a § 242 violation was a misdemeanor.

The United States District Court ruled on several critical pre-trial motions in February 1965. Favorably to the government, the Court ruled that the August 3, 1964 search warrant was valid under the Fourth Amendment, refusing to exclude evidence derived from the search of the Old Jolly Farm. The defendants' motion for separate trials was denied. But, another ruling substantially delayed the federal prosecution. The court granted the defense motion to dismiss the § 241 conspiracy and the substantive § 242 misdemeanor counts in the 1965 indictment against all defendants except Neshoba County Deputy Price and the other law enforcement defendants. The dismissal caused an over two-year delay while the Department appealed.

Ultimately, the United States Supreme Court upheld the entire 1965 indictment in *United States v. Price*, 383 U.S. 786 (1966). The Supreme Court held that all of the non-law enforcement defendants, the civilian Klansmen, could be prosecuted for violating §§ 241 and 242, if they conspired with and aided and abetted law enforcement officers who were acting under the color of law to deprive a person of life and liberty without due process of law, a right protected by the Fourteenth Amendment.

In February 1967, nineteen defendants were indicted on a single § 241 conspiracy charge in a superseding indictment by another federal grand jury in the Southern District of Mississippi. The number of indicted defendants changed to nineteen because one of the 1965 indicted defendants (Jimmy Lee Townsend, the then seventeen-year-old defendant left behind with Posey's disabled car) was removed from the 1967 indictment (see discussion regarding Townsend in Section VII.C.2.a), and two other defendants, state Klan leader Sam Bowers and former Neshoba County Sheriff Ethal Glenn "Hop" Barnette (to be distinguished from H.D. Barnette), were added. Under this superseding 1967 indictment, the Department proceeded to trial in *United States v. Price*.

IV. *United States v. Price* Evidence Summary

A. Overview

The trial of *United States v. Price* was held in Meridian in the Southern District of Mississippi, commencing on October 9, 1967. One hundred and fifty-one witnesses testified. Approximately twenty percent of the witnesses presented the government's evidence of the crime, while the remaining eighty percent of the witnesses offered character and alibi evidence for the defendants. The jury returned its verdicts on October 20, 1967.

- 13 -

The 1967 federal prosecution trial team focused its evidentiary presentation on those defendants who participated in the shooting deaths of the three victims and on the top Klan leadership, Mississippi Klan leader Bowers and Philadelphia Klan leader Killen. All of the primary targeted defendants were convicted except for Killen. Accordingly, the prosecution team concentrated less on the secondary defendants, who had helped arrange, facilitate, and organize the murders and the burials, but had not actually participated in the killing. Given the available evidence and the political climate surrounding the trial, this strategy can hardly be faulted and proved largely successful.

A mix of witnesses – civilians, local law enforcement officers and officials, FBI agents, and forensic experts – portrayed the victims and their activities for the jury, described the recovery of their vehicle and bodies, and identified the bodies. Also among this first group of government witnesses were civilians, highway patrol officers, and jail personnel who established that Deputy Price arrested the three civil rights workers on the afternoon of June 21, 1964, detained them in the Philadelphia jail, and released them that evening. African-American colleagues and the victims' family members established that Schwerner and Chaney were in Mississippi working with the African-American community on voter registration efforts and were planning on using the Mt. Zion Methodist Church as a Freedom School. After the church burned, the civil rights workers returned to investigate the burning, speaking with African-American victims. Highway Patrol and Neshoba County jail personnel witnesses recalled the arrest, detention in the Philadelphia jail, and the release of the three civil rights workers on June 21, 1964. Highway Patrolman Earl Robert Poe (deceased) testified that, sometime after 10 p.m. on Highway 19 just south of Philadelphia, Posey approached his patrol car and asked where Price was.

As set forth further below, cooperating Klansmen Carlton Wallace Miller and Delmar Dennis thereafter testified about the defendants' Klan affiliations and their targeting of Michael Schwerner. James Jordan, who pled guilty and cooperated as a government witness, testified from personal knowledge regarding the events of June 21 after the three victims were released from the jail. He also testified to state Klan leader Bowers' approval of the murder. Another witness, Joseph Michael Hatcher, provided testimony that repeated some of what Miller and Dennis provided to the jury and related a key admission by Killen. The government's case ended with H.D. Barnette's confession, which was necessarily redacted to eliminate statements implicating other defendants in order to comply with the Sixth Amendment's right to confront witnesses.

As previously noted, seven defendants – Price, Roberts, H.D. Barnette, Posey, Arledge, Snowden, and Bowers – were convicted of the federal criminal civil rights conspiracy. Eight defendants – Burrage and Harris, as well as Bernard Akin, Travis Barnette, Herndon, Rainey, Tucker, and Willis – were found not guilty. Mistrials were entered by the court after the jury could not agree as to three defendants, Killen, Sharpe and "Hop" Barnette.

B. Carlton Wallace Miller (deceased)

Miller, now deceased, testified that he was a police officer in Meridian in 1964, and also a member of the Klan, sworn in by Killen, whom he had known most of his life. He testified that

- 14 -

he personally saw other defendants attending Klan meetings prior to June 21, 1964, including Harris, Akin and Herndon (Meridian Klan Chapter leaders), Killen and Bowers, and Roberts, Arledge, Snowden, and H.D. Barnette (all present at the killing) and H.D. Barnette's brother Travis. Miller also testified that he was present at the meeting when Harris was sworn into the Klan in April 1964.

Miller further testified that he attended a joint Philadelphia/Meridian Klan meeting at which the "elimination" of Schwerner was discussed, explaining that "elimination" was a Klan term for murder, and that all eliminations needed to be approved by the state Klan leader. According to Miller, Killen and Herndon, who ran the particular meeting where elimination was discussed, represented to the group that Bowers, who was the state leader of the Klan in Mississippi, had approved the elimination of Schwerner.

Miller testified that he had just returned to Meridian on June 21 from National Guard duty and thus learned nothing about the murders on the day they were committed. However, after the murders, Miller had separate discussions with Killen, Herndon, and Akin, all of whom divulged certain aspects of the murders to him.

According to Miller's testimony, Killen provided the most information about the events of June 21, explaining that the civil rights workers were chased in their car down Highway 19, then shot and buried in a dam about 15 feet deep. According to Miller, Killen advised that the Klan burned a church to lure Schwerner to Philadelphia. Killen also told Miller of his own involvement on the night of June 21, 1964, saying that when he received the news that the civil rights workers were arrested in Philadelphia, he traveled to The Longhorn Drive-in restaurant in Meridian to meet Herndon. Together Killen and Herndon organized a group of Klansmen at the Longhorn to travel to Philadelphia.

Miller testified that Herndon told him a similar story about organizing Klansmen with Killen at the Longhorn, and that Akin provided a comparable report about the Klan burning the church to lure Schwerner to Philadelphia. Miller also told the jury that on the day the FBI recovered the station wagon, Herndon said to Miller that "someone goofed up, that they were supposed to carry the car to Birmingham."

During the cross-examination of Miller regarding his motives, the defense raised the question of whether Miller provided information in order to obtain reward money. Miller denied receiving reward money, but admitted that the FBI paid him $2,400 to remain as an informant in the Klan and to report what he witnessed. Miller was also cross-examined on the reliability of his memory.

C. **Delmar Dennis** (deceased)

Another former Klansman, Delmar Dennis, also now deceased, corroborated much of Miller's testimony. Dennis testified that he was sworn into the Klan in March 1964 by Killen at the Cash Salvage store in Meridian, and that Harris, Roberts, and Herndon were present along with Killen. Killen told Dennis at his swearing-in that the Klan "was an organization of action,"

- 15 -

and that "elimination" meant killing. Dennis testified about Klan meetings, secret codes, and Klan doctrine.

Dennis further testified that he attended three separate meetings in which the Klan discussed the elimination of Schwerner. The first meeting was at Cash Salvage and the same defendants present at Dennis's swearing-in were again present, along with Akin. Dennis testified that Killen said that the elimination of Schwerner had been approved.

The second meeting took place in early May 1964, in Herndon's trailer home. There, Klan members discussed the fact that the elimination of Schwerner had been approved, but nothing had been yet done about it. Dennis told the jury that Harris was present at this meeting.

The third Klan meeting took place at a gymnasium in Neshoba County. During that meeting, it was announced that there was activity at the Mount Zion Church and that civil rights volunteers might be there. Klan members left their meeting, assaulted the African-American parishioners at the church, and returned to report their actions. According to Dennis, Harris was also present at this Neshoba County Klan meeting.

Dennis was cross-examined regarding the money that he received from the government. He admitted that he received $15,000 for his work as a confidential informant.

D. Joseph Michael Hatcher

A second Meridian police officer, also a Klansman, Joseph Michael Hatcher, testified and corroborated some of the testimony of Miller, Dennis and Jordan. Hatcher testified that he had attended Klan meetings, including a meeting led by Killen and a meeting where it was discussed that civil rights workers "needed to be done away with."

Most significantly, Hatcher testified that on the afternoon after the murders, Killen spoke alone with Hatcher. Killen told Hatcher that "the three had been taken care of," the bodies were buried in an earthen dam, the car had been burned, and that Killen had established an alibi at a funeral home.

E. James Jordan (deceased)

James Jordan was perhaps the most critical government witness because he provided a narrative of what happened on June 21, 1964, from personal knowledge. He testified that he was an early member of the Meridian Klan, and was brought into the Klan by Miller. On June 21, he went to The Longhorn Drive-In and Harris and Herndon were present at the Longhorn when he arrived.

Jordan testified that Killen arrived at The Longhorn from Philadelphia. According to Jordan, a Philadelphia Klansman, whom he knew only by his last name, Sharpe (acquitted

- 16 -

defendant Jerry McGrew Sharpe), drove Killen to The Longhorn and another "young man" from Philadelphia, Jimmy Lee Townsend, accompanied the other two Klansmen. [13]

Jordan told the jury that Killen spoke with Herndon upon arrival at the Longhorn. After speaking with Herndon, "he" (it is unclear from the testimony whether "he" is Herndon or Killen) solicited "some help on over in Neshoba County" and "some men to go with him" because "two or three of those civil rights workers were locked up and they needed their rear ends tore up." Jordan also testified that one of the civil rights workers was Schwerner.

When asked what action the men took in response to Killen's request for assistance, Jordan responded, "we started calling them on the telephone trying to line up some more men to go with us." Notably, Jordan identified Harris as one of the men making those telephone calls to recruit other Meridian Klansmen and that Harris had a particular Klan job as "an Investigator."

As the group grew in numbers, Jordan testified that it moved from The Longhorn to Akin's Mobile Homes, Bernard Akin's business. During the move between Klan locations, Jordan rode with Killen and Sharpe in either Harris' car or in the Philadelphia Klansmen's car. Jordan added at this point that Harris was known to him by the nickname "Pete."

Jordan testified that once the group assembled at Akin's Mobile Homes, Killen said that they would need six or seven men. Killen sent Jordan to pick up Roberts and to buy rubber gloves. Killen told Jordan to find gloves at Warner's grocery store. [14] Jordan testified that Harris was present at Akin's Mobile Homes, but he did not relate what Harris did, said or might have witnessed while there. Jordan testified that Killen said "we" had to hurry to get the three civil rights workers who were "locked up" and "pick them up" at "the outskirts of town" [Philadelphia] and "tear their butts up." Jordan testified that, when the group left Meridian for Philadelphia, Harris did not join them. [15]

Later in his testimony, Jordan told of an earlier important conversation between Harris and state Klan leader Bowers. Jordan testified that in May 1964, he went with Harris to meet with Bowers at a restaurant outside of Laurel, Mississippi (Bowers' hometown). At that meeting, Bowers said to Jordan and Harris that Schwerner "was a thorn in the side of everyone living, especially the white people and that he should be taken care of." Jordan testified that a third man, "Akin's son," was present at the Laurel meeting." [16] Jordan also told the jury that he

---

[13] Although Townsend was not a defendant in the 1967 *Price* trial, defense attorneys cross-examined Jordan about Townsend by name in an effort to suggest to the jury that Jordan had mistaken Sharpe for Townsend.

[14] Oliver Richard Warner (deceased), another Meridian Klansman, was charged in preliminary charging documents, but was not charged in the final Indictment and was not a defendant at trial.

[15] In an FBI interview, but not at trial, Jordan explained that Harris told the group that because of his status as an "Investigator" for the Klan, he was not allowed to go on jobs of any kind.

[16] Bernard Akin's son, Earl, worked with him at Akin's Mobile Homes. Earl Akin was charged in 1964 in a federal criminal complaint for suborning perjury related to this case. That charge

- 17 -

and Harris met again with Bowers about a month after the murders. At that subsequent meeting, Bowers told Jordan and Harris that "the best thing to do was not to talk about it, that everything was well done, it was a job to be proud of, if there were any instruments involved they were to be gotten rid of."

Jordan's testimony was most explicit about what occurred after leaving Meridian on the evening of June 21, 1964. He testified that Killen left first, along with defendants Roberts and Sharpe, because "he had to get on back there fast as he could and to make the arrangements." Thereafter, Jordan traveled to Philadelphia, with Meridian Klansmen Arledge, Snowden, H.D. Barnette and his brother Travis. They met Killen in Philadelphia where Killen showed them the jail and instructed them where to wait until the civil rights workers were released. At this time, Jordan testified that another Barnette brother, known to him as "Hop" [former Neshoba County Sherriff Ethal "Hop" Glenn Barnette (Hop)], met them, told them someone else would come to instruct them, and left.[17]

Jordan testified that Killen was taken to a Philadelphia funeral home to establish an alibi. Thereafter, a police car approached the Meridian Klan car and a Philadelphia city policeman reported that the three civil rights workers had been released from jail and were driving on Highway 19. Jordan failed at trial to name or identify acquitted defendant Richard Andrew Willis whom he had previously identified to the FBI as the policeman.

Jordan testified that Posey, Roberts, Sharpe, and another Philadelphia man were all in a second car (Posey's Chevrolet). The two cars were joined by defendant Price in his patrol car when those three cars left Philadelphia on Highway 19. According to Jordan, as the cars drove to catch up to the victims, Posey's car broke down. Jordan testified that Roberts and Posey, and then Sharpe, abandoned Posey's car and rejoined the group. Of significance to our later investigation, Jordan testified during cross-examination that the "other young man" from Philadelphia – who not only went to Meridian with Killen and Sharpe, but also was later left behind on the highway to repair Posey's disabled car – was named Townsend.[18]

Jordan testified that when Deputy Price caught up to and stopped the three civil rights workers after they turned off Highway 19, he ordered them out of their station wagon and into

---

was dismissed and Earl Akin was not indicted in 1967 nor prosecuted for any charge related to the murders (see further discussion of Earl Akin later in Section VII.C.2.b).

[17] Jordan further testified that Hop Barnette recruited and led men from the June 16 Klan meeting to go to the Mt. Zion church. An African-American church member corroborated Jordan with testimony that Hop Barnette was one of the Klansmen present during the beating at the church.

[18] In an effort to convince the jury that Jordan had mistaken Sharpe for Townsend, the defense elicited conflicting testimony from Jordan in *Price* about Townsend. Ultimately during cross-examination, however, Jordan somewhat confusingly affirmed that Townsend did go to Meridian and was later left on the highway to repair Posey's car.

- 18 -

his patrol car. Posey then got into the driver's seat of the station wagon and followed Price as they drove back toward Philadelphia.

The cars then turned onto a gravel road (Rock Cut Road) off Highway 19. Jordan testified that he got out of the car to be a lookout before it drove up the gravel road. According to Jordan, he heard the sound of car doors slamming, loud talking, and then gunshots. Jordan then testified he walked up the road toward the noise and saw the victims lying beside the gravel road. Jordan testified that the bodies were loaded into the victims' station wagon and Posey then stated, "Just follow me; I know where we're going." Jordan testified that Price, Posey, Roberts, Arledge, Snowden, H.D. and Travis Barnette, and Sharpe were all present at the shooting.

Jordan testified that, following Posey, the cars then drove to a dam site, where they "opened the back of the station wagon, took the boys out, and took them down in this hollow" where there were two bulldozers. Posey sent Jordan back up the road to listen for the bulldozer operator, who was not there yet. Snowden told Jordan that he had seen a man who must be the operator and then they heard the bulldozer "crank up." Jordan heard the machine working for about twenty minutes. Jordan added that Posey told them that the bulldozer operator would take care of the station wagon, claiming that "Herman" (acquitted defendant Herman Tucker) would take the victims' car to Alabama and burn it.

Jordan testified that he next went to a "warehouse and office building and gas pump." There, Jordan saw a man that he had never seen before, whose photograph he had thereafter viewed. Asked to identify the man, Jordan pointed to "a gentleman sitting next to Mr. Price" in the courtroom. Presumably, Jordan pointed to Burrage, rather than to another defendant. Otherwise, one would expect Burrage's counsel to have informed the jury about a misidentification. However, the record does not reflect to whom Jordan pointed.[19]

Jordan was vigorously cross-examined regarding the accuracy of his account and confronted with his prior inconsistent statements about various issues in addition to a possible confusion of Sharpe for Townsend. He was impeached by a prior inconsistent statement in which Jordan did not indicate that Travis Barnette went to Philadelphia with the other defendants.[20] He was further impeached by a prior inconsistent statement in which he named an officer other than Willis as the Philadelphia policeman who delivered the message that the victims' had been released. After presenting a self-serving characterization of the money paid by the FBI, Jordan admitted a $3,000 one-time payment and weekly payments from $25 to $100 by the FBI. Jordan was inconsistent in his willingness to admit parts of his substantial criminal record that included fraudulent conduct.

---

[19] Throughout the trial, government counsel neglected to indicate on the record which defendant was identified when witnesses made identifications by gesture.

[20] H.D. Barnette's unredacted confession also identified his brother, Travis Barnette, as having been present for the murders, but that information was redacted from H.D. Barnette's confession as it was admitted in trial.

- 19 -

F. H.D. Barnette (deceased)

The Price trial concluded with a trial exhibit – H.D. Barnette's redacted November 20, 1964 confession. As previously discussed, H.D. Barnette's unredacted confession was largely corroborative of Jordan's testimony. However, because H.D. Barnette was a defendant and did not take the stand, in order to comply with the Sixth Amendment right to confrontation, the names of H.D. Barnette's codefendants as well as any language that might identify any of them were redacted from the version of the confession introduced at trial. However, because Jordan testified for the government at trial, references to him were not redacted – a fact that focused attention on the glaring difference between Jordan's account of his own conduct (lookout) versus H.D. Barnette's recounting of it (shooter).

Because of redactions, the trial exhibit version of H.D. Barnette's confession was incomplete and confusing (for the reader's aid the redacted names and information are included inside brackets):

> [Travis Barnette] called [Arledge] at his house and said "the Klan had a job" to do and [Arledge] asked H.D. Barnette to go. They went to Meridian [specifically Akin's Mobile Homes] and were met there by Jordan and [Killen, Bernard Akin and Roberts].

> [Killen] told H.D. Barnette and the others that the three civil rights workers would be released from jail; they would catch them and give them a whipping. H.D. Barnette drove in his car with Jordan and [Arledge and Snowden] to Philadelphia. When they arrived in Philadelphia, [Killen] said that there was a "place to bury them," and "a man to run the dozer to cover them up." According to H.D. Barnette that was the first time that he understood the civil rights workers would be killed.

The description of the car chase, the abduction, the journey to Rock Cut Road, and the events after the shooting of Schwerner, Chaney and Goodman in H.D. Barnette's confession, while generally consistent with Jordan's testimony, are considerably less persuasive after redaction. Of particular note, the description of the events surrounding the break-down of Posey's Chevrolet is completely redacted from the trial exhibit, thus there is no reference to "someone from Philadelphia" (Townsend) left behind.

As to the shooting itself, H.D. Barnette's redacted confession recounted that:

> [Roberts] pulled Schwerner from the car, spun him around, and asked, "Are you that nigger lover?" Schwerner replied, "Sir, I know just how you feel." With his left hand on Schwerner's shoulder, [Roberts] raised a pistol in his right hand and shot Michael Schwerner. He then turned toward the patrol car and pulled out Andrew Goodman, and shot Andrew Goodman.

> Jordan said, "Save one for me." Jordan got Chaney out of the car. As Chaney backed up toward the ditch on the side of the road, Jordan was standing in the

- 20 -

middle of the road facing Chaney. Jordan shot James Chaney, and then said, "You didn't leave anything but a nigger, but at least I killed me a nigger."

Also redacted from the confession was H.D. Barnette's affirmation that the dam was "on Burrage's property." Additionally, the redactions excised the activity at the dam site, including that H.D. Barnette saw Burrage and two other men in a car near the dam. Similarly, because of the redactions, Burrage is not identified as the person who provided the gas to burn the victims' car. Thus, H.D. Barnette's redacted confession made no reference to Burrage, his conduct, or the killers' presence at his business.

H. D. Barnette's unredacted confession also related that when the killers returned to Philadelphia after the murders, Neshoba County Sheriff Rainey warned them that anyone who talked would be killed. That information, too, was redacted.

G. Defense Witnesses

As previously indicated, the defendants' witnesses far outnumbered the government witnesses – by approximately four to one. They provided alibi and character testimony for all the defendants. Particularly germane to the recent "Emmett Till Act" investigation, defendants Harris and Burrage presented the following witnesses in their defense.

Burrage called eleven witnesses in total. The combined testimony of the first eight witnesses explained that defendant Burrage hosted relatives and friends at his home during the afternoon on June 21. According to the witnesses, Burrage then attended church services in the early evening. At about 8:30 p.m., Burrage's witnesses testified that he traveled to the home of his sister-in-law, Ruby Davis, in downtown Philadelphia to pick her up and bring her back to his home. Mrs. Davis and Burrage's wife testified that Burrage did not thereafter leave the Burrage home that evening and that, in fact, Burrage was at home on the telephone speaking with Ruby Davis' husband at about 1:00 a.m.[21] The remaining three witnesses called by Burrage testified that he enjoyed a good reputation in the community.

Harris called four witnesses, including his brother, Clarence Harris. Harris's brother testified that Harris came to his home on the afternoon of June 21, and worked with him on a car until about 8:30 or 9:00 p.m. Harris's other three witnesses testified that he enjoyed a good reputation in the community.

H. *Price* Trial Conclusion

Jury deliberations concluded on October 20, 1967, with the seven guilty verdicts previously mentioned. The District Court imposed the legal maximum ten-year prison sentence on two defendants – Roberts, one of the shooters, and Bowers, the state Klan leader who

---

[21] This part of Burrage's alibi established that Burrage was awake in his home just across a country road from his business buildings at 1 a.m. According to both Jordan's testimony and H.D. Barnette's unredacted confession, that is approximately the same time when Burrage was at his business buildings assisting the killers.

authorized the killings. The other convicted defendants were sentenced to shorter terms of incarceration – Price and Posey were sentenced to six years; and Arledge, H.D. Barnette and Snowden were sentenced to three years. Jordan, who testified for the government and was, according to H.D. Barnette's confession the other shooter, pled guilty and was sentenced to a four-year prison term. The defendants, who are all now deceased, began to serve their sentences in 1970 when their appeals were exhausted.[22]

V.   2000 Price/Posey Proffers and State Murder Investigation

This matter was revived in 2000, initially because of new information obtained from Cecil Price before his death. After completing his term of federal incarceration, Price returned to the Philadelphia area and worked at various different jobs, including employment with Burrage's Trucking Company. In the 1990s, he began working as an independent third party Commercial Drivers License (CDL) Examiner, conducting road driving tests for persons attempting to obtain their CDL. Price was caught selling passing test results for personal profit without actually performing the road test.

Because Price's fraudulent scheme involved the filing of false federal government forms with the Mississippi Department of Public Safety (CDLs come under the jurisdiction of the United States Department of Transportation), he was charged with violating Title 18 United States Code § 1001, false statements. After he pled guilty on December 6, 1999, he was sentenced to three years of probation in February 2000 in return for his agreement to cooperate with the Mississippi Attorney General's Office by providing information about the 1964 murders of Schwerner, Chaney, and Goodman.

In the summer of 2000, Price proffered information during interviews with the Mississippi Attorney General's investigators and attorneys. Price said he advised Killen of the arrest through Posey. Later, Killen called Price after dark and told him to come to Jolly's car lot in downtown Philadelphia. There, Price heard Killen tell a group of Meridian Klansmen that Price would release the victims, who would be stopped by highway patrol officers on their way back to Meridian and turned over to the Meridian Klansmen.

Price admitted in the proffer that he later agreed to stop the victims after releasing them from jail and did so. He insisted that he thought they would only be beaten. Price confirmed that a car broke down during the chase and speculated that it was Posey's car. He identified Roberts, Jordan, Posey, Arledge, Snowden, and H.D. Barnette as present at the murder scene. He corroborated H.D. Barnette's contention that the shooters were Roberts and Jordan, adding that most of the individuals present had guns.

Price stated that Killen gave the order to release the "boys" from custody, organized the group, set up the meeting at the car lot, and then attended a wake for his uncle at a funeral home to create an alibi. Price said he later learned from Killen that Killen knew the victims were buried in a dam at a pond.

---

[22] There were no sentencing guidelines in the 1960s and federal judges had wide sentencing discretion.

In May 2001, Price died after falling from a piece of heavy equipment while working in Neshoba County. Rumors that Price's death was not accidental have never been confirmed.

In the spring and summer of 2000, State authorities approached all the other surviving *Price* defendants and many witnesses. Most of them – Harris, Arledge, Snowden, Sharpe, and Townsend – gave general denials when interviewed, claiming to have no information about the murders. Burrage complained of chest pains and went to the hospital. Bowers claimed the only thing he knew about the murders was what he read in the newspapers.

Posey also proffered information to the Mississippi Attorney General. At the same time, Posey insisted that his memory was faulty regarding a number of key facts. He confirmed that Price sought out Killen through Posey so that Killen could get a group together to beat the victims. He claimed that someone whom he could not remember contacted him later on June 21 and told him to go to Jolly's car lot. Another person whom he claimed to be unable to remember told the waiting group that the victims had been released.

Posey stated that he drove with Sharpe in his car south on Highway 19 following the victims. After his car broke down, he got into the victim's station wagon which had already been stopped. Posey said the station wagon was being driven by a Meridian Klansman, whom he claimed he did not know. According to Posey, the victims were shot while he was still inside their station wagon. He identified Price, Jordan, Roberts, H.D. Barnette and Sharpe as present at the shooting scene. After the shooting, he heard Jordan say "killed me a nigger."

After the bodies were loaded back in the station wagon, Posey related that he drove with Sharpe and Jordan. He stated that Jordan said that the group was going to Burrage's pond where they had a bulldozer. He stated that Jordan was at the dam and that he and Sharpe then drove to Burrage's nearby trucking company, where they reconnected with Jordan.

Posey's memory was self-serving as to his own conduct. With the exception of Sharpe and Jordan, he related little of substance about the conduct of, or, in some cases, even the names of, anyone then still alive. Specifically, he did not acknowledge that Townsend was in his (Posey's) disabled car or that Burrage was at the dam site and at Burrage's trucking company. Additionally, Posey maintained that he could not remember whether he saw Killen and Price at Jolly's Car Lot.

Most incredible was Posey's contention that Jordan, not he (Posey), was the one who led the group to Burrage's dam. Jordan, who was from Meridian, was far less familiar with the Philadelphia area than Posey. Posey had a business relationship with Burrage at the time in the small rural town of Philadelphia where they were both life-long residents. Also, Posey had ample motive to falsely implicate Jordan, who had betrayed the Klan and testified in the federal trial against Posey and his codefendants.

Over the next few years, the Mississippi Attorney General and District Attorneys who had jurisdiction over the murders, with assistance from the FBI, were able to supplement previously known evidence with sufficient new evidence (discussed below) to support a state murder indictment. In January 2005, a Mississippi grand jury indicted Killen with three counts

- 23 -

of murder. Despite Posey's self-serving, but still incriminating, proffer the grand jury did not also indict Posey, who died in 2009. Nor were any of the other potential then-surviving subjects indicted. Arledge and Snowden died in 2008, after Killen was convicted.

VI. *Mississippi v. Killen* Evidence Summary

State prosecutors in Mississippi tried Edgar Ray Killen for the murders of Michael Schwerner, James Chaney, and Andrew Goodman, beginning on June 13, 2005, in Neshoba County. The trial lasted for eight days, and on June 21, 2005 (41 years to the day of the murders), a Neshoba County jury convicted Killen, a lifelong resident of Neshoba County, on three counts of manslaughter.

The case focused on the role of Edgar Ray Killen in planning and facilitating the killings and secret burial of the bodies. The most incriminating evidence against Killen came in the form of recorded testimony from the *Price* trial. Carlton Wallace Miller, Delmar Dennis, and James Jordan, had all died by 2005, but prosecutors introduced their testimony from the *Price* trial as it related to Killen's involvement in the murders.

The state also called two surviving FBI Special Agents. One testified that he was one of the agents who recovered the burned station wagon; he identified photos of the car and the recovery scene. Another testified that he was one of the agents present when the bodies were recovered in the earthen dam; he identified the photos of the victims' bodies at the burial scene.

Joseph Michael Hatcher, who testified in the *Price* trial, testified again, and was more valuable to the government in the *Killen* trial. Hatcher's testimony was consistent with his testimony four decades earlier, but he provided greater detail regarding Killen's incriminating statements regarding the killing and burial of the victims. Hatcher additionally testified that Killen gave him a handgun the day after the murders and asked him to return the gun to the man who had given the gun to Killen. Hatcher added further that Killen boasted that the FBI would not be able to trace any telephone calls to him because he travelled to Meridian to gather Klan volunteers rather than making telephone calls.

The state also called Mike Winstead, who testified that as a ten-year-old boy he overheard his grandfather speaking with Killen. Specifically, he heard his grandfather ask Killen whether he had "anything to do with those boys being killed." According to Winstead, Killen replied, "Yes," and that he was "proud of it."

Family members of each of the victims also testified to their loss. Schwerner's widow testified that COFO's civil rights organizing efforts were not welcomed by many in the community, and that she and Schwerner had previously been threatened.

Killen offered five witnesses in his defense. His brother and sister each testified that Killen was present at a family event until 4:00 p.m. or 5:00 p.m. on June 21, 1964. Killen's brother, Kenneth Killen, further testified that he saw Killen later that evening between 7:00 p.m. or 8:00 p.m. at a funeral home. The defense called David Winstead to testify, and he offered that he believed his brother, Mike Winstead, was lying about hearing the conversation between

- 24 -

Killen and his grandfather. Killen's remaining two witnesses each testified that Killen enjoyed a good reputation in the community.

The jury found Killen guilty on three counts of manslaughter. Thereafter, the court sentenced Killen to twenty years for each count, to be served consecutively for a total of sixty years. Killen remains incarcerated in the Mississippi prison system. The state trial against Killen produced no new evidence against Willis, Burrage, Harris, or Townsend.

VII. Federal "Emmett Till Act" Investigation Summary: 2010 through 2016

A. Emmett Till Act Investigation Overview

Our goal with the federal Emmett Till Act investigation was ultimately to assist the Mississippi Attorney General by seeking additional admissible evidence against persons potentially prosecutable under the state murder statute. Beginning in 2010, we initiated a careful review of the massive federal MIBURN file, particularly its confidential source files. Later, we also reviewed the state's investigative files from the late 1990s/early 2000s, which led to Killen's conviction in 2005. We searched the files with a focus on identifying the universe of known witnesses, as well as other potential witnesses who had not previously been interviewed, or not fully or robustly interviewed. Additionally, we searched for witnesses who might help resolve the credibility of witnesses who might be concealing relevant facts. We further examined potential leads and rumors proffered by non-governmental sources. The FBI thereafter expended considerable effort determining which potential subjects and witnesses were alive and which were deceased. Next, surviving persons had to be physically located.

The FBI determined that only five of the individuals originally identified as participants in the murder conspiracy remained alive in 2010 – Willis (who died in July 2011), Burrage (who died in March 2013), Killen, Harris, and Townsend. As previously indicated, Killen was successfully prosecuted by the state in 2005 for his role in the murders. Regarding the remaining four subjects, we suspected the following: Willis was alleged to have notified the Klan killers that the victims were being released from jail; Burrage owned the land on which the victims were buried and allegedly assisted with their burial and the disposal of the car; Harris allegedly received prior authorization to kill Schwerner and helped in the early evening before the murders to recruit the killers from Meridian; and Townsend was identified as one of the Philadelphia men who came with Killen to Meridian and then later, before the victims were abducted, stayed with Posey's disabled car.

The FBI, often along with Department attorneys, interviewed or attempted to interview every living, competent witness and potential defendant who could be located. Additionally, witnesses who might have information relevant to the credibility of other witnesses were also interviewed. Witnesses who purportedly had competency deficiencies were personally contacted to corroborate the reported mental condition. Some witnesses were re-interviewed several times and vigorously confronted with information that suggested they were not completely forthright.   In certain cases, we obtained additional relevant information from reluctant witnesses. We followed every lead to its logical conclusion and queried every potential witness until we were satisfied that we had attained the full extent of their knowledge and willingness to cooperate.

Additionally, beginning in 2011, the FBI commenced several covert operations aimed at discovery of information relevant to the murders. These covert operations targeted the individuals believed to have knowledge of the murders and were conducted at various times during the course of the investigation under the supervision of Department attorneys and, in one case, pursuant to a sealed federal district court order. While the covert operations revealed some relevant information, they produced neither inculpatory admissible evidence against any subject, nor any reliable, credible exculpatory evidence. We have shared the substance of that information with the Mississippi Attorney General.

As set forth in detail below, we questioned the veracity of the statements that certain witnesses made to the FBI in 2010-11, within the statute of limitations. Accordingly, we utilized a federal grand jury to investigate violations of 18 U.S.C. § 1001. For § 1001 subjects, the knowledge that they were subjects of a federal grand jury investigation could strengthen their concern that federal prosecution was a reality and might thereby motivate truthfulness. Grand jury also permits testimony under oath from subject witnesses and from witnesses with information that might bear on the truthfulness of statements by the § 1001 subjects. Additionally, truthful information relevant to material false statements could have collateral value to the murder investigation. Finally, if false material statements, which were supported by sufficient evidence to bring prosecution, were made in this important federal investigation, federal prosecution would be warranted.

B. **Legal Authority, Issues, and Limitations**

1. **Murder**

As mentioned previously, because the federal statute of limitations on the then existing and applicable federal criminal civil rights statutes was five years, any federal prosecution for these offenses is time-barred.[23] Nonetheless, the United States properly reopened the investigation into the murders pursuant to the Emmett Till Act, which specifically authorizes the federal investigation of unresolved criminal civil rights violations that occurred not later than December 31, 1969 and resulted in death. The Attorney General, through the Assistant Attorney General for Civil Rights, and the Director of the FBI are obligated to "expeditiously investigate unsolved civil rights murders . . . [and] provide all the resources necessary to ensure timely and thorough investigations in the cases involved." The Act further encourages the federal government to coordinate with state and local law enforcement, and to refer cases to state and local prosecutors for evaluation of prosecution under state laws. Thus, our investigation was

---

[23] A federal prosecution of Harris, who was acquitted in the *Price* trial, is also barred by the Double Jeopardy Clause of the Fifth Amendment. U.S. Const., Amend. V. "To permit a second trial after an acquittal, however mistaken the acquittal may have been, would present an unacceptably high risk that the Government with its vast superior resources, might wear down the defendant so that 'even though innocent, he may be found guilty.'" *United States v. Scott*, 437 U.S. 82, 91 (1978) (quoting *Green v. United States*, 355 U.S. 184, 188 (1957)).

- 26 -

primarily aimed at seeking evidence that might support a state murder charge. As noted above, we have shared all relevant information with the Mississippi Attorney General for his review and assessment.

2. False Statements

We also explored whether several material witnesses in our investigation may have committed more recent federal crimes – within the statute of limitations – for willfully providing material false information to the FBI in violation of 18 U.S.C. § 1001.

18 U.S.C. § 1001 makes it a crime when a person "in any matter within the jurisdiction of the executive, legislative or judicial branch of the Government of the United States, knowingly and willfully makes any material false, fictitious, or fraudulent statement or representation." *Id.* at § 1001(a)(2). The term "false, fictitious, or fraudulent" means that the statement "must have a natural tendency to influence, or be capable of affecting or influencing a government function." *United States v. Shah*, 44 F.3d 285, 288 n.4 (5ᵗʰ Cir. 1995) (quoting *United States v. Markham*, 537 F.2d 187, 196 (5ᵗʰ Cir. 1976)). The government agency need not have actually been misled, *id.*, but "the concealment 'must simply have the capacity to impair or pervert the functioning of a government agency.'" *United States v. Swaim*, 757 F.2d 1530, 1534 (5ᵗʰ Cir. 1985) (quoting *United States v. Lichenstein*, 610 F.2d 512, 514 n. 5 (5ᵗʰ Cir. 1980)).

The elements necessary to establish a violation of § 1001 applicable to these facts are:

(1) whoever, in any matter within the jurisdiction of the executive, legislative, or judicial branch of the Government of the United States;

(2) knowingly and willfully;

(3) makes any materially false, fictitious, or fraudulent statement or representation.

Interviews conducted by the FBI in an Emmett Till Act investigation are within the jurisdiction of the executive branch because Congress has charged the FBI with conducting such investigations. To establish beyond a reasonable doubt that a material statement is false, the government must prove that the contradictory facts are true. Obviously, an investigation of whether witnesses in this case made material false statements overlapped the effort to seek material facts probative of the murders. Thus, many of the same difficulties facing our Emmett Till Act murder investigation confronted the investigation of § 1001 violations. Unlike the murders, barred from federal prosecution by the statute of limitations, recent material false statements are prosecutable federal offenses that a federal grand jury could properly investigate. In the end, as discussed below in the summaries for the relevant witnesses, we have concluded that we lack sufficient admissible evidence to charge any witness with violating 18 U.S.C. § 1001.

- 27 -

C.   Emmett Till Act Investigation Witnesses

We interviewed and, in some cases, re-interviewed surviving witnesses with the ultimate goal of obtaining additional information that might build a prosecutable state murder case against a surviving subject. Some witnesses had not been interviewed in prior investigations. Most witnesses had previously been interviewed and were re-interviewed in an effort to ensure that they revealed all relevant information, especially information that we suspected might have been withheld in the past. Some witnesses were interviewed more than once or under proffer agreements or given polygraph examinations. All reasonable efforts were taken to induce complete candor from witnesses to determine whether further state prosecution was warranted, as well as to determine whether there were prosecutable federal § 1001 violations.

1.   Individuals with Indirect Knowledge Regarding the Murders

a. Meridian Source

The Emmett Till Act investigation initially produced some fresh evidence in December 2010, when the FBI case agent and a Department attorney interviewed a newly discovered source, who lived in Meridian in 1964 and is now over 70-years-old and living outside of Mississippi. The Meridian Source had a close relationship with Harris during the summer of 1964. The Meridian Source had never been previously interviewed and we believed that Harris might have revealed relevant information to the source. In fact, we learned that Harris had boasted to the Meridian Source that he had planned the murders.

The witness would not acknowledge a relationship with Harris until promised that the source's identity would not be publicly revealed, unless and until the source was needed as a witness in a criminal trial. Even then, the source initially denied knowledge of anything related to the murders. In March 2011, after persistent questioning, the Meridian Source admitted concealing information from the FBI. The Meridian Source signed a written statement that declared that Harris admitted (1) "he hated Blacks and liked to hurt them," (2) "those three civil rights workers were killed by the Klan," and (3) "they got what they deserved." Most significantly, the Meridian Source reported that "Pete told me that he was involved in the planning of the killings of the civil rights workers but that he was not there when it happened."

This information is consistent with prior information incriminating Harris. Significantly, Harris's admission to the source that he was "involved in the planning of the killings . . . but that he was not there when it happened" corroborates Jordan's testimony in the 1967 *Price* trial, which would also be admissible against Harris. Specific to Harris, Jordan testified that Harris made telephone calls from The Longhorn Restaurant to recruit Meridian Klansmen to go to Philadelphia with Killen to abduct and assault the civil rights workers who were jailed there. Jordan added that Harris did not go with the killers from Meridian to Philadelphia. These facts about Harris are also confirmed by H.D. Barnette's unredacted confession. Finally, Jordan further testified that Harris had received instructions weeks before June 21, 1964, from Sam Bowers, the state Klan leader, to "eliminate" Schwerner.

- 28 -

242

The Meridian Source appears credible, given the nature of the relationship with Harris, the initial reluctance to reveal that relationship, the circumstances under which the source ultimately revealed the incriminating information, and Jordan's corroborating testimony under oath in 1967. We are unaware of background information that would raise questions about the witness's credibility. The Meridian Source has nothing to gain by fabricating this information.

However, the Meridian Source is extremely reluctant to testify as a witness in a public trial. Already, since signing the written statement, the source has begun to equivocate, claiming memory problems because of age. While the witness' demeanor belies this suggestion, it would not be difficult for an over-seventy-year-old reluctant witness to convincingly assert a failed memory. It is our best assessment that the Meridian Source could – and probably would – likely claim failed memory if subpoenaed to trial.

b. *Klansman Source*

In the fall of 2012, we re-connected with an 80-plus-year-old Klansman, an FBI confidential source since 1964. The Klansman Source has demonstrated excellent mental acuity, good physical health, has been consistent, and, appears to be candid. However, the FBI promised that the source's identity would be protected in order to gain his cooperation in the 1960s. Based upon their long-standing relationship and prior assurances necessary to obtain information and to protect the witness, the Klansman Source has a reasonable expectation of anonymity unless the source consents to public exposure.

In September 2012, the Klansman Source related information that was consistent with his 1960s reports to the FBI. Most significantly, he advised that in 1964: (1) Harris was one of 30 Klansmen present at a Klan meeting when Miller announced several weeks before the murders that Bowers had authorized the elimination of Schwerner; (2) a still living Meridian Klansman attended and also led local Klan meetings before the murders; and (3) Harris and the Meridian Klansman were friends and may have attended Klan meetings together. Alone, the evidence that this witness has to offer is somewhat limited. The source simply places Harris at meetings where "elimination" of Schwerner was addressed by someone but not by Harris. The source does not provide information regarding Harris' conduct on the night of the murders. Further, he provided no information regarding the Philadelphia subjects, with whom he was not personally acquainted.

On the other hand, the Klansman Source could provide live testimony to unequivocally corroborate the former testimony from *Price* witnesses Jordan, Miller, and Dennis. Specifically, the source would confirm that Harris attended Klan meetings where the elimination of Schwerner was discussed. The source would further confirm that Harris was present at a Klan meeting from which Klansmen left to assault African-American churchgoers and civil rights workers. At the same time, the Klansman Source would only establish that others, not Harris, spoke about the "elimination" of Schwerner.

As discussed later, the Klansman Source's primary value to the investigation was the information about the Meridian Klansman. The source had observed the Meridian Klansman leading Klan meetings at his own business establishment before the murders and knew him to be friends with Harris (see discussion of Meridian Klansman in Section VII.C.1.d.).

The source appears authentic and reliable. However, the Klansman Source has never been publicly identified and the FBI wishes to fulfill its 1960 promise to protect his identity, which was necessary to obtain useful information and to protect the source from harm. Accordingly, the source expects not to be subpoenaed to testify unless he agrees to do so. We have a good rapport with the witness, who appeared to enjoy talking about his past experiences, and he may choose to testify. However, our best assessment is that the Klansman Source will likely continue to elect anonymity. Moreover, the probative value of the admissible evidence that the Klansman Source provides is insufficient to override the legitimate interest in honoring a long-standing commitment to a trusted source.

c. *Joseph Michael Hatcher*

Joseph Michael Hatcher, a 1960s Meridian police officer and Klansman, was an important, but somewhat reluctant, witness in the *Killen* trial, and he had previously testified in the *Price* trial. His testimony covered what he learned from Killen after the murders. According to information from a variety of sources, Hatcher was believed to be a "trusted" Klansman in the summer of 1964. Consequently, we anticipated that Harris and the Meridian Klansman might have confided in Hatcher as Killen had. As a police officer/Klansman, he served as the doorman for the meetings. His regular hangout was The Longhorn Restaurant. As an indication of Hatcher's trusted Klan status, the day after the murders, Killen gave Hatcher a gun, told him where the bodies were buried, and stated that the FBI would not trace any phone calls to him because he went to Meridian personally to gather the Klan group there. Hatcher attended Klan meetings with Harris and the Meridian Klansman.

Hatcher is in his 70s and still works for the city of Meridian, although no longer in law enforcement. When approached by the FBI in 2010 and 2011, Hatcher insisted that he had no relevant information to offer.

Later, in September 2012, Hatcher agreed to speak with the FBI and Department attorneys. He claimed to have difficulties remembering things that he had expressly told the FBI in the 1960s, even after he reviewed records of his prior statements. After further interview, Hatcher subsequently signed a statement to the FBI admitting that he had seen Harris and the Meridian Klansman attending the same Klan meetings. Soon after signing the statement, Hatcher asserted that his memory was again uncertain about both Harris and the Meridian Klansman and their Klan activity in the 1960s, going so far as to claim he is no longer sure if he knew Harris.

Hatcher has exhibited a suspiciously selective memory, providing no firm information about any person who could still be prosecuted. Hatcher was in a position to learn inculpatory information about Harris and he should know that the Meridian Klansman was an active participant in the Klan in the summer of 1964. He does not otherwise behave like a person suffering from a deficient memory. Nonetheless, Hatcher has nothing new to offer as a witness for the government. Further, we have no admissible evidence to prove that Harris or anyone else actually confided in Hatcher, nor do we have any admissible evidence to disprove Hatcher's claimed memory failures regarding participants in Klan meetings that took place 50 years ago. Thus, it cannot be established that Hatcher violated 18 U.S.C. § 1001.

d. The Meridian Klansman

The investigation revealed that in the 1960s the Meridian Klansman was Harris's friend, hosted Klan meetings, led some of those meetings, and was present when the killing of Schwerner was discussed. When interviewed by the FBI shortly after the murders, the Meridian Klansman denied being in the Klan or knowing anything about the murders. However, the Meridian Klansman was observed by FBI agents leaving a meeting at The Lamar Hotel in Meridian with the co-conspirators, including Harris and Bowers, after the defendants were indicted. He was persistently hostile toward FBI agents. For these reasons, and other reasons provided by confidential sources, we explored whether the Meridian Klansman had heard incriminating information, including possibly admissions from Harris.

On January 14, 2012, the FBI interviewed the Meridian Klansman. His demeanor was antagonistic. He maintained that (1) he never joined the Klan, (2) if Klan meetings were held at his place of business, he did not know about them and an employee who had a key must have hosted the Klan, (3) Harris only "got tied up with the wrong group," and (4) he knew nothing regarding the murders.

Because other evidence contradicted these statements, in February 2013 the Department advised the Meridian Klansman by letter that he was a subject of a federal § 1001 investigation. The Meridian Klansman retained counsel and on February 20, 2013, he and his attorney met with the FBI case agent and Department attorneys. During a lengthy conversation, the Meridian Klansman conceded that he had permitted the Klan to hold meetings at his business. He claimed that he attended some meetings along with Harris and other *Price* defendants, but insisted that he was not an official member of the Klan. The Meridian Klansman further maintained that he never knew of plans to commit the murders and would have stopped them if he had known. He advised that only Jordan told him about the murders afterwards. Most significantly, the Meridian Klansman persisted in his contention that Harris never admitted involvement in the murders.

It appeared that the Meridian Klansman had relevant information but was reluctant to be a witness against an old friend and the Klan, so he was granted use immunity from criminal prosecution for information provided. Thereafter, the Meridian Klansman engaged in proffer sessions with counsel present, but he continued to vacillate about what he actually knew. Accordingly, the Meridian Klansman was offered transactional (complete) immunity from § 1001 prosecution, if he provided truthful information pursuant to a written agreement, which included a provision that federal and state prosecutors would not use anything the Meridian Klansman said during the subsequent interview against him in a criminal prosecution.

On March 6, 2013, the Meridian Klansman was again interviewed under the terms of the written agreement and affirmed that he had been deliberately withholding information. He agreed to dictate a written statement relating that which he had been withholding. Thereafter, he signed that written statement, even making a change in it that he initialed.

- 31 -

In the March 6, 2013 signed written statement, the Meridian Klansman divulged that Harris had admitted to him his role in the murders. The statement revealed that Harris specifically told the Meridian Klansman (1) "he [Harris] had been OKed to eliminate Schwerner," before the murders, and Harris said (2) "the FBI was after him [Harris] for organizing the men who went up to Neshoba to kill the boys" after the murders. This information was consistent with Jordan's testimony and H.D. Barnette's confession, as well as with the admission that the Meridian Source, who had a close relationship with Harris, revealed a year earlier.

Immediately thereafter, the Meridian Klansman began to equivocate about the truthfulness of the written statement. At the direction of the Department attorney, the FBI agents asked to continue the interview to seek further detail to expand upon the written statement. Counsel objected to continuing at that time, but agreed to schedule a follow-up interview which would include the Mississippi Attorney General because the information in the written statement presented critical admissions by Harris about his participation in the murders. Thereafter, the parties agreed that the Meridian Klansman would continue to proffer under a grant of transactional (complete) federal and state immunity in return for continued truthful information and testimony. On the morning of the date of the next planned proffer, the Meridian Klansman was hospitalized, complaining of heart symptoms.

After further delays, the Meridian Klansman and his counsel met with the Department attorney, the Mississippi Attorney General, and the FBI on April 2, 2013. Through counsel, the Meriden Klansman advised that his written signed statement was not truthful and that he had signed it merely to be able to terminate the interview. At one point in this meeting, the Meridian Klansman spoke directly to Mississippi Attorney General Jim Hood and firmly avowed that the written statement was a lie and he would not so lie under oath.

It is our best judgment, based upon all the surrounding circumstances and other available information, that the Meridian Klansman did – as he related in the signed written statement – hear Harris admit his involvement in the planning of the 1964 murders. However, it is abundantly clear that the Meridian Klansman will continue to refute the truth of that written statement.

Although two inherently inconsistent statements to federal authorities can suffice as evidence of a § 1001 violation, they do not under the circumstance of this case. The Meridian Klansman's written statement pursuant to the government's agreement does not allow for the government to use anything said during the interview against the witness in a criminal prosecution. Thus, the resulting written statement is not admissible. Accordingly, we are left with only the Meridian Klansman's subsequent statements that Harris made no admissions, and no admissible way to refute that claim.

We also considered whether the Meridian Klansman should be charged with making a false statement for his January 14, 2012 denial that he was a "member" of the Klan. Although witness testimony and the witness's own admissible statements raise questions regarding that denial, the evidence is not sufficient to establish a violation of § 1001. First, the fact that other

- 32 -

witnesses and the Meridian Klansman himself ultimately agreed that he "attended Klan meetings" does not prove that his statement that he was "not a Klan member" is false. He could have attended Klan meetings without being a member, as he claimed, in which case the statement would be true. Second, whether the Meridian Klansman was a "Klan member" as opposed to a person who attended Klan meetings is not necessarily material to an investigation seeking information relevant to the involvement of other persons in the 1964 murders. Third, the Meridian Klansman is over 70 years old and has confirmed health problems. We could not prove beyond a reasonable doubt that his statements regarding fifty-year-old events were intentionally false, as opposed to the product of failed or imperfect recollection. Thus, we have concluded that there is insufficient evidence to support a federal prosecution of the Meridian Klansman under § 1001.

2. Witnesses with Direct Knowledge of Murders/Murder Plan

a. Jimmy Lee Townsend

At the outset of the Emmett Till Act investigation, it appeared from all available information that Jimmy Lee Townsend had knowledge about the murders; specifically, he likely observed Harris's conduct in Meridian and heard admissions from Burrage. According to both Jordan and H.D. Barnette, a third person from Philadelphia accompanied Killen to Meridian to obtain Harris's help in recruiting Meridian Klansmen and then remained with the coconspirators until Posey's car failed them during the chase of the victims. Jordan's interviews with the FBI unequivocally identified that young man to be Posey's employee Townsend. Based on this information and Townsend's inability to provide an alibi, he was arrested and charged in December 1964 and indicted in the original *Price* indictment. He was dropped from the superseding indictment and never re-charged.[24]

Thereafter, additional information further linked Townsend to the Klan conspirators. Other 1960s FBI sources claimed that Townsend accompanied Posey when he paid Klan money to defendants as the *Price* trial approached. While Townsend persisted in his inconceivable claim that he could not remember what he did the night of the murders, he contradicted himself about the few facts that he did provide federal and later state investigators. Also, when we examined real estate records in 2010, we learned that in the 1970s Townsend purchased land from Burrage, contiguous to Burrage's own property. And, Townsend later became a minister at Burrage's church.

Because, according to the accounts of Jordan and H.D. Barnette (both deceased), Townsend remained with Posey's disabled car, the evidence suggested that Townsend was a teenaged tag-a-long and was not present at the murders. As a result, Harris and Burrage appeared more culpable in the conspiracy, and we hoped to persuade Townsend to divulge his

---

[24] John Doar, former Assistant Attorney General for Civil Rights and one of the prosecutors in the 1967 *Price* trial, advised a current Department attorney that, while he had no specific recollection of why Townsend was not included in the 1967 indictment, he believed that Townsend's role in the events and his status as a juvenile at the time of the murders mitigated against his prosecution.

- 33 -

knowledge regarding the murders in order to develop sufficient evidence against Harris and (when he was alive) Burrage. If Townsend would cooperate with prosecuting authorities and give truthful testimony, his cooperation could fairly warrant immunity from prosecution. Nonetheless, Townsend persisted in his implausible contention that he cannot recall his actions on June 21, 1964. There is no reason to expect that Townsend will ever retract his denials or incriminate anyone.

In 1964, Townsend was a 17-year-old high school student working for the summer at Posey's gas station outside of Philadelphia on Highway 19. When interviewed by the FBI in 1964, he denied knowledge of the murders but articulated no specific account of his whereabouts on June 21. He denied knowing any of the Meridian Klansmen, including Harris. Over the years in different interviews, he has admitted working at Posey's gas station during the day, but consistently denied recalling his activities that night. In 2000, for the first time, he told state investigators that he was absent from work part of the day to visit his father in a local hospital. There was no such visit on the day of June 21. Hospital records establish that his father, Tom Townsend, was not at the hospital on June 21, but rather was admitted into the emergency room of Neshoba County Hospital in the early morning hours of June 22 at 2 a.m., soon after the bodies of the victims had been buried.

Townsend's professed lack of memory about his action on the night of June 21 warrants heavy skepticism for several obvious reasons. First, June 21 was perhaps the most momentous occasion in Townsend's life; the day the country's attention was turned to his small town. Second, Townsend was arrested in December 1964 and charged in the notorious triple homicide along with nineteen others, including his boss and well-known individuals in his town. Third, it was the Father's Day on which Townsend's own father was rushed to the emergency room. Hospital records established that his ailing father was admitted into the Neshoba County Hospital with heart attack symptoms (a medical condition from which he died within a year) within hours after the coconspirators completed the burial of the victims and left the Old Jolly Farm on June 22. And, while Father's Day was not as widely celebrated in 1964 as it is today, it is reasonable to believe that the coincidence of Townsend's father suffering an apparent heart attack on Father's Day would trigger some recollection of the event in his son's mind. The FBI learned in 1964 that Tom Townsend's now deceased doctor reported that Mrs. Townsend (Tom's wife and Jimmy Lee's mother) encouraged the doctor to falsely recall Jimmy Lee being at the hospital.

Townsend continued to maintain a relationship with Burrage and the other Philadelphia Klansmen over the years. In the early 1970s, Townsend bought land that abutted Burrage's own property and has lived there since. Townsend became a minister at the Center Ridge Church, the church attended by Burrage and his family. After the federal charges were initially lodged, 1960s FBI confidential sources reported that Townsend travelled with Posey and others to collect monetary funds for the Klansmen facing trial. One visit was to Bowers allegedly seeking money to ensure the silence of Herman Tucker, Burrage's bulldozer operator who allegedly helped bury the bodies on Burrage's property. Townsend was in an obvious position to hear admissions from either Burrage or Harris or incriminating information about them.

On December 6, 2011, the FBI interviewed Townsend, who again claimed to know nothing about the murders. He advised that he had been home that night and over the

- 34 -

248

intervening years had never heard Burrage or anyone admit involvement in the murders or burial. This time, Townsend agreed to a polygraph examination, but he indicated deceptiveness when he denied hearing that Burrage claimed responsibility for the burial of the bodies on his property.

On September 6, 2012, a Department attorney and FBI agent met with Townsend at his home and spoke with him for two hours. We advised him that we suspected that his December 6 statement to the FBI was not truthful and were seeking to establish sufficient evidence to prosecute him for false statements to the FBI. We further advised that, if he instead provided truthful information, we would forego the prosecution of a federal false statement charge and that the Mississippi Attorney General was also willing to forego prosecution for the 1964 murders. Townsend was provided a prepared written "Proffer Agreement" that, if signed by Townsend, would guarantee him immunity from prosecution. Townsend responded that he was not interested in the proposed agreement because he had been truthful. Rather, he insisted that "some boy" confused him with someone else (echoing the defense used by Sharpe in *Price* that Jordan confused him with Townsend).

In the same interview, Townsend again expressed an inexplicable lack of memory about his activities on the evening of June 21-22. He stated that he "thought" his grandfather drove him home from work, but he could not remember specifically being home or even whether he drove his father, with whom he claimed to have a good relationship, to the emergency room or whether he went to the hospital to see his father after he was admitted. Townsend was thereafter confronted with the implausibility of his lack of memory. Townsend offered no explanation for this improbability.

Interestingly, whenever Townsend was pressed about whether Olen Burrage made admissions, regardless of how the question was phrased, Townsend always peculiarly answered with the same words, "Burrage never said [anything] to me or to anyone else in my presence." Carefully repeated phrasing is often an indication that the assertion is true only when framed as the speaker has framed it. Additionally, although arrested, arraigned and present at numerous court hearings with Harris, who has been associated with this celebrated case for as long as Townsend, Townsend claimed that he did not recognize a 1964 picture of Harris and claimed he did not know Harris.

The failed memory is further suspect because Townsend easily recalled the details of a land transaction with Burrage a few years after the murders – reciting without notes the lawyers' names, the dates, the boundaries of land involved, and other innocuous details. Townsend similarly recalled exact details of other contemporaneous events on occasions other than June 21, 1964. When confronted with this anomaly, Townsend could provide no explanation.

In late 2012, the Department sent Townsend a letter that explained his potential criminal exposure and advised him of his right to legal representation. In January 2013 Townsend retained counsel. Assurances from Attorney General Hood regarding immunity from state prosecution and recurring negotiations over the next couple of months with Townsend's attorney did nothing to change Townsend's account.

In February 2013, through counsel, Townsend reiterated that he remembered nothing differently than he had previous expressed, and that, even if he were prosecuted for false material statements to federal investigators, he would continue to maintain that he has no information relevant to the 1964 murders. As Townsend emphatically told us, "Burrage never said anything to me or to anyone in my presence" and "I am satisfied that there is nothing I did wrong that I need to explain when I pass on." It is our best assessment that Townsend's expressed lack of memory will not change.

We have concluded that, absent additional evidence, Townsend's December 2011 and September 2012 claims that he does not recall his activities on the night of June 21, 1964, while far-fetched, are nonetheless not prosecutable as a violations of § 1001. There is no admissible evidence available to contradict Townsend's account. Jordan is deceased, and his *Price* trial testimony – where Townsend was not a defendant – and his account to the FBI that it was Townsend who accompanied Killen to Meridian and in Posey's car are all hearsay and inadmissible. The doctor who told the FBI that Townsend's mother asked him to provide a false alibi is deceased and his account is also inadmissible hearsay.

We are not aware of any admissible evidence that conclusively establishes where Townsend was on the evening of June 21, 1964, or that he ever heard any relevant information about the murders. The implausibility of one's memory alone, especially the memory of someone over 70 years old regarding events that occurred nearly fifty years ago, is insufficient to sustain a criminal conviction for making knowingly and intentionally material false statement under § 1001. Moreover, Townsend has not provided any information over the last 50 years that incriminates Harris, Burrage, or any other person in the murders.

b.   Earl Akin

As previously noted, Jordan testified that "Akin's son" accompanied Harris and Jordan to Laurel, Mississippi, several weeks before the murders at which time state Klan leader Sam Bowers provided authorization to Harris to eliminate Schwerner. When interviewed by the FBI in 1964, Jordan specifically identified the person who went to Laurel with Harris by his full name – Earl Akin. During our investigation, Earl Akin confirmed Jordan's assertion that he was present with Harris in Laurel and heard the instructions from Bowers to Harris regarding the killing of Schwerner. His account, however, otherwise diverged significantly from Jordan's.

Earl Akin was charged in 1964 by the federal government with misprision of felony, a violation of Title 18 United States Code § 4, based upon his 1964 FBI interviews in which he denied any knowledge of who was involved in the murders. That charge was dismissed and the statute of limitations now obviates any federal prosecution. His father, Bernard Akin, was one of the now-deceased 1967 defendants acquitted in *Price*. In 1964, Earl Akin was working for his father at Akin's Mobile Homes (which also employed *Price* defendants Jordan and Herndon). Akin's Mobile Homes was a Klan hangout where Meridian Klansmen, including Harris, gathered. However, there is no evidence that Earl Akin was a member of the Klan or that he was present on June 21 when Killen organized the group who would later commit the murders.

- 36 -

Earl Akin is now in his mid-70s. He has been incarcerated in Mississippi for recent, serious state convictions for fraudulent activity unrelated to the murders.

The FBI interviewed Earl Akin on several occasions in 2012. Initially, he denied any knowledge of any information related to the 1964 murders, except that which was in the public domain and only implicated dead persons. For example, he acknowledged that he knew that Roberts, who had been convicted and was already deceased, shot the civil rights workers (a fact established at the *Price* trial), but he claimed that although he knew Burrage, he knew nothing regarding Burrage's connection to the murders.

In a subsequent interview, Earl Akin signed a written statement in which he admitted that he had a relationship with Harris; knew that his father and Harris were Klansmen; and went with Harris on the trip to Laurel, Mississippi to meet with Bowers. He said that Bowers "gave Pete Harris the authority to get rid of the civil rights workers, which I knew meant to kill them." Earl Akin stated that only he and Harris flew in a private airplane to Laurel.[25] Significantly, he did not include Jordan as a fellow traveler with Harris to Laurel.

Over the course of several interviews, Earl Akin provided more detail about the Laurel meeting. He advised that his father, Bernard Akin, asked Earl Akin to accompany Harris to meet someone in Laurel and to report back to Bernard Akin. Earl Akin and Harris drove to Laurel together. Akin insisted that Jordan did not accompany them. Once in Laurel, Earl Akin and Harris met with Bowers, and the three spoke in a restaurant. Bowers gave Harris an unequivocal order for the Klan to kill Schwerner. Although Earl Akin's initial written statement uses the words "three civil rights workers," he later clarified that Bowers' order concerned only Schwerner.

Earl Akin maintained that he and Harris had no relevant conversations either during the drive to meet Bowers, or on the drive home. Back at Akin's Mobile Homes, Harris spoke privately to Bernard Akin. Then, Bernard Akin spoke privately with Earl Akin, asking only what the man in Laurel looked like. It seems unlikely that this was the extent of Earl Akin's conversations with his father and with Harris.

Earl Akin's insistence that Jordan did not go to Laurel, raises at least three possibilities. First, perhaps the passage of nearly fifty years has impacted the accuracy of Earl Akin's memory on this point. Second, perhaps he has deliberately not included Jordan to create a conflict that would diminish Akin's value as a government witness and, at the same time, discredit a key government witness. Finally, perhaps Jordan was not present, but falsely claimed to be present for the Bowers meeting in an attempt to increase his value to the government and thereby lessen his time in prison.

Of further significance, Earl Akin sent the FBI bizarre written allegations, and asserted that Harris buried one of the victims' bodies at the dam site. No other source contends that that Harris was at the dam site on June 21-22.

---

[25] When shown records proving that his private airplane was purchased after the killings, Earl Akin withdrew that contention.

- 37 -

While it appears that – just as Jordan claimed – Earl Akin likely heard Bowers give Harris authorization to kill Schwerner, Earl Akin will continue to insist that Jordan was not present for the conversation that he claims to have heard. Earl Akin's credibility on key points is highly suspect and his criminal history includes crimes that would impeach his credibility as a witness. Earl Akin would be an extremely problematic witness and it is difficult to place confidence in his factual assertions.

c. Edgar Ray Killen

We contacted the attorney representing Edgar Ray Killen in October 2012 to seek his client's cooperation. We advised that a reduction in sentence was unlikely, but we suggested that it was worth discussing the possibility and advantages of federal custody for his client should Killen provide information useful to the investigation. We asked for an opportunity to meet with Killen to talk about his potential cooperation.

Killen's attorney contacted his client and responded that Killen advised that he knew nothing about the 1964 murders and that he was unwilling to meet with us. Killen's attorney further advised that nothing, not even a potential nominal state sentence reduction, would alter his client's position. A November 2012 letter to Killen's attorney memorialized his rejection of our offer. Based upon Killen's consistent denials for the past 50 years that he has any knowledge regarding the murders and the current representations of his attorney that nothing will alter Killen's position, we concluded that further efforts regarding Killen would not be fruitful.

3. Attempts to Develop Evidence Through Recently Identified Witnesses

a. James Billy Burrage

James Billy Burrage (known as Billy), Olen Burrage's younger brother, did not testify in *Price*. In the summer of 1964, Billy Burrage had recently moved from Philadelphia, Mississippi to Houston, Texas. In Philadelphia, he had lived in a house on Olen Burrage's Old Jolly Farm. After the murders, a witness who knew the Billy Burrage family in Texas told the FBI that Billy's wife had said that Billy was involved in the Philadelphia murders. Billy Burrage was working as a long distance truck driver in the summer of 1964 and thus could have been in Philadelphia on June 21. We speculated that he could have been one of the two unidentified men whom H.D. Barnette claimed to have seen with Olen Burrage in the car near the Old Jolly Farm. Moreover, Billy Burrage has a criminal record unrelated to the 1964 murders.

Billy Burrage was interviewed by the FBI and claimed that he was in Houston on June 21, 1964, and that he had never heard his brother say anything regarding the murders, other than to deny that he (Olen) was involved in them. We have discovered no direct information to contradict any of Billy Burrage's contentions. In fact, we determined that Olen Burrage did not appear to trust Billy Burrage and it was unlikely that he would have made an admission to him.

- 38 -

b. Harris' Relative

We received a tip from an NAACP official that a family relative of subject Harris had heard Harris make incriminating statements about the murders. The hearsay was rather vague and required clarification from the alleged source.

We contacted the estranged relative by telephone on several occasions in the fall of 2012. He was initially unreceptive, but eventually agreed to meet. Thereafter, he would not answer his telephone to arrange a meeting time and place. We additionally learned that Harris' Relative was receiving medical treatment. Even if the purported witness was willing to meet with us and were to provide relevant information, his strained relationship with Harris suggests a potential bias against Harris and his reported medical condition could raise competency issues. Accordingly, we determined that this potential investigative lead would not lead to information that could be useful in a criminal prosecution of Harris.

c. Jailhouse Sources

Two jailhouse sources surfaced during this investigation – Larry Ellis and James Stern. Both sources made public claims that each had separately developed a close relationship in prison with Edgar Ray Killen, a relationship in which Killen supplied each of them with information inculpating Killen and others in the June 21, 1964 murders. One witness, Stern, was an unlikely confidante of Killen's as he is African American.

The FBI interviewed and collected documents from both sources. Despite their public claims, neither the individuals nor the information they supplied were credible or substantively useful to our investigation. In short, what was advertized publically – that Killen had made relevant admissions incriminating others – was not what was delivered by these self-promoting witnesses.

d. Choctaw Women

The FBI interviewed two women from the Choctaw Indian Tribe who were with Deputy Price when he visited Posey's gas station on the afternoon of June 21, 1964. Neither of the women had any information relevant to any surviving subjects of our investigation.

e. County Coroner's Juror

A surviving member of the Neshoba County Coroner's jury that conducted an investigation of the murders was also rumored to have been a member of the Philadelphia Klan chapter in 1964. The FBI located the surviving County Corner's Juror in 2013 and attempted to interview him. He was a resident of a Neshoba County nursing home and, according to his daughter, he suffered from dementia. The FBI attempted to speak with the County Coroner's Juror and found nothing to contradict the daughter's contention.

- 39 -

253

4.   **Attempts to Develop New Evidence Through Previously Identified Witnesses**

a. Catherine Tucker

Catherine Tucker is the widow of Herman Tucker, an acquitted *Price* trial defendant who worked as a bulldozer operator for Olen Burrage during the spring and summer of 1964 building the dam on the Old Jolly Farm. At the *Price* trial, Jordan testified that, although he did not see the bulldozer operator who buried the bodies, he heard him referred to as "Herman." H.D. Barnette's confession described a man matching Herman Tucker's general physical description as the bulldozer operator who accompanied Burrage to the burial site. Katherine Tucker testified in *Price* as an alibi witness. She claimed that Herman Tucker arrived home at 9:00 p.m. after working at the dam site on June 21, 1964, and remained at home all night.

Confidential sources claimed that Herman Tucker received money from the Klan to keep silent. In October 2013, the FBI and Department attorneys interviewed Mrs. Tucker to explore whether she might now provide a different account than what she provided at the *Price* Trial. However, Mrs. Tucker continued to insist that her husband did not leave their home on the evening of June 21, 1964, and that she knew nothing to inculpate Olen Burrage in the murders or burials. She also acknowledged that she had been employed by Burrage Trucking subsequent to the murders and that she and Olen Burrage share grandchildren from the marriage of their children.

b. Burrage Family "Alibi" Witnesses

Of the eight witnesses Olen Burrage presented in the *Price* trial, three were still alive and interviewed pursuant to the Emmett Till Act investigation – Burrage's wife, Audine, his then sister-in-law Ruby Davis, and Clifton Leon Myer, who later became an in-law by the marriage of the two men's children. Each provided information consistent with their 1967 testimony.

The *Price* testimony, and consistent recent statements of Audine Burrage and Davis put Olen Burrage at his home across a country road from his trucking business talking on the telephone to R.P. Davis (Ruby Davis's husband, whom they claimed was in Indiana at the time of the call) at 1 a.m. on June 22, 1964, approximately the same time that Jordan and H.D. Barnette claim they saw Burrage at his business complex supplying gasoline to the killers after the burial. These witnesses thus establish that Burrage needed only to cross the road to participate in the crime.

Myer, who had visited Burrage earlier in the day, but was not present at the relevant time, did not report seeing any of the coconspirators at the Burrage home or business complex when he visited during the afternoon. We have no admissible evidence to contradict or challenge what these witnesses have consistently stated.

c. Mrs. Cecil Price

The FBI visited former Deputy Cecil Price's widow at her home in 2010 in an attempt to interview her. Mrs. Price would not speak with the agents. We have no specific reason to believe that Price confided anything about the murders to his wife.

d. Additional Meridian Source

An additional surviving Meridian 1960s FBI confidential source was re-interviewed during the Emmet Till Act investigation to determine if the source had any information relating to Harris or other relevant information. The source convincingly claimed to know nothing relevant beyond what was previously provided to the FBI that does not advance our investigation. We have no contradictory information to question the truthfulness of that assertion. Moreover, the source has serious medical problems that prevent him from leaving his home.

D.   Emmett Till Act Investigation/ Subjects

As previously discussed, we considered four individuals alleged to have participated in the events related to the murders as the initial subjects of our Emmett Till Act investigation. Richard Andrew Willis died soon after the investigation was commenced. For the reasons discussed in Section VII.C., we focused on Jimmy Lee Townsend as a subject of our § 1001 investigation with the goal of persuading him to proffer information related to the surviving Emmett Till Act subjects, Harris and Burrage. In the course of the investigation, we also attempted to interview Harris and later, through their counsel, we provided Harris and Burrage opportunities to present their accounts.

1. James Thomas "Pete" Harris

James Thomas "Pete" Harris has never acknowledged to the FBI or to state investigators any involvement in or knowledge about the murders. As discussed in the summary of the *Price* trial, Harris presented an alibi through his brother. That alibi was inconsistent with what Harris had told the FBI soon after the murders (that he was at home rather than with his brother).

During the recent Emmett Till Act investigation, Harris demonstrated a continued resolve to remain silent. The FBI visited Harris at his home in Meridian to seek an interview on January 12, 2011. Harris stated that an attorney had advised him "not to speak to anyone." Harris did not indicate whether he was represented by this attorney.

In November 2012, the Department sent Harris a letter inviting him to meet with a Department attorney, along with his legal representative, should he have one, to answer our questions and to provide his account of the events. The letter also advised Harris that he had a Fifth Amendment privilege to decline to engage in such an interview. A paralegal/investigator from the Department called Harris at his home to confirm that he had received the letter after he did not respond. Harris advised that he had received the letter. When asked if he had any questions regarding the matter, he said he did not.

- 41 -

After exhausting other investigative leads, in October 2013, the Department sent a letter to a Meridian, Mississippi, attorney representing Harris, offering Harris an opportunity to provide information to this investigation. Thereafter, Harris's attorney advised a Department attorney by telephone that he would convey the message to Harris but that he would recommend that any conversation with the government was not in Harris's interest. In a November 2013 letter, the Department reiterated its willingness to hear a proffer from Harris, but Harris's attorney declined to respond. Our letter of January 17, 2014, to Harris's counsel memorialized our understanding that Harris is not interested in an opportunity to relate his version of events.

2. Olen Lovell Burrage

Olen Lovell Burrage denied knowledge of the murders when the FBI executed the warrant to search the Old Jolly Farm back in 1964. Later, when state investigators attempted to interview him in 2000, Burrage went to a local hospital with heart attack symptoms.

In November 2012, an attorney representing Burrage contacted the Department. He had learned that we were interviewing Burrage family members. We met with the attorney and offered Burrage an opportunity to present his account. After consulting with his client, in December 2012, the attorney responded that, due to Burrage's age and health, an interview was not possible. Burrage died in March 2013.

E. Potential Forensic Evidence

We received rumors regarding the possible continued existence of the guns used during the murders. The FBI explored every allegation. Based upon all available information related to the murders and the cover-up thereafter, we believe that all guns were likely disposed of or destroyed. In any event we found no reliable information that might lead to the discovery of a relevant weapon.

Forensic medical examiner Dr. Michael M. Baden stated that he was consulted by state prosecutors prior to the *Killen* trial. He said that, based upon the 1964 medical examiner's report, bullets still in James Chaney's interred body could be matched to the gun that fired them. However, the government has no gun associated with the murders. All efforts to track down the whereabouts of a murder weapon have been unsuccessful.

Moreover, all the individuals known or suspected to have been present for the murders are now deceased. Thus, even if we located a gun used in the murders and positively matched it to bullets extracted from Chaney's body, it would not advance a prosecution against any living subject.

VIII. Analysis of Evidence Regarding Surviving Subjects

The decision regarding the initiation of a state murder or other state criminal prosecution is properly the province of Mississippi State authorities. As such, although we proffer observations about the strengths and weaknesses of the existing evidence relevant to Townsend

- 42 -

and Harris, we do not make any recommendation. Further, an analysis of the evidence related to the now deceased Willis and Burrage would be an unproductive exercise as no prosecution could result.

A. Jimmy Lee Townsend

Our investigation focused on Jimmy Lee Townsend as a potential witness to inculpate Harris and, before his death, Burrage. Because of the limited extent and nature of Townsend's believed involvement in the murders, the Mississippi Attorney General and the Department were willing to grant him immunity from all prosecution should he have provided truthful information. Nonetheless, Townsend consistently maintained that he knew no information related to the murders and was not involved in them. No further admissible evidence was discovered during our investigation to inculpate him.

Unlike the other living subjects Killen and Harris, Townsend was not included as a defendant in the final *Price* indictment. Because he was not a trial defendant, deceased witness Jordan's testimony in *Price* regarding Townsend's conduct, as well as his unequivocal incriminating information provided to the FBI that Townsend accompanied Killen to Meridian to recruit Klansmen and that he was later left on the roadside with Posey's disabled car – is hearsay not admissible under the former testimony hearsay exception.

Accordingly, the only information of Townsend's involvement in the murders remains: (1) the account of the deceased cooperating government witness James Jordan, in which he maintained Townsend accompanied Killen and later the killers, but was not at the scene of the murders (hearsay, not admissible under the former testimony exception); (2) Townsend's own inability or unwillingness to account for his conduct on the night of the murders; (3) his relationship with known participants in the murders; and (4) confidential source hearsay information that Townsend was present when financial payments were made to defendants in the *Price* prosecution. During the course of our investigation, we were alert for any new information that would establish Townsend's own involvement in the events of June 21. However, we discovered no other witness or admissible evidence relevant to the prosecution of Townsend for the murders or for false statements to federal officials.

B. James Thomas "Pete" Harris

Regarding Harris, much of the information discussed in this report, while incriminating, would be inadmissible in a state murder trial against him or has been provided by aging, reluctant witnesses who have begun to assert memory problems. Other information would have limited probative value, merely establishing his presence at Klan activities.

The single most incriminating evidence is provided by the deceased government cooperator, Jordan. While Jordan testified in *Price* that Harris received state Klan leader Bowers' authorization to kill Schwerner, no evidence demonstrates that Harris ever conveyed that instruction to anyone else. Rather, Jordan and several other witnesses heard other Klansman, not Harris, speak about killing Schwerner, in some cases in Harris' presence. Moreover, the only sources who attribute incriminating conduct to Harris on the day of the

- 43 -

murders, Jordan and H.D. Barnette, also maintained that they did not learn the victims would be killed until Harris was no longer present.

The Mississippi Attorney General is uniquely aware of what former testimony from the *Price* and *Killen* trials would be admissible, as he faced the same issues in the prosecution of Killen. Some information, such as H.D. Barnette's confession, would be excluded in trial because the deceased source of the information never testified at trial against Harris. Other information would be excluded because that source is now deceased or is a protected confidential source, like the Klansman Source, and therefore may not be available to testify.

Jordan's *Price* trial testimony would likely be admissible against Harris under the former testimony hearsay exception. However, while Jordan testified that Harris made telephone calls to recruit Meridian Klansmen for Killen, he also testified that Killen was looking for volunteers to "whup their asses" not explicitly to abduct and kill the civil rights volunteers. Jordan's testimony that Jordan did not know that killings were planned until they actually occurred is undercut by his own testimony that he was present when Bowers conveyed an order to Harris to have Schwerner eliminated. At the same time, Earl Akin is a living witness who, if believed, would contradict Jordan's former testimony. Earl Akin claims to have overheard the same conversation between Bowers and Harris but insists that Jordan was not there. As discussed, Jordan and Earl Akin each present their own credibility concerns. We are aware of nothing that would definitively credit the account of one witness over the other.

The *Price* trial testimony of Carlton Miller and Delmar Dennis would also likely be admissible against Harris. They testified that Harris was at Klan meetings where others announced the "elimination" had been approved or complained that it had been delayed too long. But, neither witness testified that Harris himself spoke at those Klan meetings. In fact, none of the former testimony includes any admission of culpability by Harris to any witness.

As set forth above, certain surviving witnesses admit to knowing information that incriminates Harris. Most significantly, the Meridian Source provides an admission by Harris that corroborates Jordan's testimony that Harris helped plan the abduction and killings. The Klansman Source corroborates the testimony of Jordan, Miller, and Dennis that Harris was present at meetings when "elimination" was discussed by others, but not by Harris. We have discussed the issues that impact the Meridian Source's value as a witness. Further, even if the Klansman Source could be persuaded to testify, his testimony would have limited probative value. The source corroborates the former testimony by Jordan, Miller, and Dennis, which is limited to Harris's presence at Klan meetings where others, not Harris, discussed Schwerner's "elimination." Such qualified evidence must be balanced against the long-standing promise to protect a trusted source's identity.

Earl Akin, Michael Hatcher, and the Meridian Klansman raise other issues impacting their value to a state prosecution. Earl Akin presents substantial reliability and credibility concerns. Hatcher may well know more than he has admitted regarding Harris. After equivocation, Hatcher emphatically denies knowing any incriminating information regarding Harris or any living person. Finally, the Meridian Klansman has emphatically retracted the incriminating information that he at one time provided against Harris.

- 44 -

The evidence against Harris appears now to include: (1) Jordan's former testimony, restricted as it was presented in *Price* to Bowers' "elimination" authorization (this time impeached by Earl Akin's testimony) and Harris' actions in Meridian at The Longhorn and Akin's Motor Homes; (2) the former testimony of Jordan, Miller, and Dennis that Harris attended Klan meetings where the killing of Schwerner was discussed by others; (3) potentially the Klansman Sources' testimony to corroborate the former testimony of those witnesses; and (4) possibly, although not certainly, the Meridian Source's testimony that Harris admitted that he helped plan the killings. Only Mississippi authorities have the necessary understanding of Mississippi law to determine whether the available admissible evidence is sufficient to meet the burden of proof required to establish murder or another prosecutable state criminal charge.

IX. Conclusion

It has been our goal in this Emmett Till Act investigation to assist the state in the critical decisions it must make. This report is intended to provide as fair an analysis of the available evidence as is practical to help the Mississippi Attorney General make a fully informed decision. We have assessed the evidentiary strengths and weaknesses of the information related, the probative value of what a witness has said, the likelihood that the witness will be willing to testify in public, and if so, our best view as to whether a witness's account will remain firm should the witness testify at a public trial. Obviously, the willingness of surviving witnesses to cooperate fully rather than minimizing their knowledge with false denials or feigned memory problems is a factor to consider in analyzing the strength or weakness of a potential prosecution. Finally, nothing contained herein is intended to favor either state prosecution or declination of prosecution.

It is appropriate to close this report with an observation made in its Introduction. With the passage of nearly fifty years, few persons with any direct knowledge of the facts relevant to the June 21, 1964 murders still remain alive. Most of the original cooperators and confidential sources are deceased. Many of these elderly witnesses have understandably imperfect recollections. Other witnesses are reluctant to provide information. Some witnesses, despite comprehensive efforts – including pursuit of evidence to support federal prosecution for false statement, nonetheless appear to have accomplished their intention to continue to conceal crucial relevant information. These realities impacted our investigation and the current prospects of uncovering any further information useful for prosecutive purposes.

But, it should also not be forgotten that nine men have been held accountable for this crime. Heroic efforts by the FBI and Department's Civil Right Division enabled the successful federal prosecution of eight Klansmen, none of whom would otherwise have been brought to justice by the civil rights era Mississippi State authorities. Thereafter, an equally remarkable 2005 effort by modern era Mississippi prosecutors resulted in yet one more criminal conviction in these tragic murders. Seven Klansmen who directly participated in this horrific killing and the state Klan leader who authorized the murders were incarcerated and have now passed on. The Klansman who, as much as anyone, facilitated these racist murders will spend his remaining years behind bars. Regardless whether all those responsible have or can be held accountable, the deaths of Michael Schwerner, James Chaney, and Andrew Goodman have been thoroughly and

- 45 -

aggressively investigated and reinvestigated and have thus received some measure of vindication.

Attachment A
Defendants, Witnesses and Others Related to June 21, 1964 Murders
(in alphabetical order)

Arledge, Jimmy deceased – (Meridian) convicted *Price* defendant, present at murders.

Akin, Bernard L. deceased – (Meridian) acquitted *Price* defendant, owner of Akin's Mobile Homes, allegedly present when Killen came to Meridian to recruit Klansmen.

Akin, Earl – (Meridian) Bernard's son, allegedly at meeting with Harris where Bowers authorized "elimination" of Schwerner.

Barnette, Ethal Glenn "Hop" deceased – (Philadelphia) mistrial *Price* defendant, former Neshoba County Sherriff.

Barnette, Horace Doyle "H.D." deceased – (Meridian) convicted *Price* defendant, confessed he was present at murders.

Barnette, Travis Maryn deceased – (Meridian) acquitted *Price* defendant, brother of H.D. Barnette, conflict whether present at murders.

Bowers, Sam Holloway deceased – (Laurel, MS) convicted *Price* defendant, leader Mississippi Klan, authorized "elimination" of Schwerner.

Burrage, James Billy – (Philadelphia) brother of acquitted *Price* defendant Olen Burrage, residing in Houston in 1964.

Burrage, Olen Lowell deceased – (Philadelphia) acquitted *Price* defendant, owner Old Jolly Farm where bodies buried, allegedly assisted burial.

Burkes, Otha deceased – (Philadelphia) police officer charged, but dismissed, as *Price* defendant.

Chaney, James deceased – (Meridian) local volunteer, Mississippi Congress of Federation Organizations, killed June 21, 1964.

Dennis, Delmar deceased – (Meridian) Klan leader, testified in *Price* about Klan meetings and discussions.

Goodman, Andrew (New York) – recent volunteer, Mississippi Congress of Federation Organizations, killed June 21, 1964.

Harris, James Thomas "Pete" – (Meridian) acquitted *Price* defendant, allegedly recruited Meridian Klansmen on June 21 after obtained Bowers' approval to "eliminate" Schwerner.

Hatcher, Joseph Michael – (Meridian) 1964 police officer, testified in Price and Killen about Klan meetings and Killen admissions.

Herndon, Frank J. deceased – (Meridian) acquitted *Price* defendant, allegedly recruited Meridian Klansmen for Killen on June 21.

Jordan, James Edward deceased – (Meridian) convicted *Price* defendant, testified for government at *Price* trial & present at murders.

Killen, Edgar Ray – (Philadelphia) mistrial *Price* defendant, convicted *Killen* defendant, recruited Meridian Klansmen

Klansman Source – (Protected ID) attended 1964 Klan meetings with Harris and Meridian Klansman when "elimination" discussed.

Meridian Source – (Protected ID) 1964 Harris friend, heard admission by Harris.

Miller, Carlton Wallace deceased – (Meridian) 1964 police sergeant, attended Klan meetings when "elimination" discussed.

Posey, Billy Wayne deceased – (Philadelphia) convicted *Price* defendant, present at murders.

- 47 -

Price, Cecil Ray deceased – (Philadelphia) convicted *Price* defendant, Neshoba County Deputy Sheriff.

Meridian Klansman – (Meridian) 1964 Harris friend, who attended Klan meetings.

Rainey, Lawrence Andrew deceased – (Philadelphia) acquitted *Price* defendant, Neshoba County Sherriff.

Roberts, Alton Wayne deceased – (Meridian) convicted *Price* defendant, present at murders.

Schwerner, Michael deceased – (New York) volunteer, Mississippi Congress of Federation Organizations, killed June 21, 1964.

Sharpe, Jerry McGrew deceased – (Philadelphia) mistrial *Price* defendant, allegedly accompanied Killen to Meridian, conflict whether present at murders.

Snowden, Jimmy deceased – (Meridian) convicted *Price* defendant, present at murders.

Townsend, Jimmy Lee – (Philadelphia) allegedly accompanied Killen to Meridian and remained with Posey's disabled car.

Tucker, Herman deceased – (Philadelphia) acquitted *Price* defendant, bulldozer operator Old Jolly Farm

Warner, Oliver Richard deceased – (Meridian) storeowner originally charged, but dismissed, as *Price* defendant.

Willis, Richard Andrew deceased – (Philadelphia) acquitted *Price* defendant, policeman allegedly helped Deputy Price alert Klansmen in Philadelphia.

Meridian *Price* Defendants

Arledge, Jimmy deceased
Akin, Bernard L. deceased
Barnette, Horace Doyle "H.D." deceased
Barnette, Travis Maryn deceased
Harris, James Thomas "Pete"
Herndon, Frank J. deceased
Jordan, James Edward deceased
Roberts, Alton Wayne deceased
Snowden, Jimmy deceased

Philadelphia *Price* Defendants

Barnette, Ethal Glenn "Hop" deceased
Burrage, Olen Lowell deceased
Killen, Edgar Ray
Posey, Billy Wayne deceased
Price, Cecil Ray deceased
Sharpe, Jerry McGrew deceased
Tucker, Herman deceased
Willis, Richard Andrew deceased

Laurel, MS *Price* Defendant

Bowers, Sam Holloway deceased

ABOUT THE AUTHOR

Brian Boney was a full-time law enforcement officer for twenty-five years, from 1989 to October of 2014, when he retired at the rank of sergeant. He served with the Rapides Parish Sheriff's Department, the police department in the town of Ball, Louisiana, and went to work in June of 1993 for the Alexandria, Louisiana police department. During his tenure in law enforcement, he worked as a patrol officer, a DWI enforcement officer, was a SWAT member, DARE officer, police academy instructor, hostage negotiator, internal affairs investigator, street narcotics supervisor, and patrol supervisor. This is his first book.

20919606R00155

Made in the USA
Lexington, KY
08 December 2018